THE KAY ALDRIDGE STORY

By Jim Manago

THE THRILLS GONE BY: THE KAY ALDRIDGE STORY

The Thrills Gone By: The Kay Aldridge Story by Jim Manago
© 2016, ALL RIGHTS RESERVED
No part of this book may be reproduced in any form or by any means, electronic, mechanical, digital, photocopying, or recording, except for inclusion of a review, without permission in writing from the publisher.

Published in the USA by:
BearManor Media
P O Box 71426
Albany, Georgia 31708
www.bearmanormedia.com

ISBN: 978-1-59393-186-5
BearManor Media, Albany, Georgia
Printed in the United States of America
Cover photo by Strauss-Peyton, New York City
Book design by Robbie Adkins, www.adkinsconsult.com

Table of Contents

Acknowledgements v
Dedication vii
Introduction viii
Part One: Kay Aldridge's Life
Chapter One: From Farm Gal to Glamour Girl 3
Chapter Two: America's Cover Girl and Starlet 16
Chapter Three: Window Dressing at Fox 22
Chapter Four: Sexy Sextet at Warners 48
Chapter Five: Serial Queen at Republic 57
Chapter Six: From Broadway Footlights To Poverty Row 73
Chapter Seven: "I Got to Get a Husband and Some Children!" . 82
Chapter Eight: The Fans Rekindle the Thrills 133
Chapter Nine: Good Night, Good Looking! 139
Part Two: The Serial Thrills
Chapter Ten: *Perils of Nyoka* (1942) 146
Chapter Eleven: *Daredevils of the West* (1943) 163
Chapter Twelve: *Haunted Harbor* (1944) 170
Chapter Thirteen: Afterword 181
Appendix 183
Bibliography 183
Foreword by Carey Cameron to the Scrapbook,
"Memoirs of a Southern Belle" 185
Letter by Kay Aldridge to her mother Cornelia Ward Aldridge ... 188
List of Magazine Covers 192
Print Advertising 193
Film Studios 193
Credits 194

THE THRILLS GONE BY: THE KAY ALDRIDGE STORY

Acknowledgements:

I am most indebted to Carey Cameron for providing me with the PDF of the reassembled scrapbook that came from her mother's original books. The scrapbook, "Memoirs of a Southern Belle," is a compilation of the materials that Carey assembled years after her mother's death in 1995. I am thankful that she allowed me to reprint portions of the material contained therein. Carey offered a valuable understanding that made my job of telling her mother's story less trying.

As her scrapbook is not available to the general public, the copies that were made received limited circulation to Aldridge's family and friends. However, the Foreword to that scrapbook is reprinted in the Appendix to this book.

When I first contacted Carey she explained why she never wrote a book about her mother: "[My mother's] story has plenty of drama, but the reason I didn't try to write something (I am in fact an author myself!) more marketable is because her career was so brief. There are of course all the side aspects (the Powers Agency, the studio system, the movies featuring line ups of show-girls, the story of Republic, etc. etc.)

"But perhaps her daughter is the least capable of writing about her. She was a great puzzlement to me, and to all her children. At least now, thanks to the delving into the material that I did, her career, at least, is less of a puzzle to me. Her career was emblematic of the careers so many woman at the time—who had looks, needy families, and few options."

Thanks to James Ricotta, who shared his love of the serials with me so many years ago.

I offer a very special thanks to Donna Manago for her research assistance as well as her help in reviewing the manuscript.

Also, many thanks to Randy Bonneville for always being a reliable source for creating the list of credits that appear in the Appendix.

I owe my publisher my deep appreciation. Ben Ohmart said "yes" to my idea without hesitation. Thanks to him for making this book a reality.

Finally, I owe so many wonderful memories to a special friendship that stretches back over forty years. Thanks forever to the late Joe Franklin who enriched my life with his love of the movies. I will miss him dearly.

DEDICATION:

To serial fans everywhere; &
to Dee, my love and best friend,
especially for bringing laughter to my life
with her comical
visitor from another galaxy.

I hope the world will know of him
someday . . .

Introduction:

Her name is forgotten today with a career that lasted just nine thrilling years. At the height of her fame, showman Billy Rose called Kay Aldridge "the most beautiful girl in the United States!"[1]

First and foremost, she excelled as "America's most famous model." She quickly became the most recognizable face in the late 1930's as noted by the *New York Times* (hereinafter referred to as *NYT*). By 1944 Aldridge had appeared on at least 50 national magazine covers, including *Life, Ladies Home Journal, Redbook* and *Look* magazines.

It was not long before the magazine cover girl got a Hollywood contract to make movies. She tried to make it as a star and actress, but the studio system seemed to fail her. The glamour chill parts she was given in eleven Twentieth Century-Fox films did not make her a star. The studio did not renew her contract. Simply put, she did not register as an actress or as a bankable star for them. Then she made three films for Warners. But her greatest success came with a serial for the B-movie studio, Republic Pictures. This followed with two more serials, a stint on Broadway, and two films for Poverty Row's PRC Studios. Then her career in films ended when she quit the business.

Aldridge continued to model between the minor movie roles. It was six years after her start as a model that she seemed to hit pay dirt with her role as a heroine and Serial Queen. Yet all this did not mean much to her.

Even though she seemed to be stuck with secondary roles, Kay Aldridge may not have achieved much more in films as her limitations as an actress are readily apparent. Of course, one might suggest that perhaps with the right acting coach or better casting and career supervision she may have found her place in the movies or later with some steady work in the new medium of televi-

---

1 Feg Murray's "Seein' Stars . . " strip noted: "Kay Aldridge, according to famous showman Billy Rose, is 'The Most Beautiful Girl in the United States'!" Also, the quote attributed to Rose has been reported as: "The Most Beautiful Girl in America!" and "The Most Beautiful Girl in the World!"

sion. However, when she made the life-long choice to be a wife and mother, her career did not matter anymore as she focused on raising her four children.

Nevertheless, Aldridge's fragile and unforgettable beauty did not preclude her from her greatest success as the iconic serial heroine, and that is what she is best remembered for today; namely, the title character in *Perils of Nyoka*. Her two other serials, *Daredevils of the West* and *Haunted Harbor*, did not enhance her reputation at all. Nevertheless, her role in *Perils of Nyoka* proved she could hold her own against any man as being strong and tough.

An explanation for this book is necessary for it chronicles the life of a performer who was seen by audiences for a brief time in just twenty-one rarely seen movies (five of them uncredited), three serials (one not seen for sixty-five years until recently) and several short subjects.

No, Aldridge did not become a big-name success in Hollywood movies, and sadly so. Perhaps one could say that she never got a part that could show she could surpass the label of being so photogenic and so beautiful to look at.

Today the fact remains that Aldridge, if remembered at all, is remembered only as Nyoka. Few of her movies offered her a substantial role that would develop her star presence or acting any further. Almost all of the productions were primarily using her beauty to prettify the scenery. Simply put, why devote an entire book studying the life of an actress with such a limited career?

The answer to this question is because Aldridge had a magical impact with that one serial then, and even now. One does not have to watch many serials to realize how she stood above the typical female serial character. She rose above almost all of the females in the 266 sound serials as they were male-dominated productions.

Certainly, by no means is the serial a form that excels in anything except in offering many exciting and enjoyable action sequences. In particular, Republic Studio's special effects and miniature work of the Lydecker Brothers, Howard and Theodore, offered more convincing effects than those done by the major studios of that day.

In short, it is the cliffhanger at the end of each chapter which offered the sole reason for watching these shorts. Everything else about serials, including the plots, set design, dialogue, and so forth, is quite limited and undoubtedly aimed at the non-discriminating juvenile audiences. Serial "acting," if you can even call it acting at all, is mediocre at best, and embarrassingly amateurish at its worst.

My fascination with Aldridge began many years before in the 1960's when I discovered the world of the serial film. Then, when I was seven years old, I viewed chapters of *Buck Rogers* on New York television (WOR-Channel 9). The strange futuristic world of 'Killer' Kane with his mind-controlling helmets and the desperate struggles of the 'Hidden City' inhabitants (Buck Rogers, Buddy Wade, Wilma Deering, and Prince Tallin) intrigued me. At that moment, I was hooked.

Finally, in my early teens, I got to see the oft-talked about three *Flash Gordon* serials thanks to Public Television, WNET-Channel 13. By then there was no escaping the desire to watch and study every serial production ever made.

A fuller awareness of the "serial world" came when a local individual named James Ricotta answered my ad to sell my Super 8 film collection. He informed me of his love of the serials. Then for a period of time he shared his serials on VHS that he rented weekly from a store in New York City.

Then my horizon widened with *The Adventures of Captain Marvel, Mysterious Doctor Satan, The Purple Monster Strikes, The Crimson Ghost*, and others. One of the most influential and memorable serials for me was *Perils of Nyoka*. Besides being fascinated with the heroine, I loved watching Nyoka's nemesis, Vultura (Lorna Gray), who added to the thrills I experienced. Moments from *Perils of Nyoka* have stayed with me. The lasting impact of that serial gave me a life-long desire to pursue this biography so that I can tell Aldridge's story in detail.

Back in 1979, I happened to be one of those few who purchased the first book written about Aldridge by film teacher and collector Merrill T. McCord. Although the many photographs therein were endearing (many from Aldridge's collection), and the fact that Mc-

Cord's interviews got some apt reflections about Aldridge's own career that I found priceless, I was then disappointed and wanted more than a large booklet about Aldridge as it was just sixty-four catalog-sized pages. That book, *Perils of Kay Aldridge* (Alhambra Publishers, Washington, D.C.), offered one thing to me - the saving grace of receiving a book by mail autographed by the star.

My intention here has been to give the reader the text missing from McCord's book that would have given Aldridge's fans a more detailed examination of her life as a model as well as an actress.

The fact remains that in almost all of Aldridge's films her character role is a bit part. Also, most are rarely seen and/or are hard-to-obtain. Some may still expect an in-depth study of them, or at least a description of the few moments with Aldridge. However, my goal here was not to seek the esoteric. I wanted to inform readers with the most complete factual biography, and to share my love of her one iconic role. I am convinced that this is what most readers will come to regard as her movie career.

My hope is that this book will satisfy Kay Aldridge's fans as well as encourage interest among those unfamiliar with her contribution to entertainment history. The pages that follow chronicle the newspaper coverage of Kay Aldridge's career and preserve the memory of our Nyoka now and forever.

I invite you to relive some of the thrills gone by that both serial audiences and Kay Aldridge personally experienced.

Jim Manago
November 2015

Part One:
Kay Aldridge's Life

Chapter One:
From Farm Gal to Glamour Girl

> "Though only in the 5th grade, the attention she receives from male classmates (in the form of stealing her tam-o'-shanter and throwing it up a tree so that her male classmates can look up her skirt as she climbs to retrieve it) 'introduces [her] to the power of being a girl.'"
> - Carey Cameron,
> "Memoirs of a Southern Belle"

If you could use only one word to best describe the general public's perception of Kay Aldridge back in her day, then it would be "Photogenic" with a capital "P." From the first photograph that appeared in a newspaper reporting an accident she suffered a few months before her eighteenth birthday, it is understandable that she was undoubtedly destined to be seen on magazines covers and in newspapers ads.

Then when she appeared in films, often it seemed as though she was acting more like a model endorsing a product in a commercial. It was like she played the pretty cover girl or the magazine ad girl coming to life.

An article that appeared in *Vogue* magazine remarked that old Paris would call her an "Un-Classic Beauty," as "Miss Aldridge's figure is too Junoesque, her face too circular." This would mean nothing to the public tantalized by the ravishing five feet-eight cover girl, advertisement model and Hollywood starlet.

Aldridge's career as a well-known model began in 1936, and her movie career started in 1937. By mid-1945, she traded in her career for life as a wife and mother: retiring from her career at the youthful age of 27. Though it is a professional career that lasted a mere nine years, the press coverage as documented in the pages that follow is impressive in any estimation, especially considering that Aldridge is very much forgotten now.

Throughout her modeling and movie career her name appeared as Kay Aldridge, Kitty Aldridge, Katherine Aldridge, and Katharine Aldridge. She was born as Katharine and she modified it during her career to Kay. All other variants are errors of the studio publicity and the press. In this text, she will be referred to oftentimes by her last name. However, I have taken the liberty to simplify the text by not preserving all of the name variations offered by printed quotes.

Aldridge's daughter Carey Cameron (hereinafter referred to simply as "Carey") referred to her mother as "K.A." in her scrapbook. Although in early newspaper references I do preserve the name variations, eventually I too simplify matters by using "K.A." whenever a quote mentions one of the variants of her name.

Carey explained: "Her birth name was Katharine, an old-fashioned spelling of the name (like Katharine Hepburn). But this was somehow really a challenge for journalists, film credit people, etc. to get right. I thought it was one of the reasons she opted for Kay for some purposes. Hard to get that wrong. But she said she adopted Kay because she thought it was trendy."

Katharine Aldridge was born on July 9, 1917 in Tallahassee, Florida. As the fourth child of her parents, John and Cornelia Ward Aldridge; her father came from Maryland, her mother from Virginia, they lived in Florida due to her father's business of raising and selling fruit trees. Her mother was an artist and writer.

She never knew her father, as he died in 1922 from stomach cancer. Some incorrectly reported that it was when Kay was just two years old. Aldridge was next to the youngest. Her sister and brothers were under eight years old at the time of their father's death.

Aldridge's daughter Carey best tells what happened next to the widowed mother and Aldridge's siblings; an older sister Clelia (Cornelia); brothers John, Ran (Randolph), and Bill (William).

Carey: "As she has no means of support, Cornelia has no choice but to return to her family home, Bladensfield, in northeastern Virginia. Bladensfield is inhabited by Cornelia's 3 maiden aunts [Evie, Lucy and Fonnie]. It is this historic but dilapidated house – a house without electricity, plumbing, or any heat source other than fireplaces – that K.A. spends an 'unforgettable' childhood, attending classes taught by her great-aunts, who are retired school teachers, playing in its surrounding fields and woods and resolving to somehow 'save' herself, her family and Bladensfield itself from the depredations of poverty."

Aldridge: "The claims that growing up there have on me are still so strong that they are almost an obsession with me. Always from the time that I was a very young child I have felt a sense of mission about saving the old place and all my fantasies were based on something that would happen to enable me to have the money needed to restore Bladensfield . . . always in my dreams I would come home with a handsome prince . . . and he and I would make everything right . . . for the family. This is a romantic southern version of inculcating me with the aspiration of catching a rich husband but nothing so crass as this was ever verbalized . . . still I was given this sense of mission and the only possible way of making a lot of money was to be discovered.

"My childhood, while impoverished, was very, very good and I enjoyed it."[2] Reportedly, her mother struggled to raise her family on less than $20 per week.

To better understand Aldridge, one needs to acknowledge the supreme importance of the mysterious allure of the family mansion at Bladensfield. It mattered much to a young girl as this is where she grew up having the ambitions and dreams to return there one day to make it better. As a woman, it meant the chance to relive her memories tied intrinsically to the mansion as well as to be in the position to restore and preserve Bladensfield as the family's most precious heirloom.

In Evelyn S. Ward's *The Children of Bladensfield*, Aldridge's letters are quoted by her author/cousin Peter Matthiessen. Ward's book is maiden aunt Evie's memoir of life as a child at Bladensfield during the Civil War. Aldridge: "Many of Cousin Betty's maternity outfits ended up as my regular clothing. Once when Aunt Fonnie heard me inquire why these dresses had such peculiar extendable waistlines, this expression of what she termed 'lewd

---

2 Interview by Boyd Magers and Bobby Copeland, Serial Report: Chapter Forty-Six: "The Perils of Kay Aldridge," westernclippings.com.

curiosity' convinced her anew that I was a 'lascivious and licentious child with a definitely common streak.' She was wont to walk around the dining table and on general principles stop at my chair to give me a thump on my head . . . just in case.

"Once she detected that I rouged my cheeks and, therefore proceeded to 'box my jaws.' To this day I avoid any sort of physical fight encounter but that morning I gave Aunt Fonnie a now-famous uppercut. Incidentally, the source of my rouge was the tiny first-born oak leaves that are such a delicious shade of red. Aunt Evie had told me about this trick of the belles of the day. She also told me that her Mama used to use pokeberries crushed juicy and placed in a hollowed-out pumpkin as a source of dye for their homespun clothes during the Civil War.

"Another idea I enjoyed was that of wrapping a coiled switch of hair around a rag and then (after covering it for protection) burying it in a pan of dough and cooking it a while so that the moist heat would produce one of those bean-catching neck coils that girls used to attach to their chignons. I was always frantic to have curly hair, and went so far as to eat out of the garbage in the hope of getting typhoid fever and having my straight hair fall out entirely and a new crop come in curling. Aunt Evie said that this happened to someone she knew after typhoid fever, and so I had high hopes,

"It always strikes sister and me that our mother and aunts, and a very few other of the era's Virginia 'gentlewomen,' personified the profoundest meaning of that word. They were totally incapable of coarseness of any description. Isn't it amazing that in that old house back in the woods and without money, plumbing, heat, radio or phone, the aunts and mother somehow conveyed a sense of confidence in the unassailability of our social position. There was never any posturing or affectation in their attitude, just a consciousness of not dropping standards; that we children must not ever behave in such a way that we would be a disappointment to our ancestors or hurt those who were nurturing us.

"In my own case, modeling had its common aspects, so did Hollywood, and certainly getting myself extricated from my first marriage was a sordid experience, but somehow through it all I have felt at the core uncontaminated because of what I was given by my mother, the aunts, and the total ambiance of Bladensfield."

The home in Virginia is a place that always stayed close to Aldridge's heart. Later on when she was a busy model/actress the press coverage seemed to often detail her goal of improving the family's ancestral home.

"Bladensfield" had been built around 1690. For Aldridge, the more than 200-year old, 575-acre plantation in Lyells, Virginia proudly stood as one of the oldest frame homes still standing in the state. Despite its allure to Aldridge, a critic Kyle Crichton (*Collier's*, October 24, 1942) called it simply "a 24-room wreck with no lights or plumbing but plenty of atmosphere and land."

The property eventually got added to the Virginia Historic Landmarks Commission. It probably got its name to honor Thomas Bladen, Governor of Maryland from 1742 to 1747. Aldridge's ancestor, the Reverend William Norvell Ward, known primarily as "Norvell," acquired the property in 1847, which he used to run a female academy there.

Matthiessen noted that the many eventual improvements made to Bladensfield; including telephone, heater in the dining room, a downstairs bathroom toilet, and the home's outside painted white, did not satisfy Aldridge.

Aldridge wrote to Matthiessen: "Sadly you are too late to talk with three very remarkable women (Aunts Lucy, Evie and Fonnie) who dominated my mother and Uncle William's lives and then took us on . . . all five father-less Aldridges when 'Poor dear Cornelia' was widowed. It was they who gave the place its fascination for me and I miss terribly their determination that Bladensfield should remain authentic even if shabby and rundown. For instance, the patina that had over the several hundred years given the old clapboard its silvery mossy tones has all been replaced and painted, thus revealing the lack of architectural design of the original house, plus the off-balance addition put on by my great-grandfather – your great-great, I believe.

"Just as too much make-up in old age reveals and distorts more than it enhances, so it is with renovations. And even the very necessary steps that have been taken to heat the old house and provide plumbing have for me greatly reduced its charm and challenge. In my childhood, all furniture that was common or 'tacky' was relegated to the attic. Everything was very uncomfortable and inconvenient and the gaping holes in the plaster over our beds created in me a lifetime fear of ghosts and darkness...

"I wonder if you have noticed how much Virginia boxwood smells like a cat pan...well, Bladensfield was redolent with both sources of this peculiar fragrance, for in my day the whole place was overrun with cats. My older brother John used to provoke the greatest nostalgia for the old place by reminding me how the old cushions on the hall sofas (those converted rifle-box resting places) now used as hard benches, were delightful places to lie and enjoy the summer breezes which brought out the pungent smells of the old cushions. Perhaps the nose remembers best of all."

Aldridge's motivation seemed to always hark back to raising money to restore and modernize the mansion. However, she soon realized that the priorities and material demands of World War II seemed to put a damper on construction throughout the country.

Later on, after tasting success as a model and Hollywood actress, Aldridge spoke of how hand-me-downs were the norm until she was 14. She had to work on the farm for 5 cents an hour picking tomatoes and digging buttercups. She admitted: "It wasn't all fun" (*Washington Post*, hereinafter referred to as *WP*, January 28, 1941).

Carey: "When K.A. is 10 years old, it is determined that she should attend a real school. Boarding with a network of relatives, she is sent first to a public elementary school in Newport News, Virginia."

Aldridge stayed with an aunt and uncle for three years when she attended grade school at Stonewall Jackson School in Newport News, Virginia. She lived with Mr. and Mrs. William Randolph Ward at 58th Street and Virginia Avenue. William Ward was her mother's only brother. There she had life-long friends, such as classmate Elsie West. The latter would be responsible for making one of the two scrapbooks that were seen by Aldridge's friends and other invitees to her homes.

Next she went to a public school in Westminster, Maryland for a year. Again she lived with her relatives. Then with the financial help from an uncle, she transferred to board at St. Mary's Female Seminary in St. Mary's City, Maryland.

There, at the seminary, she won letters in track, besides being voted the prettiest girl in the school. She was selected as Apple Blossom Princess of Winchester, Virginia.

Some eighty-years later the St. Mary's website is still proud of their famous graduate. The site notes: "Then existing as both a high school and two-year junior college, Katherine Grattan Aldridge entered St. Mary's in the Fall of 1931 as a Sophomore after attending one year of high school in Westminster, Maryland. . . . Kay was from an artistic family as Cornelia C. Aldridge, Kay's mother, notes that she is an art teacher and artist.

"While attending St. Mary's Kay Aldridge had an opportunity to act in plays, and the playbill from the January, 1933 performance of 'Sound the Horn,' preserved in the St. Mary's College of Maryland Archive, lists Katherine Aldridge as playing the part of Diane Webster, niece of 'self-made millionaire' Van Dyke. At this time there were only a small handful of men who attended classes at St. Mary's Female Seminary (the men did not live on campus), so the male parts were also played by women.

". . . Katherine Aldridge was also a member of the *Delta Phi Epsilon* sorority and played for the St. Mary's basketball team. . . ."

With clothes supplied by her school friends, Aldridge first received publicity on April 16, 1934 when she was pictured in "Attendants at the Court of Queen Shenandoah," a *Washington Post* article. As the forthcoming May Apple Blossom Festival to be held at Winchester, Virginia, the newspaper depicted: "Miss Katherine Aldridge, daughter of Mrs. John Aldridge, of Lyells, Va. Representing St. Mary's Female Seminary, St. Mary's City, Maryland. . ."

Two months later, on June 8, *WP* offered a photograph depicting the Tercentenary celebration at the Trinity Episcopal Church in St. Mary's City in Maryland. "Katherine Aldridge [among] . . . more than 1,000 Episcopal clergy and laymen celebrated the Tercentenary of the founding of Maryland and establishment of the Episcopal church in the State."

St. Mary's website explained: "Aldridge was a member of the special graduating class of 1934, which was also the Tercentenary, or 300-year anniversary, of the 1634 arrival of the *Ark and the Dove* and the settlement of the St. Mary's City colony in the New World. To mark the occasion, the class of St. Mary's Female Seminary put on an elaborate graduation ceremony. In this ceremony, Kay Gratton had the role of describing the school's function as a 'living monument' to the ideals of religious toleration that were espoused by Lord Calvert and the original colonists."

In 1933 Aldridge took her first job at age 16 as a secretary at what one source called the Federal Land Bank in Baltimore. Carey offered two other company names. Various amounts have been reported, but Carey said her mother's top pay had been $17.50 during the depths of The Great Depression.

Carey recounted how her mother, just an ordinary teen secretary, got to achieve her first professional shoot as a model, and pursue a career she never planned or even considered. Carey: "In 1935, K.A. breaks her hip in a horseback riding accident. Her photo is up on the front page of the *Baltimore News'* local section. An older distant cousin living in Baltimore, Daniel Delaney Fitzhugh Yellut, clips the photo out of *The News* and carries it folded in his breast pocket – next to his heart – at all times."

The article appeared in the Monday, March 25, 1935 issue. The picture clip, titled "Thrown by a Horse," showed a close-up of the appealingly photogenic Aldridge. Underneath the photo, the description read: "Miss Katherine E. Aldridge (above) eighteen, 2210 North Calvert Avenue, is in the University Hospital with injuries received when she was thrown from a horse against a tree near McDonogh School stables. Miss Aldridge, a niece of the late Dr. Henry Fitzhugh, came here recently from Lyells, Virginia." Actually, the article misstated her age, as she would turn 18 several months later.

Aldridge explained: "The first break in my career was a break in more senses than one. While working as a stenographer in Baltimore, I fell from a horse and broke my hip. Somehow – probably to fill up space – the story got into the papers. They printed the only available picture – a glamorous one of me in a floppy hat when I was Apple Blossom Queen of Winchester, Virginia."

Here Aldridge stands corrected as her memory of being pictured wearing a hat is not accurate.

Carey continued: "Daniel has prize-winning chickens, which he enters in a poultry show in New York's Madison Square Garden. While on the train to New York with his chickens, Daniel reads an article in *Esquire* magazine on John Robert Powers and the new profession of modeling agent. The fact (stated in the article) that the Powers Agency 'de-emphasizes sex' reassures Daniel that K.A.'s virtue would not be compromised if she should get into the modeling profession."

The article, "Broker in Beauts" by Amram Scheinfeld, appeared in the January 1936 magazine. The subtitle said: "The nation's nifties storm his office doors, but John Powers says he never was a ladies' man."

Carey continued: "As Daniel has no appointment, he is ignored by the secretaries. Undaunted, he sits in the waiting room. On his way to lunch, John Robert Powers, who is himself from a farm, sees Daniel and invites him into his office. Daniel takes out the newspaper clipping containing the photo of K.A. out of his breast pocket and shows it to Powers. Powers tells Daniel to tell his cousin Katharine to see him the next time she will be in New York City.

"K.A., who has never been to New York City, manages to get herself invited to a dance at West Point, north of New York City. Even though K.A. is no longer living with her mother, K.A.'s mother will not allow K.A., who is 18, to go to West Point without her 22-year-old sister, Clelia, along as chaperone. K.A. manages to get a date for Clelia as well.

"On their return South from West Point, K.A. persuades her sister to get off the train with her in New York City and go to Powers Agency. As they have no appointment, they are ignored. They sit in the waiting room. Powers sees them on his way to lunch. He invites them into his office.

"Powers asks the sisters why they need money. K.A. does most of the talking, and it is about her widowed mother and her great-aunts and Bladensfield, which has no electricity or indoor plumbing. Within minutes (according to K.A.) Powers is in tears.

"Clelia, who is equally attractive, does have a 'good' job (or at least a better job than K.A.) in Washington, D.C. She also has a fiancé. Powers encourages Clelia to return to Washington. Powers sends K.A. to her first professional shoot that day."

One account by Aldridge in Cue, July 3, 1943, referred to her distant cousin as her uncle. Also, Aldridge referred to her uncle and John Robert Powers: "He'd read about him in an article, 'Merchant of Beauty,' Mr. Powers said sure, he'd be glad to see me, and my uncle took that as a sign I'd have a model's career. I wasn't so sure. My mother painted and to me model meant nude, but uncle thought they could use me for hair tonic ads."

Carey: "Daniel Delaney Fitzhugh Yellut was a cousin, not an uncle. A good deal older than K.A., so sometimes older cousins are referred to, casually, as 'uncles' but he was a cousin—a distant cousin. Families were more numerous generations ago, hence K.A. had many distant cousins."

When she stopped off in New York, a cautious Aldridge: "Stayed at the Martha Washington because I'd heard it was safe and I knew this was a wicked town where men stick needles in you and then denude you of respectability. No one so much as pinched me" (Cue, July 3, 1943).

To one reporter she said: "I went to see him [Powers] with pigtails hanging down my back, in a cheap little dress, flat heels and a huge hat—all wrong for me."

Aldridge told another reporter a different version: "I got all dressed up and went to the Powers' office. The longer I waited, the scareder I got. Those girls! I could see I was corny. Mr. Powers came out of his office, gave one one look and said, 'Your face is perfectly balanced but those pigtails will have to come off.' I had a massive bun and hairpins like croquet wickets.

"That's how it started. The day my hair was cut was awful. Even the hairdresser cried and had to have a bromo. I look like a different girl in every shot. Gussied up I do the fashion work, but I haven't really the right nauseated look" (Cue, July 3, 1943).

Irene Thirer quoted Aldridge's memory of Powers' request: "I was flabbergasted. My thigh-long tresses were the pride of Bladensfield – and probably the reason why they used my photo in that Maryland local paper. I pictured myself posing for hair restorer ads and such.

"I wept – as I did what Mr. Powers suggested. But I guess he was right. Within a few months I was earning sixty dollars a day in cold cash at modeling. Then came the movies" (*New York Post*, June 19, 1943).

It all started in April of 1936.

Carey: "K.A.'s first professional photo, taken the same day she shows up at the Powers Agency. . . . The photo appears in *Vogue*. K.A. starts making 10 dollars an hour. She is paid immediately after each job. 'Some days my pockets would bulge with 80 dollars in cash and checks,' K.A. writes. K.A. never returns to Baltimore.

"The fact that K.A.'s first photo lands in *Vogue* is one of a number of significant facts preternaturally un-reticent K.A. never shared with her children. I had seen the largest photo; it had been explained to me by K.A. that it was her first professional photo, taken the first day, etc.; what I had not seen, until I went into the [scrapbook] boxes, was the article in which the photo appeared. I had to piece the article together and examine the other sides of the pages to understand the article was in *Vogue*."

She posed for the *Vogue* article entitled, "The Symptoms and Cures of a Girl with Nerves." Besides a large profile shot with her hair up, Aldridge is shown in various nervous activities, such as covering her ears from noises, chewing her pencil, wringing her hands, twitching her eyes, counting sheep in bed, clutching taxi straps, legs poised to run (not walk), and chain smoking.

One of the earliest clippings saved in Aldridge's scrapbook (date and publication unknown) had been written shortly after the start of her modeling career. "From Stenographer's Job to Become Photo Model" reported: "Already she has been 'shot' for autumn covers of two magazines and two others will use pictures of her. A major tobacco company had her photographed for a series of cigarette ads. She doesn't smoke, by the way, although she will often be depicted inhaling nonchalantly during coming months. She had to cut her hair for the latter assignment.

"The whole series of episodes has left the young lady somewhat stunned but quite thrilled. She never believed she'd make so much money, she says, and make it so easily. The prospect of Hollywood, which lures many New York models, hasn't worried her a bit. She is still the modest quietly-humorous girl, according to friends that her former class-mates of the sixth grade at [Stonewall] Jackson School knew. Her classmates remember her as a tall quiet girl, rather pretty and possessing a keen sense of humor." Carey: "Her tall frame lends itself to elegance. 5'8" is considered very tall for a girl – in 1936."

Some of her earliest advertising poses are designed to promote the sale of a product that nowadays is known to be unhealthy. Carey: "This is how K.A. starts advertising cigarettes in 1936: as a fresh-faced graduate. As K.A. is under 21, K.A.'s mother has to sign a release to allow K.A. to appear in cigarette ads. One way cigarettes are promoted is to state that they are good for health; another way is to show high society smokes. K.A. is the Chesterfield girl." Among the other brands she promotes are Lucky Strike, Old Gold, and Raleigh. The latter is the last brand she did advertising for in 1944.

Carey: "As K.A. starts modeling in April of 1936, she is just in line for the 'graduate' theme in advertising. K.A. never attends college, but she looks the part."

A *New York Sun* photo spread on June 5, 1936, entitled "All in a Summer's Day – The College Girl Chooses Her Commencement Clothes," shows and describes Aldridge wearing five different outfits, with prices offered.

Carey: "K.A. is also just in time for Kodachrome, a new, more vivid and more durable form of color film . . . . She is also just in time for the introduction of Cellophane." The latter ad with the banner "How To Glorify Christmas Gifts" shows Aldridge and a man both beaming as they are both holding a gift ready to exchange.

In short, Aldridge is suddenly and readily seen in advertising for all types of products.

John Ferris, AP staff writer, on Aldridge: "They call her Woodsy, because she thinks she looks better photographed as an out-of-doors girl. Described as radiant, needs no makeup, been offered two movie contracts" (*Baltimore Evening Sun*, August 31, 1946).

November 29, 1936: "Today she receives nearly $100 a week 'sitting' for magazine covers, cigarette ads, fashion plates, and other commercial photographs. That, she writes a friend of hers in *Newport News*, is more than she ever hoped to make.

"According to the Associated Press, Miss Aldridge is considered by photographers as a 'radiant' type of girl, who needs no makeup. She often poses for out-of-door pictures, because of her natural beauty and her appearance of vital health" (*Newport News*, "Onetime Local Girl: New Model, Gets Movie Bids").

Carey: "K.A.'s first name and/or last name will be misspelled by the press more often than not . . . . . More articles appear, putting a name to the face. Virginia newspapers are especially excited . . . . Maryland papers say K.A. is from Maryland, Virginia papers say K.A. is from Virginia . . . ."

The headlines say it all: "Maryland Beauty Boomed for Starring Role in *Gone With the Wind*," and "Virginia's Katherine Aldridge Returns Victorious from Films."

In "Virginia Movie Queen's Visit Has Richmond County Ga-Ga" (date and publication unknown), the reporter noted: "Her recent visit to her Richmond County home was almost a continuous ovation. From miles around the young people came to see her . . . . Opinion in the neighborhood is that if the movie will cast Katherine in roles in her own personality, she will grow to be one of the most popular of screen stars."

What did happen in her disappointing movie career would make this opinion prescient and significant. Yes, indeed, if only those in charge running the Hollywood studios would have paid heed to such common-sense opinion and cast Aldridge correctly . . .

Chapter Two:
America's Cover Girl and Starlet

"I am thrilled and frightened. I feel that the course of my life is changing and am a scared little girl tonight."
- *Kay Aldridge diary entry,*
Monday, March 1, 1937

Sometimes the best things in life seem to come by accident. However, there are few accidents. The pivotal point in Aldridge's early life came when in her teens she had an accidental injury. That seeming accident forever changed her life, and set her on a path to great success, a way to achieve her dream of being discovered and become wealthy. This led to a financially rewarding career which lasted for just nine years. Those nine years are enviable by anyone's standards, and many would be blessed for life if they could have lived just one year in the limelight as did Aldridge.

Her career led Aldridge to realize her ultimate dream—to be discovered by someone who would become her husband and provide her with a family. As will become evident that though her marriage would not last long, it did help sustain her own success with certain financial freedom and security.

Hollywood's call came rather simply. Carey: ". . . K.A. signs a contract to appear in the film *Vogues of 1938*. The film features a line-up of beautiful girls – all Powers Agency models."

Aldridge writes in her Monday, March 1, 1937 entry of her diary: "Slept till about nine. . . Signed my contract with Walter Wanger at 4:30 p.m. A momentous decision in my young life! Wired mother and wrote Elia and Cousin Fitz. . . Phoned Ed. I am thrilled and frightened. I feel that the course of my life is changing and am a scared little girl tonight."

Almost three years after being pictured as a representative from her school, Aldridge received newspaper mention as a favorite among commercial photographers in a photo piece entitled "11 Most Photographed Models Visit Chicago." Aldridge is named among "... America's most photographed models, eleven girls en route from New York to Hollywood stopped for a few hours yesterday at the Hotel Sherman. They will appear in *Vogues of 1938*" (*Chicago Daily Tribune*, hereinafter referred to as *CDT*, March 12, 1937).

In that time span, Aldridge became elevated from local news bit to be the most photographed model, and then to appear in a feature-length movie.

In the article "Train Hustles for Hollywood With a Private Car Full of Pulchritude": "The most beautiful gals in the world left Grand Central today for Hollywood . . . . All of the models are going to get famous in Wanger's *Vogues of 1938*" (Publication Unknown, by Arthur "Bugs" Baer, March 16, 1937). Aldridge is one of the Powers models chaperoned by press agent Monte Prosser.

Her entrance into films came about as an inevitable career progression related to her modeling career. Aldridge: "It was really through my modeling. In 1937, I was chosen as one of the ten most photographed girls in the world. Some of the girls were selected to go to Hollywood to appear in the film *Vogues of 1938* (1937 U.A.). That was my first film."

Aldridge could be proud to be named among the few picked out of so many applicants. The press explained: "The prize mannequins were chosen from an army of applicants in a nation-wide search. More than 1,000,000 photographs were looked at, 6000 girls interviewed and 500 given screen tests to determine the twelve final selections."

The April 1937 issue of *Ladies Home Journal* featured Aldridge on the first of two covers by famed American photographer Edward Steichen.

The headline "Blackened Optic Explained by Girl," by Read Kendall, *Los Angeles Times* (hereinafter referred to as *LAT*), June 4, 1937, gave audiences the explanation for Aldridge's recent disturbing appearance: "The mystery of the black eye and swollen jaw sported for several days by Katharine Aldridge, one of the models in *Vogues of 1938*, was explained by her yesterday. As a matter of fact, the girl had her entire explanation printed on paper which she handed out to everybody who asked her. A refractory wisdom tooth, so goes her story, is entirely responsible. While injecting a pain deadener the dentist accidentally struck a tiny blood vessel which caused the blackening."

In reference to the models in *Vogues of 1938*, there happened to be an optimistic view that the studio had regarding Aldridge. "The company feels that Katharine Aldridge particularly is a definite find, with star possibilities. She is the Virginia horsewoman, old-family type, and a curious coincidence is that she actually comes from an old Virginia family and can ride a horse" (B.R. Chrisler, *NYT*, June 27, 1937).

Hal Horne, production head for Walter Wanger said *Vogues of 1938* "represents a new approach to color in films, with neutral sets correctly rendered instead of blinding rainbow combinations that detract from the people and incidents of the story. A new perfection of make-up is another factor – a Max Factor, to be exact – a facial impasto so good, so natural that ladies may now walk directly from before the cameras into the street without altering an eyelash. The secret seems to be lighter shades in complexions, with pale lipstick and the merest soupcon of penciling for eyebrows" (B.R. Chrisler, *NYT*, June 27, 1937).

A journalist asked, "Is there something familiar about the features of these attractive young women? There should be – for they are among the most photographed girls in the world. Their photographs have been used to advertise soap, cigarettes, automobiles, dresses, hats – almost everything. Now they are appearing in the movies playing in Walter Wanger's *Vogues of 1938*, which will be shown in Detroit soon. . . ." Pictured were Ruth Martin, Dorothy Day, Ida Vollmer, Libby (Elizabeth) Harban, Olive Cawley, Frances Joyce, and Katharine Aldridge (*Detroit News*, August 8, 1937).

CDT, August 15, 1937, describes the highly paid models under contract to Wanger: "Katharine Aldridge spends most of her salary in the upkeep of her family estate in Virginia, known as Bladensfield. It is near Warsaw on the Northern Neck. She is only 19 and is said to possess the perfect oval face. . . . [Wanger] instituted a talent school for them under the direction of Harold Clurman of the noted New York Group theater. A special classroom has been put on the set and the girls are drilled in the rudiments of acting and screen technique."

Even when entertainment news was about other actresses, Aldridge managed to be mentioned glowingly among others in *NYT*, September 15, 1937: "a long line of 'Miss Americans' – a list which includes the most beautifully gracious of modern young girls: . . . Katharine Aldridge . . . among others."

Aldridge was pictured in "Artists and Models," *LAT*, September 29, 1937: "Katherine Aldridge, left and Ida Vollmar, right, models in cast of *Vogues of 1938*, discuss styles in Technicolor film which opens today . . ."

On September 17, 1937, Aldridge's first movie, *Vogues of 1938*, hit the theaters through United Artists with Aldridge not significant enough to get billed in the credits. Also on that same day: "Miss Katharine Aldridge, a former employee of the F.C.A. of Baltimore, is rumored to be a candidate for the role of Scarlet O'Hara in the motion picture version of *Gone With the Wind*. She left the F.C.A. to become a model in New York and already has had a role in one movie, *Vogues of 1938*" ("The Federal Diary," Reg. U.S. Patent Office).

It has been said that David O. Selznick saw her *Life* cover and sent a wire asking her to try out for the part – for both Scarlett and Melanie. Years later, Aldridge told Magers/Copeland how she got the chance to try-out for the hotly desired role of Scarlet. Aldridge: "Yes, David Selznick saw my picture on the cover of a magazine and wanted to test me for the part. Unfortunately for me, I didn't get it. But then I was signed by 20th."

Carey: "K.A.'s appearance in *Vogues of 1938* is used to sell everything from water heaters to furs. . . . K.A. is also just in time for the wide use of Technicolor in feature-length films. *Vogues of 1938* is the first film to show scenes of New York City in Technicolor."

By this time, Aldridge began receiving frequent press attention as regards to modeling. *LAT*, October 17, 1937 ("Seeing Favorite Fur Fashions," Isabel Sheldon), Aldridge is pictured: "Sleek Formality evolves by combining two luxury furs. Above a wrap-round skirt section of black broadtail, Labrador mink carries the slim lines on to the jacket-like upper part of the coat. There is further elegance in the square muff of mink. Worn by Katherine Aldridge. Designed in a local shop."

On December 24, 1937, Aldridge would appear in another movie – again unbilled. She got the offer from MGM to do this one as soon as she finished *Vogues of 1938*. Carey: "While in Hollywood, K.A. appears in a second film, *Rosalie*, starring Nelson Eddy and Jeanette McDonald."

"I do hope," Katharine stammered, "that when *Rosalie* comes to Virginia my family won't be able to tell me from the other girls in the court scene. I don't think they'd approve of this costume I have on" (clip from K.A.'s scrapbook, publication and date unknown).

In an interview with Roy Kinnard for *Films in Review* (Vol. 45, Issue 9/10, Sept/Oct 1994), the Northern Neck beauty noted: "In my modeling work, I appeared in *Life* magazine several times, and in *Redbook* and *Ladies' Home Journal*. I knew all the great photographers of that day, that's how I was discovered."

The September 5, 1938 issue of *Life* had 21-year old Katharine Aldridge on the cover. The description to *Life*'s cover noted: "The demure brunette framed on a background of quilted white taffeta on this week's cover is 21-year old Katharine Aldridge of Bladensfield, Virginia. She is wearing one of the romantic new evening dresses with hoops described on page 42. This picture was taken while Miss Aldridge lay on the floor completely surrounded by the huge circle of her wide skirt. Miss Aldridge's ambition is to be a female Noel Coward, i.e., write and act her own plays. She has written several, but so far none has been produced."

The next issue of *Life* offered a letter written by Aldridge. It read:

"Sirs:

Inasmuch as you chose to describe me as a 'demure brunette ... [whose] ambition is to be a female 'Noel Coward,' I feel in duty-bound to submit to you an outline of the following play:

Act I: *Life* puts Katharine Aldridge on its cover.

Act II: Things begin to happen. She receives: a). four telegrams from four motion-picture companies asking her to call on their New York representatives; b). a dozen or so letters from various New York cleaners assuring her that 'no cleaner is too good' to do justice to the dress she wore on the cover of *Life*; c). assorted invitations including from a West Point cadet to attend the Army-Notre Dame football game; d). 25 proposals of marriage including one from a man who states by way of recommendation that he 'loves vegetables, hates meat and cannot abide the Republican party.'

Act III: Katharine Aldridge undergoes a screen test and hopes for the best.

All of the above occurred within five days after the appearance of *Life*. The next five years will be the hardest.
KATHARINE ALDRIDGE
New York, N.Y."

In a scrapbook clip (date and publication unknown) called "The Hollywood Grapevine," Aldridge is pictured with the caption: "Kay Aldridge ... wants to write autobiography when she's old enough." The article noted: "Kay Aldridge, former model now seeking out a movie career: 'When I get old enough, I will write my autobiography. I already have started it. At least I have the first sentence and it's a whopper-dooper: 'My father and mother married beneath themselves.' The trouble is that everybody wants to read what comes after that, and I can't think of anything to top it.' However, she still has 50 years to work on it."

Carey: "I have read one fragment of a play she wrote, based on her experience as a naive in showbiz. It was terrible, and the rejection letters said as much."

Chapter Three:
Hollywood Window Dressing at Fox

"K.A. appears in 11 Fox films, all of them forgettable, except in her home town and in Serbo-Croatia."
Carey Cameron,
"Memoirs of a Southern Belle"

Aldridge's second *Life* cover appears with the March 27, 1939 issue. The magazine had her wearing rainwear and on another page wearing a hooded rain cape.

Life described it as follows: "This is the second time that pretty Katharine Aldridge has been on *Life*'s cover. Last September she modeled a hoopskirt evening dress. Now she appears in rainwear of Pliofilm, Goodyear's transparent waterproof fabric. A Pliofilm cover keeps her handbag dry, 'mitty's' protect her suede gloves from rain spots. Pliofilm umbrella is interesting not only for transforming a dreary necessity into a thing of glamour but also because you can look through it to see where you are going."

Carey: "*Redbook* plans to send K.A. and Georgia Carroll on a photographic trip around the world. It is, however, 1939, and because of world tensions, they only make it as far as Hawaii. They travel through San Francisco on their way to Hawaii and through Los Angeles on the way back to New York."

San Francisco's *Graphic* picture staff observed Aldridge and Carroll as they "perused San Francisco by way of a vacation from it all.... Because she has this kind of smile, plus an elusive quality called verve, Kitty Aldridge has landed a movie contract."

In a magazine spread "*Redbook* Covers Go to Hollywood," Aldridge is pictured with a new Powers model and life-long friend Georgia Carroll meeting the stars; namely, Hedy Lamarr, Mickey Rooney, Bette Davis, Spencer Tracy, Ginger Rogers, Robert Taylor, Robert Young, Elsa Maxwell, Richard Greene, and Robert Montgomery.

Redbook: "Once more we present those two indefatigable travelers – Miss Katharine Aldridge and Miss Georgia Carroll, who have carried the *Redbook* as far as Hawaii. This time we find them in Hollywood, of all places, rubbing elbows with the stars."

This hobnobbing with the stars does not matter to Aldridge's family. Carey: "What counts at Bladensfield is the Sears Roebuck catalogue."

In a scrapbook clip (date and publication unknown): "Miss Aldridge was amazingly successful from the first. You've seen her girlish face from the covers of well-known magazines (she's done a lot of work for *Redbook*, especially) and in the most famous advertisements. The folks back home, however, didn't fully appreciate her success until Sears Roebuck catalogue containing her picture was sent to Bladensfield, Miss Aldridge's old home. Then Richmond County knew that the Aldridge girl really had arrived."

The catalogue pictured ads with Aldridge and Carroll modeling together.

Carey: "*Redbook* arranges for K.A. and Georgia [Carroll] to tour Fox studios. Elsa Maxwell (1893 – 1963), gossip columnist, author, songwriter and professional hostess, persuades Fox to put K.A. under contract, so that K.A. can appear in a film that Maxwell has screen-written, *Hotel for Women*. K.A. thus becomes part of 'the studio system,' receiving a regular salary for appearing in Fox films. K.A.'s contract with Fox will last for a year and half."

Apparently Aldridge's first billed appearance came when she connected with her Los Angeles friend Elsa Maxwell, who was best known as everyone's favorite society hostess. The *San Diego Union* explained: "Elsa got busy and Kay got a part in Elsa Maxwell's *Hotel for Women* and a 20th Century-Fox contract. Funny part of it is that Elsa's movie is patterned after the hotel for women in New York City where Kay lived for two years."

Aldridge had stopped off in Hollywood on her way back from the Honolulu promotional trip. Aldridge: ". . . And Elsa Maxwell, whom we knew from New York, threw a party for us, and got us small roles in her picture, *Hotel for Women*. I was a snooty society girl." Unfortunately, that role quickly got Aldridge typecast.

Aldridge's one chance at establishing herself in a more significant role in her first film as the lead actress could not happen because of a dilemma for the enamored director, Gregory Ratoff.

Carey: "Gregory Ratoff assures K.A. that she will have the leading role in *Hotel for Women*. He is, however, asked by his boss, Darryl Zanuck, to screen test a recent discovery, Linda Darnell. Darnell, who is only 16, tests so well that Ratoff is obliged to put Darnell in the leading role and K.A. in the role of the 'Other Woman.' It is a role in which K.A. will be cast in several subsequent films."

Aldridge told Kinnard: "I am from Virginia, where I grew up as a country girl. I could be a glamour girl if I had to, but I'm more amused than I am serious about all this. As I used to say, 'Thank you very much, but I'm not an actress.' I had never thought about being an actress. I'm more literary-minded, really" (*Films in Review*, Vol. 45, Issue 9/10, Sept/Oct 1994).

One of Aldridge's many appearances in product advertising at this time included a national display ad for Camel cigarettes. She appeared with Philco engineer Richard E. Waggener. The caption on one of the panels read: "Photo Just Released, Dick Waggener directing Katharine Aldridge and Shane Kelly. Shane is one of many experts in television who find Camel's just right for steady smoking. Let up – light up a Camel, the cigarette of costlier tobaccos" (*NYT*, March 20, 1939; *WP*, March 22, 1939; *LAT*, March 24, 1939).

Aldridge is pictured in an ad for Rollins Runstop Stockings. There is a comic strip, headlined "When the lights went on . . . Was I embarrassed!" The strip says, "So from now on, I'll always wear Rollins Runstop Stockings. . . Miss Katharine Aldridge, famous fashion model, says: 'I prefer Rollins stockings because their colors are just right for my costume shades and they wear so much better, having the Runstop protection at the garter top. These stockings really do things for your legs' " (*CDT*, March 29, 1939).

On May 16, 1939, *LAT*, columnist Jimmie Fidler mentioned the name of Aldridge for the first time to Los Angeles readers. He told of what bewitched Aldridge for wanting to make movies. The answer she gave to Darryl Zanuck, the head of production at 20th Century-Fox, could not be more unexpected and atypical.

Fidler: "K.A., the New York model recently term-ticketed by 20th Century, is not only one of the most beautiful girls ever brought to film-ville, but one of the most self-possessed and original. Witness her first meeting with Darryl Zanuck. That all-powerful czar of the lot stopped her as she walked to the studio café, talked for a moment and asked her to cite her real ambition in Hollywood.

" 'May I be frank, Mr. Zanuck?' Kay asked. 'Certainly,' the great one teamed. 'Well,' said Miss Aldridge, 'I want to earn enough money to install modern plumbing in our old house in Virginia!' "

Almost a month later, Aldridge received mention in connection with a production. It simply stated that "At Fox, Lynn Bari was added to *Tin Hats* and Kay Aldridge to *Falling Stars*, which today reverted to its original title of *Hollywood Calvacade*" (*NYT*, June 10, 1939). Aldridge got assigned two scenes, which she explains in a June 11, 1939 letter to her mother (found in the Appendix): "I play an actress of the Theda Bara era." However, for whatever reason, she did not appear in the final film.

McCord told of what happened after she got a contract with a big movie studio: ". . . There were some trying moments. Shortly after signing her contract at Fox, the studio production chief, Darryl Zanuck, sent for her.

" 'I was let into his office,' she said, 'and I had to walk a long way toward him. He didn't get up. He just sat there to disquiet me and have me feel the power of him. I had to walk while he looked at my figure and me. I got there,' and he said, 'Sit down, Miss Aldridge.

" 'Everybody tells me how beautiful you are. I saw your screen test, and you are very beautiful. But in your screen test you look kinda cold to me, like a society girl. But the other night I was watching you at this party, and Mr. Ratoff tells me how funny you are, and I watched you animated. You appeal to me very much. You really do. I've never had your type.' He was setting a mood, and I didn't like it at all.

"Drawing up her nerve, Miss Aldridge told the boss that he did not really know how to cast women and that her lady-like type had an appeal of its own. Zanuck then started to make his move. Miss Aldridge jumped up, pointed her nose to the ceiling, and said, 'Mr. Zanuck, I can't imagine that you really do make passes at girls under contract.' She then walked out, but she wasn't fired."

Aldridge next gets press in reference to actress Nancy Kelly: "Her carriage is extraordinarily graceful, her manner most gracious, her conversation sprightly.... Three new girls to win contracts on just these points that have become 'musts' in today's school of winners are Linda Darnell, Brenda Joyce and Kay Aldridge. Serene moderns each and every one of them. Or, as producers put it, 'not too professional in appearance, not too glamorous in a synthetic way.' Anything that may hint of artificiality would have destroyed their chances at box office money" (*CDT*, June 25, 1939).

Along with the other potential candidates for stardom, the columns began to drop her name for any reason whatsoever, just to gain her recognition with the public. For instance, *LAT*, July 16, 1939, "Tatteletale" column reported: "Katharine Aldridge and Maisie Sharp, her roommate at the Hollywood Studio Club, found that their birthdays fell on the same day – last Sunday – so Gregory gave a luncheon in their honor in his Beverly Hills home."

In addition, Aldridge would receive mention in newspaper society columns. In regards to a Cocktail Party honoring Miss Jacqueline de Wit: "Katherine Aldridge present with others, including Mrs. Tay Garnett, Brenda Marshall, Burgess Meredith, etc." (*LAT*, July 23, 1939).

A number of other mentions by the press included the following clippings:

Louella Parsons wrote: ". . . At the Troc [Trocadero] after the *Hotel for Women* preview with Marshall Duffield; Gregory Ratoff, the director, there with pretty Katherine Aldridge, who made her debut in Elsa Maxwell's movie" (*WP*, July 29, 1939).

One of the ads for *Hotel for Women* insisted: "Girls who'll go to your head . . . girls who'll go to your heart! Young. . Smart. . Beautiful. . some dangerous. . some love-starved party girls, some just yearning for a man!" The ad listed all the stars appearing: "Ann Sothern sensation of *Maisie*, James Ellison, Jean Rogers, Lynn Bari, Joyce Compton, Elsa Maxwell, John Halliday, June Gale, Katharine Aldridge, Alan Dinehart, Sidney Blackmer and introducing the new star Linda Darnell" (*LAT*, August 21, 1939).

Another display ad for that movie, August 23, 1939 stated: "A Girl in Every Room . . . and a Man on Every Mind! Girls who'll go to your head . . Girls who'll go your heart. . Office girls in love with their bosses. . Girls on the make for fame. . Girls looking for life in a penthouse. . Girls longing for love in a cottage. and all of them BEAUTIFUL!" Elsa Says: 'Don't ever shoot a man, dears! He's worth more to you alive than dead!' And Elsa who has given a million parties throws her biggest party of fun in *Hotel for Women*."

Zanuck received press credit for discovering Aldridge: "Elsa Maxwell's *Hotel for Women*, which comes to the Roxy Theatre Friday, introduces two new Darryl F. Zanuck discoveries in featured roles. Those are Linda Darnell, acclaimed by preview critics as the discovery of the year, and Katharine Aldridge, who was once America's most photographed model" (*Wall Street Journal*, August 23, 1939).

Although *Hotel for Women* stands as Aldridge's first official appearance, she did not get any attention in the reviews. *NYT*, August 26, 1939, the reviewer mentions Ann Sothern, Linda Darnell, and Elsa Maxwell. In *LAT*, September 1, 1939, Aldridge is mentioned as the ninth name in the cast. The film is described: "Set in a smart Manhattan hostelry, exclusively for the fair sex and inhabited by glamorous models and showgirls, *Hotel for Women* is a gay story of a world of girls on their own."

Carey: "As the film receives poor reviews, there is a lot of promotion. There are also publicity tours." For instance, Aldridge made in-person appearances at theaters.

Also, Carey recalled her mother telling her: "I was photographed by Steichen once." Carey (acknowledging Steichen is now regarded as a master of 20th century photographer): "You were? When? Where? For what?"

Aldridge: "I can't remember."

Carey: "It was a mentioning, followed by a failure to recollect details, which spoke—and speaks—to many things, lack of memory not being one of them. It spoke to the cultural isolation of her upbringing, which hampered her ability to grasp the significance of what was happening to her; it speaks to the cumulative process through which the reputation of an artist such as Steichen ... is established; it spoke to K.A.'s being barely into her 20s.

"It turns out K.A. was on 2 covers by Steichen. [The second one], *Ladies Home Journal* [June 1941] cover was shot in Hawaii."

In *LAT*, September 1, 1939, Aldridge is mentioned in reference to 20th Century-Fox: "The same studio took up options on Katherine Aldridge and Lynn Bari."

After finishing her first two films for Fox, and with the second to be released later that month, *NYT*, September 2, 1939, reported: "Fox has extended the contracts of Lynn Bari and Katherine Aldridge."

Jimmie Fidler reported Aldridge's speeding off to the studio on September 9, 1939. Fidler (*LAT*): "And here's the prize chuckle of the day: K.A., the ex-model who is doing so well at 20th Century-Fox, was overhauled by a speed cop this morning on her way to the studio. 'You know,' he said, gallantly after appraising her carefully, 'You are not only the most beautiful lady I've ever stopped, but unlike most real beauties you appear to be very intelligent.' Kay sensed a reprieve and smiled her sweetest. 'In fact,' the cop continued with a smile as beautiful as her own, 'you look so intelligent that you're surely understand why I have to give you a ticket for doing forty-five in a twenty-mile zone.' "

Carey: "Gregory Ratoff (1897-1960), the director of *Hotel for Women*, who is also the director of such notable films as Intermezzo and an actor himself, writes a letter to K.A.'s mother, who is concerned about K.A.'s decision to remain in Hollywood. His reference to war breaking out is to war breaking out in Europe."

The complete letter with spelling errors reads:

"September 10, 1939
Dear Mrs. Aldridge:
   Thank you for your letter. It came to me when I was taking my first vacation in the last five years. I tried for five years to get away for at least a few weeks but it could just never materialize. As I was on my vacation I did not want to answer your letter until I got back to Hollywood; now that I am back the war has broken out and with it our studio and the entire industry is facing as many drastic problems and changes that

really before this moment I could not get myself together to write you a few lines.

I am sure your daughter Katharine has on many occasions mentioned me to you and probably in her own way has given you quite a vivid characterization of her first director. I myself say that Katharine is quite an historical figure in my life as she is the first young girl who really has attracted me. I am in this country seventeen years; as a matter of fact on the 23rd of this month it will be exactly seventeen years since I first saw the skyscrapers of New York. I came here with my wife whom I married about a year and a half before. Dispite the fact that all these seventeen years I have spent working in the theatre mostly in musicals and in pictures and have seen thousands of beautiful young girls. I passed by them as I would the windows of some fifth avenue shops, knowing that they are very beautiful and attractive but I was just not interested. Then came the dawn!

My old friend, Voldemar Vetleguin, introduced me to your Katharine and I finally met my Waterloo. I fell desperately in love with her but found myself in the army of other unfortunates who met her and fell for her. The best thing about my attitude and relationship with Katharine is that I also happen to like her very much as a person. I think that she is without doubt the finest and nicest young lady I have ever met and her qualities and virtues are equal to her physical beauty. I will flatter myself by saying that it is very fortunate for Katharine to have met me as in my own field I will be as devoted and faithful to her as my friend Vetleguin was in New York. I perdict for Katharine a very big future in this town and in this industry. She may not get there as rapidly as for instance Linda Darnell, but there isn't a doubt in my mind that within a year or two Katharine will be playing very important roles and will be a name in this industry. I want you to believe me dear Mrs. Aldridge, that I am not saying all this to you just to make you happy and encouraged for when it comes to my business I am brutally and mercilessly frank and in this regard I could just as frankly have told you that Katharine hadn't a chance. I am sure she will make the name of Aldridge known to the motion picture fans all of the world.

Katharine is blessed with the faculty of captivating people the moment they see her. There were many who did not understand at first that she was not just a New York model out here to get herself a rich husband. These people today are all very fond of her and know that she is a simple sweet girl who has every quality you would wish her to possess.

I want you to know that as long as Katharine is here I will always remain her faithful and devoted friend and if, God forbid, anything should ever happen to her I will always be there to take care of her as I would my own sister.

I am hoping to hear from you often and I may accept Katharine's invitation to come and spend a few days with you at Christmas. My kindest regards and best wishes,

Sincerely,

(signed) Gregory Ratoff"

Undoubtedly, Ratoff's prediction for Aldridge's future fame was overstated.

Nevertheless, the publicity machine kept churning Aldridge's name around.

LAT, September 15, 1939: Katharine Aldridge had been among the many attendees to see the Hollywood premiere of *The Rains Came* at the Chinese Theater.

A product promotion disguised as a feature pictured Aldridge showing her nails in Smart Set Beauty and Fashions. It read: "Katharine Aldridge (right), 20th Century Fox actress, of infectious smile and wholesome beauty, wears little brass gadgets on her fingers after the polish has been applied, and then goes about the job of reading a magazine, tucking in a curl, or anything else she chooses without danger of marring the polish on her pretty and freshly manicured nails. We think this is a clever idea and we're going to try it the very next manicure" (*Los Angeles Examiner,* September 16, 1939).

With her 6th appearance in *Redbook* (September 1939), the magazine noted: "Some call her 'Kitty,' some 'Kay,' some 'Katy,' but she has never received a fan letter that addressed her as 'Miss Aldridge.' There is something about her which makes her admirers feel as if they known her for years and years. She thinks it's because she's 'so neighborly.' We think it's because she possesses what is known to Emily Post as 'charm.'... Miss Aldridge is known for her bright sayings as she is for her radiant personality. She describes herself as wise fox, angel, and screwball."

Aldridge got pictured in *WP*, September 17, 1939, as "the ultra-feminine type in a cocktail suit of silver trimmed, gray broadcloth" (Marshall Adams, "Renaissance in Detailing Strictly Tailored Suits").

More publicity for *Hotel for Women* came as Hollywood designer Gwen Wakeling explained the tailored suits she designed for the film: "... Not every woman, even a screen star, can exploit the lines of a rigidly man-tailored suit to real advantage. Some women are too angular, some too plump. Certain very feminine stars haven't even the desire to look like a perfectly appointed tailor's dummy. They have insisted upon and gotten more feminine, more flattering, ladylike tailleurs... [Wakeling] had to take the different but uniformly feminine dispositions of Lynn Bari, K.A., and Ann Sothern into consideration" (*WP*, September 17, 1939.) *Here I Am a Stranger*, her 4th film (the second of eleven movies for 20th Century-Fox), had its release on September 19, 1939.

Almost two weeks later, Jimmie Fidler, *LAT*, September 28, 1939, questioned her simple choice in clothing: "Wonder if the psychologists can explain why K.A., America's most famous model invariably wears simple little cotton dresses...."

Not surprisingly, the display ad for *Here I Am A Stranger*, *LAT*, October 4, 1939, did not mention Aldridge: "Now He's A Star! In the story read by Millions, as a youth facing a father he has never known ... and a girl as new to love as he himself! Richard Green, Richard Dix, Brenda Joyce the sensational discovery of *The Rains Came*."

However, while it was in production a press report on May 19, 1939 claimed: "Katherine Aldridge will have a major supporting role in *Here I Am A Stranger*, in which Richard Greene and Nancy Kelly are to be co-starred." Of course, this changed as Kelly was replaced with Brenda Joyce.

LAT, October 6, 1939, mentioned Aldridge: "Twosomes of prominence included ... Katherine Aldridge and Gregory Ratoff."

The next picture that Aldridge got press coverage in the major papers would be her 6th film that was in production. *NYT*, November 13, 1939: "Marjorie Weaver and Kay Aldridge will be featured in *Shooting High* at Twentieth Century-Fox."

While in production, Jimmie Fidler, *LAT*, November 24, 1939, observed the humorous result of Aldridge's desire to do her homework for the role in this Western. Fidler: "K.A., 20th Century's beauteous best bet, learned some weeks ago that she would have to ride horseback for her role in the current Jane Withers-Gene Autry picture. Never having ridden, she worried; having worried, she spent the next 10 days taking riding lessons from a local riding academy. Yesterday, she read the script and discovered that she plays a city gal who boards a horse just long enough to fall off!"

LAT, December 9, 1939, clipping by Edwin Schallert noted that Henry Wilcoxon will be in supposed sequel to *Hotel for Women* and: "... the film will be replete with younger movie luminaries. Several have been just been added so a rehearsal of the names in the feature may be apropos. These include Joan Davis, Lynn Bari, Mary Beth Hughes, Elsie Knox, Dorothy Dearing, Joan Valerie, Katherine Aldridge."

In her third and last *Life* cover on December 25, 1939, Aldridge is about to throw a snowball. An inside photo shows her with the caption: "Red flannel skirt, red waistcoat, white sweater, ear warmers and mittens make a bright outfit. Loose, ill-fitting shoes helped land Kitty on the ice." She is smiling as she stretches her arm and hand out for someone to help her up.

Aldridge's social circle expanded in Hollywood. *LAT*, December 31, 1939, "Party Goes Wholly Feminine": Joan Davis "gave a real hen party for the women in the cast of her current picture and other feminine friends. Among the guests were Lynn Bari, Katharine Aldridge, Elise Knox, Mary Beth Hughes, Joan Valerie, Binnie Barnes, Alice Armand, Dorothy Dearing, Helen Erickson, Lilyan Porter, Iva Stewart and Irma Wilson."

The year 1940 offered seven film appearances by Aldridge; actually the most in any one year of her career. Prior to this, she had one uncredited appearance each for 1937 and 1938, and her two first credited appearances in 1939. After this, in 1941, she appeared in five movies and one short. In 1942 and 1943, she was in a serial each year as well as one uncredited role in 1942, and two uncredited roles in 1943. In 1944, she did her final of three serials. She closed her film career out in 1945 with the co-starring roles in two PRC productions.

Jimmie Fidler's *LAT* column regularly monitored whatever Aldridge was doing, for example:

January 12, 1940: "Southern Belle Katharine Aldridge planes today to Sun Valley for her first try, at skiing..."

February 1, 1940: "Time out for Katharine Aldridge – she sat on a nail."

February 6, 1940: "A piled-high hair-do makes Katharine Aldridge look years older."

LAT, January 28, 1940, Maxine Bartlett reported: "Katharine Aldridge and Alfred Wright, Jr. among the many celebrities to attend Alice Faye's party at the Trocadero after the Hollywood preview for Twentieth Century-Fox's *Little Old New York*."

Ed Sullivan in "To the Ladies: It's A Leap Year," *CDT*, January 28, 1940, wrote: "Anita Louise, Carole Landis, Wendy Barrie, Lucille Ball, Dorris Bowdon, Katharine Aldridge, and Phyllis Brooks may not be able to cook, but they'd certainly decorate a kitchenette apartment."

As regards to the numerous fans, Carey noted: "Female fans ask for advice on how to break into modeling.... As K.A. cannot reply to all the fan letters she receives, she sends some to Elsie West, her life-long friend she knew from the 5th grade. Elsie replies to the letters pretending to be K.A. The fans, encouraged by receiving a reply, write again."

Elsie sent a letter with a picture to *Life*, January 29, 1940 ("Pictures to the Editor: Glamorous Kay"):

> Sirs:
> When K.A. was a mischievous schoolgirl in 1930, I took this snapshot. Even in those days I realized this picture was a photographic insult to her Southern charm and she labeled it

'SNOBISH' herself. Although I am not one to break faith with an old friend, I feel the time has come for 'feudin.'

January marks the eleventh month that my last letter to her has been unanswered. If exposing this relic of her won't get a rise out of her, then I am convinced nothing will. In view of the three times Aldridge has appeared on *Life*'s cover, I felt you might publish this snapshot???

Elsie "May" West, *Newport News*, Va.

Carey: "K.A., chagrined at her lack of attention to her 5th grade, fan-letter-replying friend, invites Elsie to visit her in Hollywood. Elsie spends some memorable days there."

A cast update to Aldridge's 5th film for Fox came on February 4, 1940: "... and Joan Valeries, Elise Knox, Marguerite Chapman and Katherine Aldridge have joined *Million Dollar Diamond*."

More changes were announced, *LAT*, March 7, 1940 by Edwin Schallert: "Progress of Kent Taylor is again to be recorded. He will be the lead opposite Florence Rice in *Million Dollar Diamond* at 20th Century-Fox studio, which starts shooting Monday. The studio last had the actor for Ramona. Judy Gilbert and Katharine Aldridge have also been cast in *Million Dollar Diamond*." The film eventually became titled *Girl in 313*.

A reader to *CDT*, March 17, 1940, asked about the cast of Aldridge's first film appearance, *Vogues of 1938*. The columnist responded by offering the credits, with K.A. listed as playing Melinda Craig.

Fidler in *LAT*, March 19, 1940, revealed the reason why 20th Century billed Aldridge in the film credits as "the girl on a hundred magazine covers." Fidler: "Audience reaction to date has shown that she distracts attention from the principal players, because people who vaguely remember her mag covers, are so tantalized that they spend all their effort trying to recall where they've seen her before and who she is."

NYT, March 26, 1940, Douglas W. Churchill writes: "Katharine Aldridge and Elise Knox will join Jane Withers in a remake of *The Brat* which Otto Brower will direct." That film was later released under the title *A Girl From Avenue A*. As production zoomed ahead on the latter title (her seventh for Fox), *Free, Blonde and Twenty-One*, her third for Fox, is released on March 28, 1940.

Hedda Hopper, *LAT*, April 2, 1940, told readers about a humorous experience, which exposed Aldridge in a white lie. Hopper: "K.A. dressed herself up for an awful letdown when she went to dinner the other night wearing elaborate costume jewelry which she uses in *Girl in 313*.

"To an admiring guest she said, 'Yes, aren't they nice? They're family heirlooms, you know!'

"To which her host replied, 'What a coincidence! Because just three weeks ago I made some jewelry like that for a 20th Century picture.'

"Kay swears she'll never wear another prop as long as she lives."

The fact that Aldridge's talent extended beyond modeling got revealed by the "Tattletale" column, *LAT*, March 14, 1940: "Katherine Aldridge, former Powers model, proved herself efficient as well as decorative and cooked a festive dinner to celebrate her settling in a new apartment. Younger brother Bill has come from Virginia to join her and John Aldridge, so larger quarters were in order. Guests at the housewarming included Mary Jane Barnes, Marguerite Chapman and Ray Ferguson."

At times Aldridge received press coverage via a photograph when she attended a premiere or a party gathering of luminaries, such as a wedding. ("Couple Takes Bridal Vows," *LAT*, April 15, 1940).

Since her screen time tended to be quite limited, as well as her speaking lines, almost all of the press coverage of her films rarely said more than just dropping her name as being in the picture. For instance, *LAT*, April 18, 1940: "In *Shooting High*, young Miss Withers connives successfully in breaking the feud between the Carsons and Pritchards. Autry is a Carson and Marjorie Weaver a Pritchard, and in the end love conquers all. The players include Katherine Aldridge and Robert Lowery. There are some songs."

Shooting High, Aldridge's 4th film for Fox, opened in theaters on April 26, 1940. Gene Autry was borrowed by 20th Century-Fox Studios.

An Associated Press clip told of a Virginia town where the residents attended a screening of the Autry film despite the bad weather, as they believed Aldridge was born and attended school in nearby Richmond County. AP reported: "Despite a near blizzard that toppled telephone and telegraph poles and partly disrupted communications, residents of Tappahannock packed the theatre here last night to see a 'home town' girl, Katharine Aldridge, on the screen in *Shooting High*. . . . Sleet and snow fell throughout this section, accompanied by a high wind" (clip from K.A.'s scrapbook, publication and date unknown).

Ed Sullivan in his May 11, 1940 (*CDT*) column stated correctly: "Beauty, popularity or other contests launched Margaret Weaver, Katherine Aldridge, Elise Knox, Linda Darnell, Helen Wood, Linda Hayes, Gail Patrick, Susan Hayward and Lona Andre on their screen careers. Even when they crash pictures most contest winners have very brief careers, being used only while they have freak exploitation value."

On May 31, 1940, her fifth film for Fox, *Girl in 313*, opened at theaters. Aldridge played a member of a gang. In the Bosley Crowther's review (*NYT*, June 6, 1940), Katharine Aldridge is billed fourth after Florence Rice, Kent Taylor, and Lionel Atwill. Crowther criticizes the film for an: "unhappy finale tacked on to a modestly diverting piece of jewels and top-halted thieves. . . . When a lady thief, in the person of Florence Rice, is really in the employ of the police and the detective, alias Kent Taylor, is her quarry, the opportunities for cross and double-cross are practically limitless. Thus, when a highly valued diamond disappears at a fashion show, Mr. Taylor in no time at all is furiously pursuing Miss Rice and vice versa. . . . Ultimately justice triumphs, but romance doesn't. Call us a turncoat, Mr. Zanuck, but we think Mr. Kent rated a reprieve. In trivia like *Girl in 313* it is well and fitting that boy gets girl. T.S."

A typewritten scrapbook clip penned by Aldridge offered her own opinion of her acting abilities and her films. The 'Bill' she refers to here is her younger brother. Aldridge: "We all went to see me in *Girl in 313* the other evening and somehow seeing me up there acting so silly in such a dumb movie gave us the giggles and Bill laughed so hard at one point that the usher motioned him to quiet down.

"I haven't much to do in it and I still don't think this kind of part in such terrible movies under such bad direction proves I couldn't if I had a chance. The movie is so badly written and directed and the plot so confusing that none in our group seemed to understand it at all. But we did enjoy laughing at me and it is odd seeing myself being bad and I don't think even looking very well amuses me too. Don't you feel embarrassed for me as this one is not as bad as some of the others."

Actor Ricardo Cortez directed *Girl in 313*. When asked about Cortez, his biographer, Daniel Van Neste (to Jim Manago): "I am not particularly surprised to learn Kay Aldridge did not like Cortez. A number of costars, and actors he directed did not like him. He took his directorial job very seriously (to some, too seriously), and could be impatient and quite nasty on the set. For some reason he was very hard on newcomers. Glenn Ford (who made his film debut in *Heaven with a Barbed Wire Fence*) came to despise Cortez. To be fair, Cortez was under enormous pressure and experiencing personal problems during the short period he directed the Fox B's, but he should not have taken it out on his actors and other filmmakers."

Her 9th film for Fox was announced two weeks later, *NYT*, June 11, 1940: "Fox assigned Katharine Aldridge to *Down Argentine Way*."

An ad (*LAT*, June 12, 1940) for Grauman's Chinese and Loew's State Theater in Hollywood near Highland listed *Girl in 313* as the companion "B" feature to the main attraction. The ad offered the cast, including Florence Rice, Kent Taylor, Lionel Atwill, Katharine Aldridge. The banner read: "She Used Romance to Trap Broadway's Smartest Diamond Racketeers!" Of interest is Aldridge shown holding a pistol as she played a gang member involved in the jewelry theft.

Harriet Parsons, daughter of Louella Parsons, June 14, 1940, *WP*, wrote: "The whole town is primping and preparing to preen itself at the premiere tonight of *All This, and Heaven Too*... In Olivia de Havilland's party are Jimmy Stewart, Margaret Sullavan and Leland Hayward, Kay Aldridge and John Swope." Carey: "Hayward, the best agent in Hollywood, is yet another name on the roster of well-connected professionals promoting K.A.'s career."

Aldridge appeared at a fashion show to benefit Friendship House and the Red Cross held at Carmel Myers Blum's house (*LAT*, June 23, 1940).

Again Aldridge gets only her name dropped as part of the cast in her 6th film for Fox. *NYT*, June 28, 1940: "Twentieth Century-Fox's *Sailor's Lady*, which costars Jon Hall and Nancy Kelly, is today's newcomer at the Roxy. In the featured roles are Joan Davis, Dana Andrews, Mary Nash, Larry Crabbe, Katharine Aldridge and Bruce 'Skipper' Hampton...."

On that same day, *LAT* reported that the production of *Yesterday's Heroes* (what would become her 8th film for Fox), gives mention to K.A. as being in the cast. The press reports: "What with *The Life of Knute Rockne* at Warners and *Touchdown* at Paramount, it seems that 20th Century-Fox executives also feel it is well to be 'hep' to the football situation, come fall. So a new subject has been set called *Yesterday's Heroes*, written by William Brent, and adapted by Irving Cummings, Jr. and William Conselman Jr. to present Robert Sterling, Katharine Aldridge and Jean Rogers in the cast. Herbert I. Leeds will start directing July 8."

Aldridge received attention in local "home town" ads, such as the one for the Palace Theatre. It read: "An All-American Football Story Featuring Newport News' Own Katharine Aldridge."

Sailor's Lady officially opened a week later on July 5, 1940. A negative review appeared in the *LAT* two days before ("Anchors Go Awry in Navy: 'Comic' Opus"). It said that Nancy Kelly, Jon Hall, Joan Davis, Dana Andrews, Mary Nash, Larry Crabbe, Katharine Aldridge, etc. were "among the victims of the travesty... for it practically turns the service of the sea into a burlesque, with the sailors depicted as zanies and rowdies. The film undoubtedly was made some little while ago, but that is no reason why it shouldn't find a quiet resting place on the shelf. Its entertainment value is next to nothing.... It's no Pinafore, this affair of the screen, for even its comedy, when there is any, is pretty blatant. Wally Vernon, Larry Crabbe, who is a partner in the fisticuffs, Katharine Aldridge, Harry Shannon and Charles D. Brown are among those appearing."

A display ad for *Sailor's Lady*, *LAT*, August 1, 1940, reads: "A thousand gobs on the loose ... the war games all balled up...and still these two found LOVE!"

Aldridge's appearance in *Sailor's Lady* is a case in point of how her actual film time is so limited in the Fox entries. Undoubtedly this is a film in which someone else other than Aldridge is given much more to do. Here it is Nancy Kelly. The film opens as several women (including Aldridge and Joan Davis) are chatting and putting on their makeup. Aldridge endears herself quickly as she is clearly photogenic, but she seems to be playing her scene as if she is doing a promotion for a beauty product.

Aldridge's seeming lack of training is evident here as she is given some lines, but she could not do much with them, though she is physically perfectly appealing. She shows she has no problem being easily liked by the viewers - but this is not convincing as far as film acting goes. Later, she is seen again briefly – but again she has no important connection to the film's plot. As with her other appearances, Aldridge does not prove she could really do much as an actress. She appeared in the Fox films as simply window dressing, and it seemed that she could not get away from looking like she was only just a model.

A scrapbook clip (date and publication unknown) entitled "Model Writes Play": "Katharine Aldridge, lovely photographer's model, who recently completed roles in *Shooting High* and *Sailor's Lady*, has written a play which she will adapt for the screen. The play is entitled 'The Subject Is Alive.'"

Two months after the release of *Sailor's Lady*, Aldridge's seventh Fox release, called *A Girl From Avenue A*, opened on August 9, 1940. A local "home town" ad read: "Girl From Avenue A -with- Lovely Katharine Aldridge of Newport News, Va."

NYT, September 5, 1940: "Casting at the studio ... and Katharine Aldridge in Tin Pan Alley." This is another film that Aldridge was supposed to appear in, but did not do.

A week later, the studio announced the cast additions for her 10th Fox film on September 11, 1940. Douglas W. Churchill (*NYT*) reported: "Katharine Aldridge and Buddy Pepper have *joined Golden Hoofs*."

When it comes to a discussion of Aldridge's acting, it rarely got mentioned in the reviews. If it did, the accolades were for playing the "other woman" well. *Yesterday's Heroes*, is an exception. *LAT*, September 13, 1940: ". . . the production doesn't leave one with much of that lift which football stories should generate. . . . Something is lacking in the spirit of the piece . . . Acting by the youthful cast is strictly okeh . . . Katharine Aldridge is a winsome 'other women' and performs creditably."

On the same day as that reviewer's boost, a reporter at the same paper was told by Aldridge that it was onions, yes I said onions, that got her into pictures, if albeit indirectly. However, this did not get explained in this article.

Yesterday's Heroes, Aldridge's 8th film for Fox, opened officially on September 20, 1940. *LAT*, October 8, 1940, offered the cast, Gary Cooper as 'Westerner' "with Jean Rogers, Robert Sterling, Katharine Aldridge, Ted North and Russell Gleason."

LAT, September 29, 1940, reported that Aldridge planned to participate in a China aid benefit. "Gene Tierney, Brenda Joyce, Mary Healy, Katharine Aldridge, Mary Beth Hughes, Dorris Bowden and many other feminine celebrity will be in various booths, lending their aid and figures in wearing the fabulously rich gowns loaned by Gumps for the occasion."

On October 11, 1940, *Down Argentine Way*, Aldridge's 9th film for Fox, is released. Two days later, *CDT*'s reviewer does not specify Aldridge by name, but the movie is given high marks. "Technicolor-ally speaking *Down Argentine Way* is a gorgeous thing. NEVER, it seems to me, have I seen such luscious reds. It has lots of gay music, arresting dances, and so far as the story goes –pouf! – That's just so many yards of fictional chiffon, embroidered by excellent acting. . . . Excellent cast throughout. Dialogue has sparkle and the director knew how."

Another positive review appeared in *LAT*, October 17, 1940 ("*Down Argentine Way* Spirited Musical"): "Charlotte Greenwood heads an excellent supporting company, along with J. Carrol Naish, Henry Stephenson, Leonid Kinsky, Katharine Aldridge and Chris-Pin Martin."

Bosley Crowther, *NYT*, October 18, 1940, offered the credits to *Down Argentine Way* with Katharine Aldridge (playing Helen Carson). As you would expect, bit-player Aldridge did not get more than a mention in film reviews. Of course, the lead star Betty Grable deservedly got all of the reviewer's attention: "We see plenty of her – singing, dancing and wearing clothes in surprising magnificence. We even see her trying to act, which is something less of a pleasure...."

In an early, brief but well-played, scene in *Down Argentine Way*, Aldridge is Betty Grable's seeming rival for affection of Don Ameche. We are told that she is Grable's best friend, but disappointingly there is no followup anywhere else in the rest of the movie.

In "Nine Models Fooled by Kay Aldridge," *The Brooklyn Daily Eagle*, October 18, 1940, revealed: "Three years ago, a group of nine John Powers models bet Powers model Kay Aldridge, then Hollywood bound, that she would not last through nine pictures. Today, at the Roxy Theater, in *Down Argentine Way*, Kay Aldridge will flash on the screen in her ninth picture for Fox. And so nine Powers models are due to pay off their lost bet – by placing a bouquet of nine orchids at the foot of the Roxy screen."

The typical exaggerations are evident in the display ads for most of these films. For example, the ad for *Down Argentine Way*, *WP*, October 20, 1940 claimed the film is: "The spectacular musical extravaganza two continents have been waiting for!"

WP, October 27, 1940, the fans got a more detailed piece explaining Aldridge's love of onions. In "Glamour Girl Credits Onions for Success," writer Franklin Arthur offers what he says is Aldridge's reasoning: "Were it not for eating onions, she wouldn't have been so healthy. Were it not for being so healthy, she wouldn't have been attractive enough to get a modeling job. And were it not for the modeling job, she'd probably still be making $15.50 a week or so as an Army secretary in Baltimore."

The *WP* review for *Down Argentine Way*, October 31, 1940, just mentions Katharine Aldridge in the list of cast credits.

LAT, November 21, 1940, "Film Stars Tell Plans For Thanksgiving Day . . ." offered that "Katharine Aldridge will have her first Thanksgiving dinner in Hollywood with her mother, Mrs. Cornelia

Ward Aldridge, who came her from Badensfield, Va., to live." Of course, the reporter erred, as he should have said "Bladensfield."

The day after Christmas 1940, Louella Parsons' column (*WP*) reported that Aldridge got a part in the film *Dead Men Tell*, her 11th and final Fox film, due to an actress' illness. "... Poor Jean Rogers will spend Christmas in bed. She is quite sick with the flu – so ill that she is out of the new Charlie Chan picture and Katherine Aldridge takes her place."

Aldridge started the year of 1941 by being crowned by California vintners as "Wine Queen." Of course, the title meant she would make a tour throughout the country in that role (*WP*, January 2, 1941).

Even Aldridge's presence at the Santa Anita racetrack did not get overlooked: "Prettiest girl in the place was Katharine Aldridge in a military blue sports outfit with swopped up hat that looked as if it had been carved out of patent leather. That swish of mink coat going by was Gladys Peabody" (*LAT*, January 7, 1941).

At this point, it seemed like the studio's publicity department worked overtime to keep Aldridge in the news. Several months after first revealing the connection of her career to onions, Aldridge elaborated in a follow-up to the article. *WP*, January 28, 1941: " 'I love 'em,' she enthuses. 'I used to eat them three times a day. I still could, but I don't think it would be wise. They don't mix well with a movie love scene and people frown upon them at the better parties. But I've dozens of ways of fixing them. I think they're best for breakfast, chopped up and peppered on toast. They're mighty fine, raw, too.'

"The way Kay had to eat when she was a girl would have bred hatred for them with many people....There were times on the 575-acre Virginia plantation where she lived that there wasn't much else." The Post columnist misstated her birthplace (which was Florida) when he said: "She was born at Bladensfield, 60 miles from Richmond, in a 24-room house built in 1690."

Aldridge: "We were always poor. Still are, for that matter, but we're proud." The reporter explained: "She's happy out here, but not satisfied. Her widowed mother ('Who can cook onions better than anybody') recently came to live with her and her two brothers, who work at an aircraft plant. But there is one thing. Katharine Aldridge: 'Down South, girls are brought with the idea that their chief mission is to find a husband. I'm definitely in the market. 'But he must like ONIONS.' "

Carey: "[With] K.A.'s salary from Fox at an end, K.A. is obliged to seek work where she can. K.A.'s agent strives to keep her as visible as possible by making sure she attends Franklin Roosevelt's 59th birthday party, dedicated to the fight against Infantile Paralysis, better known as polio."

Along with other Hollywood luminaries, she celebrated the President's birthday at the White House (*WP*, January 29, 1941). While in Washington, Aldridge attended a college football game between Georgetown and Penn State: "More than 4,500 fans including Movie Star Kay Aldridge, watched the Hoyas pull out of a 19-12 deficit to put on the season's greatest rally . . . (*WP*, January 30, 1941).

LAT, January 30, 1941: "Mr. Roosevelt will not attend the balls to be held at five Washington hotels. But Mrs. Roosevelt will, and so will more than a dozen film luminaries. Official committees and avid film fans already have welcomed Deanna Durbin, K.A., Lana Turner, Wayne Morris, Maureen O'Hara, George Raft, Wallace Beery . . ."

At times, Aldridge seemed to be treated by the press as a special attraction. As an example, for FDR's birthday *WP*, January 30, 1941, reported: "Arrivals last night included Charlotte Greenwood, Jay C. Flippen, Constance Moore, Mr. and Mrs. Clifton Fadiman and Tommy Harmon. Glamour girl K.A. slipped into town early yesterday morning."

She is named among the stars to appear at the scheduled events. The national coverage of FDR's birthday in major newspapers included a number of articles picturing Aldridge, all on January 31, 1941. In a *NYT* photo, Aldridge is prominently pictured sitting right next to the President's wife Eleanor at a White House luncheon in the Blue Room, along with over two dozen others. The *WP* offered a photograph of Aldridge in the company of Eleanor at a luncheon with Mr. and Mrs. Wallace Beery, and Laureen Robinson at the Washington Hotel.

In "War Saddens Roosevelt on Birthday," three photos made light of Aldridge. They appeared under different titles in various papers (like "Peek-a-Boo, We See You . . ."). However the copy is the same.

WP, January 31, 1941:

"1. K.A., glamorous film star, stands with a group of celebrities, including George Raft (left), having their picture made at Commissioner's Hazen's desk. But look behind the desk. – Kay's got her shoes off!

"2. SORRY, K.A., we didn't mean to surprise you. Now, all those other stars know you had your wedgees off, and it's all our fault. Deanna Durbin thought it funny and Clifton Fadiman asked. "information, please?" But wait. . .

"3. . . DON'T PULL 'EM ON! Go ahead, leave 'em off. Understand what it means to have barking dogs and we promise not to look again."

Also another WP clip, same date, she was mingling among the top talents of that time, such as Maureen O'Hara, George Raft, Red Skelton, and Lana Turner.

Columnist Don Craig quoted Emcee Clifton Fadiman on Aldridge. Fadiman: "Real reason for any threatened illiteracy in the new generation isn't the radio or the movies, it's Kay Aldridge. The boys see her picture on magazine covers and never get around to reading inside. Why should they? . . . Kay Aldridge, in a very audible aside: 'Fadiman makes his living with the inside of his head. I make mine with the outside. What's the difference?' "

Indeed, Aldridge had appeared on many magazine covers, appeared in dozens of product ads, and received plenty of publicity in the newspapers by this time. However, her movie career never really took off, as she was just window dressing in a dozen films by now. Nevertheless, she had achieved additional recognition among the public because of the movies and the special billing in the credits.

Even Aldridge's return home from Roosevelt's birthday celebration received coverage, WP, February 1, 1941: "Pretty K.A., native of Warsaw, Va., said she was going home to call on the mayor."

In her scrapbook, Carey states that "K.A. burns her bridges at Fox." McCord: "After completing the three show girl films, Miss Aldridge was 'rediscovered' by Twentieth-Century Fox. A producer who did not know her saw her in a restaurant and sent her to Fox for a screen test. Some of the Fox personnel immediately recognized her but agreed to cooperate because they liked her.

" 'I did a very stupid thing,' she lamented. 'I always felt miscast, so I got Phil Silvers to help me do it. We made our own script up, and we wrote it where I climbed in through the window in my tiger skin. And he played the part of the head of the studio. And I said, 'Oh please, Mr. Zanuck.' I didn't call him Zanuck, but I called him something like that. 'Let me take this tiger skin off and show you what I can do. I shouldn't always be cast as the rich other woman.' And with that, he looked at me, then he started chasing me around the office. We made a skit, a parody, and it was too close to home; and Zanuck didn't like it at all.' "

McCord concluded: "Our heroine did not get another Fox contract."

A newspaper clip (date and publication unknown) acknowledged that Aldridge filmed the test using her own script. The clip reported: "Kay Aldridge made a screen test at Twentieth Century-Fox that is the riot of the production rooms. Miss Aldridge wrote the scene she did with Phil Silvers, who appears in the test with her. The sequence they did is called "The Perils of Kay Aldridge," and in it, Miss Aldridge, who is a glamour girl, goes to a producer's (Phil Silvers) office for a job in pictures and she reverses the usual procedure by chasing the producer around the desk and office, and has him fighting to protect his honor.

"Kay Aldridge, after her introductory remarks, says to the producer, before she leaps toward him: 'You said you want a woman to be warm and loving. Darling, that's just how I feel when I look at you. You're so big and strong, so alive, your eyes do something to me. I love the way your nose crinkles up when you laugh. Darling, here we are alone, just the two of us. I know you are a great executive and I'm just an actress, but basically we're just boy and girl hungry for each other . . .'

Phil Silvers backing away: 'Want a cookie?'

Aldridge, 'No, I don't want a cookie. I want your love. Oh, you mad, impetuous, foolish boy, I love you so . . . I want to run barefoot through your hair . . ."

Silvers: "It's a toupee . . . ."

Aldridge: "Put your arms around me darling . . . hold me close . . . close . . . Don't ever go away . . . I want you in the morning . . . I want you at noon . . . I want you at night . . . Come to me, my darling . . . Give me my love . . . I want you . . . By now I want you."

Kay has caught Phil Silvers and is pulling him down on the couch. Silvers, as he flops down on the couch, says to the audience (which will be the executives), 'Gentlemen, I think this will give you an idea of what Miss Aldridge can do . . .' "

The article went on to say that Aldridge " . . . is tired of being a glamour girl. She wants to play roles, comedy parts. Elsa Maxwell brought her to 20th Century-Fox where she did nothing but bits in unimportant pictures. But now, in typical Hollywood fashion, she's returning to that studio to get a chance to do something, and all because she chased a producer around the desk and tossed him on the couch."

Obviously, nothing came out of this stunt played on Zanuck, as Aldridge did not get a second 20th Century-Fox contract with better terms.

Still the reason why Aldridge's contract with 20th Century Fox was not renewed is unknown. *LAT*, January 17, 1941, Jimmie Fidler claims: "The chill between 20th Century Fox and Katharine Aldridge dates from her refusal to dye her hair as ordered."

A second reason may have come a few months later. *LAT*, May 28, 1941, Fidler again offers something that may explain Aldridge's failure to become a real star over at 20th Century or anywhere, although he did not elaborate: "Too bad K.A. can't shed that air of cold dignity; without it she'd be a best-bet for stardom. . . . Some actresses keep going via stock companies, while others achieve the same result via company stock."

A third reason, or explanation connected to the studio and Aldridge's attitude/demeanor. Aldridge told McCord: ". . . Miss Aldridge believes it was because the studio was beginning to discontinue the practice of having numerous contract players and because she was so 'frivolous' about acting. 'I would get the giggles on the lot,' she said. 'I didn't take it seriously... I was never a cozy girl on the lot with anybody. I never did anything sexy to get ahead.' She also said she was not the Betty Grable-Alice Faye type of girl that Fox treasured." The thrills of being in films seemed to be all that mattered to Aldridge at the time.

Carey: "[Those are] 3 theories on why K.A.'s contract with Fox is not renewed. There is a fourth theory as well: and that is that she would not go to bed with Fox's chief, Darryl Zanuck."

Chapter Four:
Sexy Sextet at Warners

> "It seemed like a good break when she got into the *Navy Blues* Sextet, which kept the little beauties occupied for about seven months on good salary, but it really ruined any chance of a screen career because producers felt that girls as beautiful as that couldn't possibly have brains."
> - Kyle Crichton,
> *Collier's*, October 24, 1942

For now Aldridge free-lanced as Fox decided not to renew her contract. The next time the press covers Aldridge's film career, she is appearing in a Warner Brothers film. The details of her arrangement with them were not published. She made only three pictures before that studio cut her loose to find work elsewhere.

Thanks to the studio's publicity machine, Aldridge seemed to get media attention wherever she went. *LAT*, January 7, 1941: "Katharine Aldridge, her mother, Mrs. Cornelia Ward Aldridge, and her brothers Bill and John were guests at the North Verde Ranch at Victorville of Mr. and Mrs. Kemper Campbell and Kemper Campbell, Jr."

Golden Hoofs, her 10th film (the next to last) for Fox, was released on February 14, 1941. A typical fashion ad appearing in *LAT*, February 19, 1941, had Aldridge pictured modeling clothes, identified by her name and "20th Century Player . . . at a location for fashion-wise women who are shopping in a restful, unhurried atmosphere of refinement."

It is reported that Aldridge asked Hopper about how the columnist grooms her hair (*WP*, March 8, 1941). Hopper: "K.A. wanted to know how I slick my hair up the back and keep it there. Just use a spray of lacquer brilliantine, dearie, and it stays forever."

Carey: "K.A. goes on a cruise from Los Angeles to San Francisco to promote another Warner Brothers film (in which she does not appear), *The Sea Wolf*."

LAT, March 24, 1941: The publicity for *The Sea Wolf*, involved K.A. along with other luminaries (Marguerite Chapman, Julie Bishop, K.A., Georgia Carroll, Maria Montez, and others). The premiere was done on the radio with various ceremonies, at a theater in Sonoma, as well as the presentations on the S. S. America.

Her 11th and final film made for Fox was *Dead Men Tell*, released on March 28, 1941.

Louella O. Parsons, *WP*, May 23, 1941 (also *NYT*, May 22, 1941) tells of Voldemar Vetleguin " . . . a writer with an eye to beauty. He has selected the prettiest girls in America for models and magazine covers – among them K.A., Jinx Falkenberg, Peggy Diggins, Georgia Carroll, Margaret Chapman, Lorraine Gettman. Now he has written a story '*The Powers Model*' which, with Everett Freeman, he is readying for Warner production.

"Some of these beauties will be in *The Powers Model*, the tentative title, and can't you see all the roads will lead to Warners Studio? Ann Sheridan will have the lead and Ann is not so hard on the eyes, either." However, Aldridge and Sheridan did not appear in the renamed film.

As with other Hollywood celebrities of the day, Aldridge participated in shows performed for the soldiers of World War II. *CDT*, June 16, 1941: "Among the players who journeyed to the camps are Virginia O'Brien, Lewis Milestone, K.A. . . ."

A "Millionaire for a Day" contest won by a sailor, Robert N. McPheeters, provided him with a dinner date with Aldridge at the Ritz-Carlton Hotel.

Carey: "K.A. appears on the cover of *Ladies Home Journal* [June 1941] as a bride and receives thousands of marriage proposals in the mail."

John Chapman, *CDT*, June 8, 1941, succinctly chronicled her life up to this point. Chapman: "Kay Aldridge, 20-year old Virginian with light brown hair, met some models at a West Point dance, and they urged her to hit John Powers for a job. Powers put her to work, and for two years she has been a familiar magazine girl.

En route to Honolulu on a modeling job, Kay stopped off in Hollywood and was bagged for a picture by Elsa Maxwell. Miss Aldridge has a stock contract with Twentieth-Century Fox and was borrowed by the Warners for *Navy Blues*."

Carey: "Chapman is incorrect in saying she met some other models at the West Point dance and it was because of their suggestion that she went to Powers's office. What makes K.A.'s story unique is that:

"One: It was her older cousin, Daniel Delaney Fitzhugh Yellut, who read the *Esquire* article, went to see Powers and subsequently recommended to K.A. that she should consider modeling and gave her the information about the Powers agency.

"Two: K.A., who was only 18, and who, since the age of 4, had never been south of Virginia or north of Maryland. [She] used her own initiative to get herself invited to a dance at West Point, with the hidden agenda that she alone developed, of stopping in New York City on the way back to Baltimore.

"Three: "K.A., on the train back from West Point with her 22 year old sister, convinced her older sister to go with her hidden agenda and to get off the train and spend a night in New York, in order to show up at Powers the next day. I don't know what story the girls told their mother to justify their spending a night in New York. Perhaps they just said they want to do some tourism.

"Four: "K.A.'s sister was much more self-conscious than K.A. about the fact of them being out of place in New York, and having the wrong clothes, had great misgivings about going to Powers, but K.A. managed to prevail over her older (4 years older!) sister. It is the fact of K.A.'s self confidence, at such a young age, and her determination to take charge of her own destiny, with literally no help from anyone except a scrap of information from her cousin, that makes the story unique."

That trip to Hawaii served as a promotional stunt to show how "A Magazine Cover Girl Sees the World." *Redbook*, Saks Fifth Avenue and a travel shipping line sponsored the trip.

The obvious and inevitable photo-op of the pretty Hollywood star with army camp boys had the sexy smiling Aldridge being carried in the arms of a doughboy as seen in *LAT*, June 16, 1941.

WP, on that same day provided the photo, captioning the visit as "Hollywood Stars Carried Away in Maneuvers with Troops.... The troops had fun and so did the Hollywoodites." Pictured were Privates John Self, Russ Perry and George Buttgren, as they "got armloads of K.A., Peggy Diggins, and Marguerite Chapman."

The *CDT* reported that Aldridge and the other models were among 38 entertainers that put on a two-hour show organized by the movie industry's defense committee. The masters of ceremonies were Jack Benny and George Jessel. The troops were 17,000 from Fort Ord and 22,000 from Camp Hunter Liggett.

Next up was promotions for the upcoming *Navy Blues*, Aldridge's first of three films for Warner Brothers. She played a member of the *Navy Blues* Sextette.

On June 22, 1941, *CDT* pictured: "Film Beauties at the Beach..."

Again a week later, *CDT*, June 29, 1941, the Sextet beauties were pictured, this time captioned: "The Glamour Girls."

Louella O. Parsons, helped with publicity when she noted on July 3, 1941 (*WP*): "The six Warner beauties – Peggy Diggins, K.A., Georgia Carroll, Lorraine Gettman, Marguerite Chapman and Claire James are set for a trip to Honolulu. Warners are planning to preview *Navy Blues* there and these six glamorous young ladies, who are being called the Floradora Sextette of 1941, will be sent to the tropical island along with the movie. The girls are thrilled over the prospect of going. Certainly the famed Floradora girls, most of whom married millionaires, never had a chance for such exciting travel in the good old days."

Two days later, the publicity rolled on as Aldridge gave pointers on wearing perfume. "Every girl of fashion is interested in new perfume pointers to make her more desirable. And Kay Aldridge, one of the loveliest of the lovely *Navy Blues* Sextet, has them. Kay learned that many perfumes are not lasting because they evaporate with the alcohol that is part of every scent. So she lets the alcohol evaporate slightly before applying perfume, in this manner: She squeezes the bulb on her atomizer, sends a mist of perfume into the air, then walks through it. The best of the scent drops over her like a mantle" (*WP*, July 5, 1941).

Pictures abounded promoting the beautiful *Navy Blues* Sextet. *WP*, July 9, 1941: Pictured: "Six Sirens of the Sea, otherwise the *Navy Blues* Sextet ... who probably will give the gobs something to think about in *Navy Blues*. This is a forthcoming Warner Brothers film, starring Ann Sheridan, Jack Oakie and Martha Raye."

Aldridge attended dinner parties, such as one given by the Count and Countess Oleg Cassini (Gene Tierney) on July 27, 1941 (*NYT*). "Among those enjoying the buffet supper and entering into the general discussion in the Cassinis' Beverly Hills home were Ellen Drew and Si Bartlett, Katharine Aldridge with Alfred de Liagre, Linda Darnell and Bentley Ryan...."

On August 1, 1941 (*WP*), the *Navy Blues* Sextet's opinion focused on nail polish color: "Hollywood, California – Scarlet nail polish is suffering an almost total eclipse among the pulchritudinous members of the *Navy Blues* Sextet. With the exception of Claire James and Lorraine Gettman, who still prefer ruby red nails, the sextet is in favor of a meeker shade that is very new and which the girls call a "true pink." Marguerite Chapman introduced the new shade to Peggy Diggins, Georgia Carroll and K.A. and showed them her own unique way of applying it."

Almost a week later, a follow-up article did not name Aldridge. However, it again repeated information about how scarlet nail polish is no longer fashionable. In addition it was noted that, "Marguerite files her nails to perfectly round tips – also finding more favor among Hollywood girls than the pointed mandarin tips that have been so popular. She then applies a coat of white 'prolong,' followed by a thin application of the pink polish, leaving the ends of her nails untouched for a second coat of white on the tips. This new polish has a dull rather than a glossy finish" (*WP*, August 7, 1941).

Slightly over a month later, the Sextet's publicity machine turned attention to food. In "Beauties Like Salads," readers learned: "Six sumptuous salads is the order immediately relayed to the Warner Bros. commissary kitchen when the luscious *Navy Blues* Sextet comes in for lunch. All six girls prefer salads at noontime.... K.A. is true to her favorite southern salad, smoked tongue with orange cubes" (*WP*, August 12, 1941).

The pre-release publicity for *Navy Blues* continued. August 15, 1941 (*WP*): The *Navy Blues* Sextet "not only created a shortage of writing materials but also were held responsible for embarrassing the Navy with extra laundry work.... They signed autographs on every available scrap of paper when they appeared at the training station at San Diego with Warner Brothers' *Navy Blues* company. Then when the paper gave out, the sailors offered shirts, collars and caps."

WP, August 24, 1941: "... the Sextet is actually a Septet – the seventh member – Alice Talton. Alice was added as a last-minute measure. She doesn't appear in *Navy Blues*, the film that created the Sextet. But she's a much-needed substitute. If one of the others gets the migraine, has to see the dentist, has a heavy morning-after, or for any other reason, cannot appear – Alice is there.

"... But when you try to catch them in an interview all together, they are suddenly a quintet – one overslept and the other was out of town.

"Poor girls, they could do with more sleep. For the past few months, together and apart, they have had no peace – pictures every day, a bit of film acting, dramatic lessons, dancing lessons, and then, just when life looks freer, more photographing.

"As one of them said, plaintively: 'It's a joke with us now. We're all dramatic actresses – and we spend most of our lives being photographed in bathing suits!' "

LAT, August 28, 1941: "The 'streamlined Sextet,' a la 'Floradora,' has been named for *Navy Blues*, following a poll of naval stations for preferences in – well, Sextets."

CDT, September 9, 1941: In Chicago, the beauties of the Sextet made one of their many promotional appearances at a broadcasting station. The article ("Chosen by Sailors") reported: "The *Navy Blues* Sextet, adjudged the six most beautiful girls in Hollywood by sailors in the Navy, marched in last evening to join 'The Affairs of Tom, Dick, and Harry' on station W-G-N and the Mutual network. They arrived at the studio escorted by six ensigns and lieutenants in the Great Lakes Naval Training station. The trio sang, "Barnacle Bill" and the girls offered 'In Waikiki' from the Warner Brothers musical picture, *Navy Blues*, in which all six appear."

On the same day of the report of their radio station appearance, film starlet Aldridge got named to rule over a wine fete. *LAT*, September 9, 1941: "Selection of K.A., motion-picture starlet, as California's 'Sunshine Girl' to reign over the celebration of National Wine Week, Oct. 12 to 19, was announced yesterday. Miss Aldridge, possessor of light brown hair and hazel eyes, was chosen following a three months' search in key cities of the nation, with hundreds of local beauties in competition."

Carey: "Her eyes were grey, not hazel as is sometimes stated."

In a scrapbook clipping, "Kay Aldridge Becomes Highest Paid Model in United States," Carey revealed: "This article contains another piece of information K.A. never shared with her family." The clip shows Aldridge accepting a check. It noted: "Because Miss Aldridge typified the California Sunshine Girl, she received a $5000 check from Louis E. Golan, industrialist and president of the company bearing his name, to represent his firm as the 'Lango Girl' at the fiesta. . ."

After over six months of build-up, *Navy Blues* finally opened on September 13th. Richard L. Coe on September 20, 1941 (*WP*) reviewed the film. In "Gobs and Girls Mingle Gaily for *Navy Blues*, Coe finds much to be happy about in this musical comedy: "Ann Sheridan, Martha Raye and the *Navy Blues* Sextette are the charmers in this one; Jack Oakie, Jack Haley and a comparative newcomer, Herbert Anderson, take care of the gags – of which there are aplenty. . . . And that Sextette is utterly ravishing."

Bosley Crowther, *NYT*, September 13, 1941, gave his opinion: "For a picture about the Navy and sea-dogs, there is an uncommon amount of horseplay in the Warners' *Navy Blues*, which was warped into the Strand yesterday. But that's about what you would expect from a musical monkeyshine which harbors Jack Oakie, Jack Haley, Martha Raye and Ann Sheridan in its cast and which gets along without benefit of any strong assistance from its script. So you who are not averse to a lot of broad and unrestrained mugging-to a generous display of the Messrs. Oakie and Haley working harder for laughs than a bum vaudeville team in Omaha-and for those who like your musical shows noisy, this one should be all right."

WP, December 26, 1941, pictured a scene from Aldridge's second film done for Warners with the following caption: "So, That's Being in the Army! – Phil Silvers being attacked on both flanks by K.A., left, and Peggy Diggins, two of the '*Navy Blues* Sextette,' in one of the more comically inflammatory incidents in *You're in the Army Now*, which yesterday opened at the Christmas week screen feature at the Earle Theater. Mr. Silvers is costarred with Jimmy Durante and Jane Wyman in this latest of the training camp farces, with music. Its tomfoolery is exceedingly high voltage."

Despite the heavy publicity, including the many stage appearances (such as at the Hollywood Canteen), and the fact that the *Navy Blues* Sextet are voted "The Girls the Navy Would Most Like to be Shipwrecked With," many of the reviews were critical.

McCord explained what happened once the movie was released. McCord: "In the Warner films, *Navy Blues*, and *You're in the Army Now*, Miss Aldridge was a member of a musical-support group called the *Navy Blues* Sextet. The group's singing, however, was dubbed in. *Navy Blues* was such a 'lousy' movie, Miss Aldridge said, that the studio sent the Sextet on a personal appearance tour across the country to promote the film.

"In the fall of 1941, the group toured Navy bases, visited about a dozen cities, and appeared at New York City's Strand Theater six times a day for two weeks and received much publicity wherever they went. However, Miss Aldridge said, the girls were furious over the tour. 'We didn't like it at all,' she said. 'We thought it was cheap and tiresome. But we had fun.' "

A year after the *Navy Blues* fiasco, columnist Crichton understood Aldridge's plight and the damage of being promoted as a luscious doll. Crichton: "When the Sextet was in New York making personal appearances with the picture, Rose Franken was on the verge of having Kay for the Claudia company but happened to see her in makeup for the stage appearances with the Sextet and put up a faint hand and asked to be excused. 'Sophisticated,' said Franken in a horror-stricken voice"(*Collier's*, October 24, 1942).

Aldridge's second film for Warners (and 15th film of her career), *You're in the Army Now*, opened on Christmas Day in 1941. With the Navy recognizing her beauty, it was inevitable that the Army would follow suit. It has been said that *You're in the Army Now* and the earlier *Navy Blues* bear some resemblance to each other. "Both attempted to capitalize on the new interest in war-theme films. They were actually the same musical, only the cut and color of the uniforms were different. Both concerned two hapless dupes drafted into the armed forces, and the troubles they caused their superior officers. Although ostensibly comic in form, each film displayed a few moments of serious intent.

"In *Navy Blues*, Ann Sheridan explains to a naval gunner that it is unpatriotic for him to give up the navy in order to return to his farm in Iowa. *You're in the Army Now* also allows Durante and Silvers to explain the importance of the newly enacted selective service laws in song. . . . They were the last films at Warners to make light of the armed forces" (Allen Wolf, *The Hollywood Musical Goes to War*).

Louisiana Purchase, Aldridge's 16th film, her third and last one for Warners, opened on December 31, 1941. It starred Bob Hope.

Although the Navy and the Army got a Warners film devoted to them with Aldridge, the Seabees did not. However, they paid their respect to her, with a photo clip that reported: "A Seabee bracelet goes on the pretty ankle of the pretty movie star Kay Aldridge. Kay has been given the official title of Honey Bee of a Seabee battalion. The Seabees know good construction when they see it in a girl or on a fortification. They know the builds."

Chapter Five:
Serial Queen at Republic

"She never did go much for the New York model stuff and cold glamour roles. She's just a Virginia farm girl who happened to be born beautiful."
- Edwin Schallert, "Kay Aldridge Named Republic Serial Queen,"
Los Angeles Times, March 18, 1942.

The New Year of 1942 started with Aldridge's picture appearing with the caption "Toasts 1942: Meet the first beauty winner for 1942. She's Kay Aldridge, who reigns as the new Wine Queen. . . . She will visit the key cities of the country, heralding the prestige, fame and richness of the American wines. The noted model, whose beauty has graced many a magazine cover, will become the good-will ambassador of the California vintners" (*LAT*, January 1, 1942).

The press reported when Aldridge's brother Bill got married. January 8, 1942, *NYT*: "When guests called at 321 Bedford Drive in Beverly Hills one afternoon this week they were told of the betrothal of Miss Rita Jean Johnson and William Giddings Aldridge . . . Assisting at the tea were . . . Katherine Aldridge . . ."

Aldridge would appear in an illustration by the legendary Norman Rockwell on the February 7, 1942 cover of *The Saturday Evening Post*. It depicted a soldier flanked on each side by a forward-leaning lady. The woman on the left is holding a saucer. The soldier seated in the middle is holding up a cup with his right hand and a half-eaten donut with his left hand. The woman on the right wears the USO armband, and she is holding a plate of food. The inside credits (left to right) read: ". . . you have Helen Mueller, New York model, Willie [Gillis Jr.], and Kay Aldridge, ex-model, California-1942 'Wine Queen' and starlet whom the Navy picked as one of the six most beautiful girls in Hollywood."

The movie deal regarding the story of the Powers models finally seemed to come together. From the previous year, the title has been changed to *The Powers Girl* from *The Powers Model*. Aldridge at this point is still scheduled to be part of it. *NYT*, February 23, 1942: "Charles R. Rogers is seeking Richard Wallace to direct *The Powers Girl*, which United Artists will release; M. Coates Webster and Arna Lazarus are writing the scenario, and Georgia Carroll and Katharine Aldridge have been engaged for roles in the picture, which will start in April."

Released in 1943, *The Powers Girl* featured Ann Shirley, George Murphy, Dennis Day, and Benny Goodman. Why Aldridge did not appear in the film is unknown for sure, but apparently it had something to do with the fact that she got involved around the same time with another studio as she signed on for serial work at Republic Pictures.

Her movie commitment would then become reduced to just six weeks a year that she had to be on the West Coast. Now, if she chose to do so, Aldridge could spend time happily in Virginia most of the year.

With her reputation established as cover girl, fashion model, film starlet and now "Wine Queen," Aldridge would reach her pinnacle of success with the announcement of the film production that what would become her best known and lasting role ever.

NYT, March 18, 1942: "Kay Aldridge will play the lead in Republic's jungle serial, *Perils of Nyoka*, with Clayton Moore and Lorna Gray; filming will begin this week..."

Carey: "K.A.'s career opportunities diminishing, K.A. signs a contract with Republic Studios to star in serials."

McCord: "Her agent brought word that Republic Pictures was looking for a girl to play the lead in a serial, *Perils of Nyoka* and Miss Aldridge decided to seek the role for two reasons. She wanted to break away from the image of just being a beautiful girl and she needed the money. Her mother had come to California to live with her, and Miss Aldridge was also helping to support other members of her family."

Aldridge, as reported by John Todd (International News Service): "They've been casting me as the ultra-sophisticated, nasty, usually rich 'other girl,' who never gets the hero. . . . Kay insists it is just the naïve type, a role a naïve like herself should play. She doesn't think she's had her type of role before."

McCord: "At Republic Miss Aldridge was interviewed by director William Witney and studio founder Herbert J. Yates. She does not believe she had to take a screen test. 'I think I got in on the personal interview and by making lots of claims that weren't true about my being so athletic and so outdoorsy and representing myself as being just the opposite of a soignée model. I was a country girl, and I emphasized that I wanted to dress like a country girl.'"

Aldridge told McCord she thought she signed for four serials, starting at $650 a week, increasing with each serial. But then she couldn't be sure that was the amount she was paid, or why she only did three serials.

McCord: "Based on the timing pattern of her serials, she would have been due to make another cliffhanger during the first half of 1945. However, she was married in February 1945, and retired from show business."

Edwin Schallert wrote one of the first articles on Republic's acquisition: "Kay Aldridge Named Republic Serial Queen," *LAT*, March 18, 1942. Schallert: "A new Serial Queen – one of the first since Pearl White, whose fame was historic – has been captured by Republic. It's K.A., who was a member of *Navy Blues* Sextet, and she has been signed to star in *Perils of Nyoka* (remember *Perils of Pauline*?) which will be a 15-episode affair.

"No fewer than 200 young women were tested for the chapter production, which will present Clayton Moore as male lead, Lorna Gray as heavy, and will be directed by William Witney. At the time of the previous war, serials were one of the most popular cinema institutions."

The excitement over Aldridge's involvement in the rough and tumble action and adventuresome lead role as Nyoka began in earnest.

John Chapman, *CDT*, April, 6, 1942: "Thursday – To Ray Corrigan's ranch at Simi, thutty-fo'ty mile away, where Cover Girl K.A. is trying to break her beautiful neck as the heroine of a Republic serial, *Perils of Nyoka*.... Ray makes quite a thing out of his ranch, as do some of his neighbors, renting it out as a location for western, jungle, or desert pix."

The fact that Aldridge, the cover girl and sexy Sextet member, now, is showing another side to her versatility by playing a serial heroine. You would expect this to perfectly expand public interest in her.

John Chapman, *CDT*, April 19, 1942, gave Aldridge and the rest of the *Navy Blues* Sextet attention as regards to their modeling abilities. However, the article acknowledged the fact that none of them has made it big yet as actresses.

Chapman: "Each one had Hollywood at her feet, and each still has the chance to become a star; but none is a star yet. K.A. has had the most interesting subsequent career, because it's so different from what you'd expect of a cover girl. Kay has become a Serial Queen and for the last several weeks has been barking her pretty shins, falling off horses, fighting villainous Bedouins, eating box lunches on location, and wearing khaki shirt, khaki shorts, a six-gun, and a knife in a 30-reel thriller called *Perils of Nyoka*.

"*Perils* is a Republic serial. I won't burden you with a plot, but will merely give you the installment headings. From these you can write your own plot, and I'll bet it's the same one. They are: 'Desert Intrigue,' 'Death's Chariot,' 'Devil's Crucible,' 'Ascending Doom,' 'Fatal Second,' 'Human Sacrifice,' 'Monster's Clutch,' 'Tuareg Vengeance,' 'Burned Alive,' 'Treacherous Trail,' 'Unknown Peril,' 'Underground Tornado,' 'Thundering Hoofs,' 'Blazing Barrier,' and 'Satan's Fury.'

"That, friends, is a heck of a set of predicaments for a cover girl, and I went out on Republic's location I told Kay so. 'The Stork club set,' I told her as I eyed a black-and-blue mark half way between one of her knees and one of her shorts, 'would hardly recognize you.'"

Aldridge took to the part like a fly to honey, intimating that she's finally closer to her true self. Aldridge told Chapman: "But this is my dish. I was never meant to be a model. I can't walk like one yet, because I'm still pigeon-toed. I'm a farm girl from tidewater Virginia. Why, our house is the oldest frame house in that part of the country, built in 1690, and we still haven't got any money to put in plumbing and lights. Before we do that we've got to get enough money to fix up the house so it will be worth putting lights and plumbing into."

Schallert reminded readers of Aldridge's career: "Kay's career might have been nothing whatever had it not been for the wonderful accident of superlative beauty. She was a country girl. Her father had died when she was a small child, and while her mother earned money by teaching, Kay was brought up by three maiden great-aunts. Kay went to a female seminary in Maryland, won letters in track, was voted prettiest girl in the school, then became Apple Blossom princess of Winchester, Va. But she had no notion of making beauty a career, so she studied stenography and wound up with a job in the war department in Washington, D.C."

Carey: "Schallert has it really wrong. He writes that K.A.'s mother earned money by teaching. My grandmother never taught. My grandmother's maiden aunts, who lived at Bladensfield, were retired schoolteachers (they had taught at private schools in Washington, D.C.) and had their schoolteachers' pensions. They home-schooled my mother and her siblings through their early elementary school years. After that, various relatives chipped in with money and/or offerings of lodging to send the children to schools better than those in the area.

"Bladensfield, where my grandmother lived from her 30s until she was 53 years old, and the crossroads of Lyell's Corner were so remote, they presented absolutely NO employment opportunities to a woman of that age. My mother's mother was a poet, an artist and an illustrator and occasionally made money by selling illustrations. I know for sure that she sold at least one poem and an illustration to *Harper's Magazine*. She also cut silhouettes (profiles) out of black paper, which were popular in the 1920s and before and which she managed to sell sometimes. Her artistic sensibility helped her to escape the bleakness of her existence as a widow with 5 children at a remote farm, if little else."

Schallert's claim that Aldridge had a job at the War Department in Washington is incorrect and ludicrous. Carey: "My mother had two jobs in Baltimore. One was with the Production Credit Corporation, whatever that was, and the other one was with the Third

Corps Area Headquarters of the US Army. Perhaps her army job helped her to get to the dance at West Point."

Aldridge admitted in her interview with *Collier's*, October 24, 1942, that she was a "good typist, bum stenographer."

Schallert: "Somebody had suggested that she was attractive enough to be a John Powers model in New York, and she kept this in mind. In the war department a lieutenant asked her to go up to West Point to a dance, and she went. From West Point she went to New York with $6 in her purse and called at the Powers office on an off chance. Powers immediately put her to work – and that was the end of K.A., the farm girl and government stenog. In her place appeared a glamorous cover girl.

"A cover girl assignment took Kay with a group of models on a junket to Honolulu, and on the way back she naturally stopped off in Hollywood. Hollywood naturally gave her a job. Twentieth-Fox first engaged her and put her in chill parts and beautiful gowns. She didn't register. Then Warners made her one of the six honeys in *Navy Blues*. She registered, but not as an actress.

"Recently Republic began hunting for a new Serial Queen, and the choice narrowed down to Kay on the basis of looks. 'But can you show any life?' she was asked by somebody who had seen her in the chill parts. 'Just give me a chance,' said Kay. They did, and she has shown so much life that she has already injured two stunt men in fights. She hasn't yet learned to pull her punches, as good movie scrappers do.

"The life of a beauty in New York or Hollywood is extremely pleasant. Pretty clothes, publicity, compliments, parties, plenty of beaux. A hothouse life. Being a Serial Queen is something else. Most of *Perils of Nyoka* is being shot on location in Ventura County, about an hour's drive from Hollywood. Kay checks in at the studio at 6 a.m., puts on her shorts costume, and gets made up; then with the rest of the troupe she takes a bus to the ranch. Until the light fades around 6:30 p.m. it's bang-bang-bang, cramming footage into the camera, with only a few minutes out for eating a possibly dangerous box lunch.

"It's about 8 p.m. when Kay has washed the dirt and makeup and donned her own clothes at the studio. Just time for dinner and flop! into bed. For a few days Kay tried commuting to her home in Santa Monica, which she shares with her mother and two brothers, who work in an aircraft plant. A few days were enough; then she took a cabin in a motel near the studio. The movie company thought it a bit undignified for a Serial Queen to be putting up a roadside auto camp, but it didn't bother Kay.

"Of all the recent crop of four-color, slick-paper beauties I think K.A. has made herself most interesting by tackling a knock-down, drag-out job in a serial. There's no better way of learning how movies are made – and, girls, you've got to know."

As far as Aldridge's commuting to Lone Pine, Carey explained: "She gave up the idea of trying to return to Santa Monica or wherever it was she was living when she was filming *Nyoka* not only because it was far, but because there was wartime rationing of rubber and gasoline."

Aldridge liked being Serial Queen because she now had more geographical freedom with the Republic contract, which put limited demand on her time by comparison to her Fox and Warners commitments. She planned to go back to Virginia, and fix up her Bladensfield family home. Edith Lindeman explained: "All she'll have to do will be to report to the studio twice a year, go through her 15 chapters as fast as they can be shot, then go 'home,' wherever that may be."

Hopper, April 24, 1942: "K.A., formerly the Nation's leading cover... encountered some trouble in pictures till she got a chance, along with 200 girls, for lead in Republic's new serial *Perils of Nyoka*.

"They wanted a rip-snorting, fist-swinging wench for that part, and after eliminating gals through various tests, took last five to the back lot, put them to climbing trees, wrestling, jumping fences. And it was then that Kay, who was raised on a Virginia farm, proved she had 'em all skinned by a country mile when it came to taking care of herself in a free-for-all" (*LAT*, April 24, 1942; *WP*, April 30, 1942).

NYT, April 26, 1942, Thomas F. Brady on Aldridge's move to Republic Studios: "Katharine Aldridge, who has led a gilded and sheltered life as a New York model and later as a contract actress at Fox and Warners, is now face to face with reality at the Republic studios. Signed for the starring role in *Perils of Nyoka*, a jungle serial in which she will be seen as a latter-day Pearl White she was greeted by the production manager on the picture with the words, 'Always remember, you belong to Republic body and soil.' He has repeated the formula to her every day. And to check any extravagant tendencies in her, he always says, 'You might just as well be eating five-dollar bills at these prices,' when she gets her box-lunch at noon on location."

CDT, May 11, 1942, John Chapman told of an interesting incident: "K.A., the model who has become Republic's Serial Queen, went to Victory House on a bond selling expedition the other day and she wore her jungle girl suit – khaki shirt and shorts, with a real gun and a rubber knife at her belt. On the way home, the car she was in pulled alongside another at a red light. In the other car a fellow was taking advantage of the traffic pause to give his girl a hug and a kiss. In a flash the whimsical Kay leaped out of her car, shoved her real gun thru the window of the swain's car and commanded, 'Unhand that girl!' Well, before it was over traffic was snarled and a crowd of 200 had gathered."

Of course, Aldridge lived at the Studio Club when she began her Hollywood career. Hopper, *LAT*, May 14, 1942: "Tonight at the Studio Club, the old mortgage will be burned, with many of the alumnae (meaning those girls who lived there before fame caught 'em) in attendance, and Rudy Vallee. Girls they expect are ZaSu Pitts, K.A., Phyllis Brooks, Evelyn Keyes, Linda Darnell, Maureen O'Sullivan, Virginia Gilmore. Donna Reed and Barbara Britton still live there. Club now entertains about 400 men in service a month, and holds open house five nights a week for men in blue and khaki."

During the time of silent movies, females reigned supreme in the serials; woman such as Pearl White, Grace Cunard, Ruth Roland, Kathlyn Williams, and Helen Holmes. Hopper, *LAT*, May 31, 1942, spoke of this era: "We had quite a sizable escape literature in the form of the Serial Queen. Then serials suffered a decline. D. W. Griffith and Cecil De Mille discovered the 'feature film' and others were quick to follow it. Time marched on apace, and gradually the Serial Queen passed into the limbo of forgotten delights. Then, 1936, and hark! The faint rumblings of a welcome resurrection – the dawn of a beloved yesterday!

"Last year Republic again decided to take a crack at the Serial Queen. *Perils of Nyoka* was readied and the hunt was on. Two hundred beauties were given the works and the winner emerged in the shape of K.A., a former Powers model and Billy Rose's selection for 'most beautiful girl in the world.' Kay is a 'suthern gal,' Virginia born and bred; but much more important than her beauty is her ability to take it on the chin and elsewhere! These flowers of the Old South may look as if a breath would blow them away but underneath their fragile exteriors they're as tough as whipcord and will tackle their weight in wildcats once their dander's up – as many a man has discovered in his sorrow, after being taken in by that 'you-all' stuff!

"Kay neither drinks nor smokes but don't let that deceive you. She's as deadly as a rattlesnake, and when little Nyoka tightens up her belt to get herself out of a jam, stunt men turn gray under their grease paint and their lips move in silent prayer. So far, *Perils of Nyoka* is going great guns. The rushes are all that Republic ever hoped for and when it hits the screen it's my guess we're going to see the dawn of a new era for those legendary ladies of yesterday. "So look to your laurels, glamour gals; you may be exchanging your sex appeal for socks appeal, come this time next year!"

Perils of Nyoka, Aldridge's 17th production, and first of three serials Aldridge appeared in for Republic, was released on June 27, 1942.

In "Remember the Serial Queen?" *LAT*, July 14, 1942, Aldridge is pictured: "This is K.A. in a moment of repose. Most of the time she is taking a beating at the Republic lot, where she's the resilient heroine of *Perils of Nyoka*..."

LAT, July 19, 1942, Philip K. Scheuer writes: "Most curious recent fact brought to light, I think, is that the favorites of the people both civilian and military – are not the ones Hollywood fondly regards as box office. The ovations go, in descending order, to 'trademarked' players, old-timers and last of all, the glamour stars. You take a guy like Maxie Rosenbloom – everybody in this town knows Maxie – but 50 miles away they never heard of him and he didn't mean a thing.

"Neither did the late *Navy Blues* Sextette – six beauties, but the only one who stood out was K.A., who had a funny little way of winking her eyes and crinking her nose. They liked Kay for that."

Besides her eye winking and nose crinking, Aldridge's sexy charm can be seen the previous year in the *Navy Blues* trailer in a moment of pure seduction. Aldridge says: "And a cast that's super terrific and if I know anything about aisles. . ." She then does her provocative moves when she turns her shoulder to the camera, slightly tips her hat, nods her head and smiles.

LAT, July 19, 1942, Read Kendall reported: "There is more than one way to get a soldier back to camp on time after his furlough and Kay Aldridge demonstrated this yesterday. One of her friends, Sgt. Adrian Onderdonk of Baltimore, visited her from Arizona. His time was up and he wanted to hitchhike. So Miss Aldridge, in tennis shorts, drove him to Highway 66 and waited a while to see if he had any luck. Soldiers may not signal motorists but must stand to wait for their chance.

"Sgt. Onderdonk's luck wasn't good. Miss Aldridge got out of her car and suggested that she stand with him. The very next automobile stopped. Sgt. Onderdonk had to explain that Miss Aldridge wasn't going along, but the driver was sporting and it developed he was going halfway to Arizona."

LAT, August 16, 1942: Republic Pictures reported that Aldridge is scheduled to do another serial. "K.A. went to work in the serene atmosphere of the Powers models. Then Republic got her. In 15 death-defying episodes she survived *Perils of Nyoka*, but she will risk her life and limbs again in another of the ever-popular serials."

Aldridge told Kinnard: "I was in Hollywood during a very interesting period and met everybody, all of the people everyone is interested in: James Stewart, Henry Fonda, Gregory Peck. . . . And the writers I met; John O'Hara, Steinbeck, and all the movie writers. The actresses I liked as people were Claudette Colbert, Ingrid Bergman, Rosalind Russell and Margaret Sullavan; and I also liked the male comedians, Zero Mostel, Bob Hope, Red Skelton, and George Sanders. He (Sanders) was a character. I remember

Jean Rogers (Dale Arden in the serials, *Flash Gordon* and *Flash Gordon's Trip to Mars*). She was a quiet, lovely girl.

"For publicity at 20th Century Fox, a group of us were supposed to be the six girls the Navy would most like to be shipwrecked with in World War II, so I was on lots of radio programs. In the old days, they were always trying to prove pretty girls were dumber than other girls, so they'd have ten blue stocking girls up there and ten other girls who were trying to make a living with whatever else they had – besides brains. I was always one of those girls on the radio shows.

"Once, they put the microphone in front of me and asked, 'Miss Aldridge, what do you plan to do in life, what are your hopes and dreams?' I was very young and inexperienced, and so scared I was trembling. I said in a very weak voice, 'Well, thank you, but I just hope someone will marry me, and I hope he's listening in.'

"So, a nice young man in charge of the radio program delivered hundreds of letters to me later on and said, 'Miss Aldridge, our mail's been swamped with replies to your mating cry into the evening!' At that time there were an awful amount of lonely servicemen in the New York area!

"William Witney, the director of *Perils of Nyoka*, was very young, and I was only 23 or 24. I thought when I went for the interview that they wanted someone about 21, so I said I was 21. After I was chosen for the part and had worked a couple of days, Bill Witney said to me, 'You tickle me, Kay, you're not 21 yet – but I'm not gonna tell on you.' I had marked my age down, but he thought I had put it up!

"What's amusing about it is that when I made *Perils of Nyoka*, I was embarrassed about how fast it was made, and about its cheap budget. It was entirely different from the other pictures I was in, like *Hotel for Women*, *Down Argentine Way*, *DuBarry Was A Lady*, *Yesterday's Heroes* and *Here I Am A Stranger*. They were expensive movies and I was always cast as a glamorous woman. All of a sudden, I was boiling in oil and burning at the stake and being shot from a cannon or whatever. I don't know if it was a comedown, but I got into it with zest because it was such a release. The funny thing about the serials was, they were such a departure for me. Because I was from Virginia and I was always cast as a society vamp, a little bit on the bitchy side, when I was under contract to Fox" (*Films in Review*, Sept./Oct. 1994).

Aldridge told Magers/Copeland: "My contract with 20th Century Fox expired in '41, and they chose not to renew it. Republic approached me about the serials. I did it with the attitude we had in that day that to make a B-western or a serial was a comedown for a featured player at Fox. It was a comedown in one way, but it was a comeup in another way because I was the lead. They paid me about $650 a week, which was pretty good money at the time.

"My first serial was *Perils of Nyoka*. I played Nyoka in 1942 and my name has been associated with that role ever since. Nyoka was such a departure to me from what I'd been doing before that I considered it a great romp—actually a pretty rough romp. I pretended to be more of an outdoor woman than I was. I knew how to ride, but they put me on a horse that was much too wild for me.

"The first day on *Perils of Nyoka*, the horse reared up and threw me over his head toward the sound truck, with my face coming at the sound truck. But some property man gave me a push so my face didn't get smashed into the sound truck. I got kinda bruised and everything, so after that they brought Davey Sharpe in for some of those moments I wasn't quite equal to.

"David Sharpe had muscular, knotty legs with black hair and a small mouth on which he painted a sloppy lipstick job and stuck a cigar in the middle of it. He put his wig on that looked like a raggy version of my Nyoka hairdo. His walk was masculine. I didn't know about serials and stunt men, and I was so afraid there'd be some shots of him people would really think I was built like that. I thought my double had to be prettier. Davey was a great stunt man. He did all the dangerous scenes. He doubled almost everyone.

"It was also hard for me, because serials weren't shot in sequence. They do everything in the Cave of the Evil Bird one day—and the next day you're in bubbling oil actually before you've been thrown in. So, you get very confused. The dialogue is very sketchy. You can have delivered your line very badly, but they won't reshoot it unless the horse happens to simultaneously make a social error. (Chuckles) That's about the only reason for a retake on a serial. So we had to be one-take people and ready to roll.

"While at 20th Century Fox we'd wait all day to say one line. I wish I'd done the serials first, then been in 'A' movies. I might have been a little better actress in the earlier films. I tried my best, but it was very hard to learn to be an actress in serials...I think the people who come across as really holding the serial together are the fine old actors and the experienced people in small parts. I think Lorna Gray was a much better actress than myself."

Though *Perils* had stunt doubles and trick shots, Crichton elaborated. "She climbed trees and rolled down hillsides and ran incessantly for cover, cowering away from the poisoned arrows of the natives. At best she did the latter stunt badly and was reproached by the director. He asked her with some tact whether it would be possible for a lady of her obvious good Virginia breeding to unbend a trifle" (*Collier's*, October 24, 1942).

Aldridge still posed as the pretty girl at the time she was doing the serial work. One example is the composite photo by Alberto Varga, the noted painter of pin-up girls for *Esquire* magazine. Varga utilized Aldridge as one of his beauties. *WP*, October 16, 1942, photo standalone noted:– "An Easy Job – "The enviable task of blending the best features of each of these film beauties at M-G-M into a composite glamour girl drawing has fallen to Artist Varga (seated, center), assisted by Barbara Shermund and Howard Baers.

"The finished product will have these features (from left): Inez Cooper's hands, Mary Jane French's hair, Theo Coffman's feet, Ruth Ownbey's hips, Eve Whitney's waist, Aileen Haley's bust, Hazel Brook's legs, Kay William's arms, K.A.'s profile, Natalie Draper's lips, Marilyn Maxwell's ankles and Georgia Carroll's eyes."

Many of those film beauties were featured in MGM's *DuBarry Was A Lady*. Hopper reported this in *LAT*, December 19, 1942. Though unbilled again, *DuBarry* would become Aldridge's 21st film, released eight months later on August 13, 1943.

Carey, in the scrapbook, referred to a photograph strip showing a sideways view of the bottom half of a scantily clad woman lying stomach down. Her elbows, bust and stomach are seen, and lower half of her shape extending to her hips. The inscription reads: "To Kay Aldridge, The most beautiful Girl since Creation, A. Varga."

Under the title "The Varga Girl Mystery," Carey wrote in her scrapbook: "In one of the dusty cardboard boxes, I found the neatly cut scrap of paper above, featuring the bust, stomach and elbows of a 'Varga Girl' with a signed inscription from 'A. Varga.' This led me to wonder: 1.) If K.A. had been a 'Varga Girl' and 2.) if K.A. had been ashamed of or embarrassed by the image, or by the fact of being a 'Varga Girl,' which is why she saved only the part bearing Varga's signature and never showed even that part to family."

Collier's had its own question, what the magazine called Hollywood's most baffling mystery, "Why Kay Aldridge goes in for making serial pictures, of all things?" Crichton: "She is intelligent, beautiful and streamlined. She is internationally known for her face and figure, has been in Hollywood almost five years and knows everybody in the joint. Of course she can't act. But who else can, in pictures? In brief, what is she doing in *Perils of Nyoka*? 'A masochist,' says the best answer. 'With a touch of greed.'

"... When it was through, she had lacerations, contusions, cuts, and abrasions; she had strained ligaments, sprained ankles and Charley horses; she had fallen off a chariot and been singed by hot ice" ("Black and Blue Beauty," by Kyle Crichton, *Collier's*, October 24, 1942).

The injuries affected Aldridge's mother. Crichton: "Recently, with intent to badger her mother, she came home, showed some resentment and said, 'Look where a producer pinched me on the leg!'

" 'Really,' said mother, looking at the wound with greatest of interest and no disapproval whatever.

"Kay was slightly set back. 'She's been reading those fan magazines,' she said sadly.

" 'I was almost afraid to tell her a producer hadn't pinched me. It would have disillusioned her.' "

CDT, October 25, 1942: "One thing led to another for K.A. She went to school at a Maryland seminary. Became an all-around athlete. Was elected beauty queen. Went to Winchester, Va. as 'Apple Blossom Princess.' Employed as a model in New York.

Stopped in Hollywood en route from an assignment, has been in movies since. She is heroine of the serial *Perils of Nyoka*. She is 5 feet 7 inches tall, weighs 125 pounds, has brown hair and green-gray eyes." However, elsewhere she is accurately described as 5 feet 8 inches.

Aldridge made another unbilled appearance (her 18th film) in RKO Radio's *The Falcon's Brother*, which opened on November 6, 1942.

Readers learned all about the "Long-stemmed American Beauties," John Robert Powers famous models. Aldridge is a recent recruit, among the few in the $25 to $50 an hour class. Most are in the $5 to $10 an hour class.

Powers supplied models "for magazine covers, advertisers and fashion shows, [and he] has an outer office that is a girl-hive of beauty. There are girls . . .girls . . . girls. Mr. Powers frowns on the "typical" glamour girl. A girl does not necessarily have to be beautiful or even pretty to get his attention. Most successful, he says, are Southern girls, with Texas and Georgia in the lead. Recreation is limited to a 10 o'clock curfew for most models.

"Ninety per cent marry Mr. Average Man and some continue modeling. The popular conception that every model has a mink coat, diamonds and a steady supply of orchids is untrue. She's just what Mr. Powers is interested in – photogenic and natural - his idea of the All-American Beauty" (*WP*, November 12, 1942).

A radio program included Aldridge as a scheduled guest on December 17, 1942. *CDT*: "8:00 p.m. – WMAQ- Bing Crosby's show, with the Charioteers and John Scott Trotter's orchestra. Guests: K.A., Edgar Buchanan, Lt. Frances E. Shoup, Trudy Erwin, and chorus."

Aldridge's second serial and her co-star is announced in *NYT*, December 19, 1942. "Katherine Aldridge and Allan Lane will play the leads in *Daredevils of the West*, a Republic serial which will start in January. Miss Aldridge was last seen in *Perils of Nyoka*."

WP, January 2, 1943, Hopper: "What a laugh, listening to Maria Montez trying to teach K.A. how to collect jewels, because poor Kay has only one clip. . . . But what Maria didn't know is that Kay doesn't give a hoot about diamonds." In addition; *Daredevils of the West*, a serial directed by Jack English and costarring K.A. and Allan Lane goes into production Tuesday..."

January 20, 1943, Hopper referring to *Daredevils of the West*: "K.A. refused to be scalped in her present picture. Says she doesn't look well with her hair that far up."

Sometimes publicity articles are disguised as legitimate news stories. Perhaps a case might be: "Reel Scalping Role Too Real, K.A., 'Menaced by Injuns,' Slashed on Head by Tomahawk," *LAT*, January 22, 1943: "The thing that cowboys-and-Indians serial devotees never dreamed would actually happen – scalping the heroine – really occurred at Republic Studios yesterday.

"K.A., comely range gal makes the cowpokes' hearts go aflutter in episode after episode of the serial flicker, was the victim. Seems that in a scene yesterday Miss Aldridge found herself menaced by a passel of Injun varmints who made passes at her scalp with their tomahawks. There was a struggle as the heroine battled (for the cameras) against the prospect of having to go through life wearing a toupee.

"The struggling knot of actors – Miss Aldridge and the Injuns (Bill Nelson, Art Dillard and Viengar Roan) – suddenly collapsed in a heap. Miss Aldridge emitted a scream several decibels stronger than the redskins' loudest war-whoop. No wonder. She'd landed on a tomahawk, the blade of which inflicted a four-inch gash in her scalp. Miss Aldridge will be back on the job tomorrow."

Chapter Six:
From Broadway Footlights to Poverty Row

"Miss Aldridge has little to do but happens pleasantly to be one of the most beautiful animate objects in this world."
- John Maynard on K.A.'s Broadway role, "Dancing in the Streets"

CDT, January 26, 1943 (*WP*, January 30, 1943): While doing serial work Hopper wrote: "K.A. doesn't mind location. When she returned from the High Sierras, she brought back six steaks."

Aldridge's first of two appearances on the theatrical stage is announced on February 18, 1943 (*NYT*). "Rehearsals for 'Dancing in the Streets' start today with these performers, Betty Allen, Kay Aldridge, Ina Constant, Lucille Bremmer and Drucilla Strain, newly added to the cast."

Brooklyn Daily Eagle, February 20, 1943: "Kay Aldridge arrived from Hollywood yesterday to take her place in the cast of Vinton Freedley's new musical comedy, 'Dancing in the Streets,' now in rehearsal. Miss Aldridge, a model, has been starring in *Daredevils of the West*, a film serial produced by Republic Pictures, and recently completed an assignment in *DuBarry Was a Lady*, for M-G-M."

March 17, 1943, Walter Winchell: "Lint from a Blue Serge Suit: William Saroyan described Kay Aldridge (now rehearsing with 'Dancing in the Streets') as a bakery window at which all men, like little boys, press their noses..."

The stage musical opened in Boston on March 23, 1943. Aldridge was pictured the day before in the *Boston Daily Record*: "When a new musical comes to town, look for the pretty girls, and here they are, important members of the cast of Vinton Freedley's 'Dancing in the Streets,' which opens at the Shubert Tuesday night. Second from the right is the star, Mary Martin, and the others are Kay Aldridge, Constant Aina, and Peggy Moley." Unfortunately, the Boston notices were disappointing.

On February 25, 1943, Columbia released Aldridge's 19th film, Something to Shout About. Again, Aldridge did not receive screen credit.

Daredevils of the West, Aldridge's second serial (and 20th film), has an official release date of May 1, 1943. However, that is actually when Chapter Six was shown in theaters.

LAT, June 11, 1943, Edwin Schallert on Republic's upcoming serials: "...the forthcoming ones include *The Masked Marvel*, to start July 1; 20,000 *Leagues Under the Sea, Captain America, Tiger Woman of the Amazon*, which will star Kay Aldridge. Nothing if not colorful are the titles." Upon release the latter title was shortened to *Tiger Woman*.

Carey: "K.A. is saved from appearing in *Tiger Woman of the Amazon* by Mary Martin, who casts K.A. (who can neither sing nor dance) in a musical, 'Dancing in the Streets.'"

New York Post, June 18, 1943 ("Kay Aldridge, Comely Clothes Horse, Prefers Prairie Horse"), Aldridge revealed to Irene Thirer: "I'm really not the glamour girl type at all . . . I'm rugged. I'm an athlete. I'm husky enough to be believable as the heroine who gets into the most awful messes – such as falling into a vat full of burning alcohol, gun tussles, high-cliff diving – and comes out O.K.

"I enjoy smearing my face with mud, and wearing breeches and sombrero, and doing outdoor shots – not worrying about whether I'm properly lighted, or whether the cameras are focusing on my best angles or curves. It's great fun. I don't care if I never again appear as a clotheshorse in pictures. Give me a prairie horse any time."

Thirer: "Miss Aldridge does not take herself seriously as an actress, and has no ambition to become a great one – as evidenced by her appraisal of herself inside the Republic projection room, where she and this interviewer witness episodes from *Nyoka* and *Daredevils*.

"'Just look at me come! Don't I look terrible! Look at those breeches! Aren't they a scream! Will you see me ride that horse? Don't I look like a regular truck horse myself? But, my, my! Don't you think I'm the brave one?' We certainly did!"

Thirer reported that Aldridge's next shoot, *Tiger Woman of the Amazon*, is scheduled for August.

However, she had to make the decision of whether to do another film or be seen in a Broadway show. Whatever she decided, it would preclude her from making another serial for Republic. She could either sign with M-G-M after having made an appearance in *DuBarry Was a Lady* or do the stage production "Dancing in the Streets" when it moves to Broadway.

On June 29, 1943 (*LAT, CDT*), Aldridge's conflict received press in a clip entitled "Eeny Meeny Miney Moe": "K.A. is in a dilemma. She can sign with Metro or do the new Vinton Freedley show on Broadway."

WP, July 20, 1943: Pictured "Kay Aldridge, come to think of it, does seem to be dressed, more or less, for a shower! Anyhow, Artist Vargas exercised superlative judgment in selecting Miss Aldridge for one of the months – it wouldn't make any difference which – in the "*Esquire*" number in Metro-Goldwyn-Mayer's forthcoming production of *DuBarry Was a Lady*, costarring Red Skelton and Lucille Ball – or the other way around, if you prefer." This film opened on August 13, 1943, and it would be Aldridge's 21st film, and her second for M-G-M.

Her decision to be on Broadway first got announced on August 21, 1943 (*CDT*): "K.A., Republic's Serial Queen, who's back in New York, will be in Vinton Freedley's new musical."

Interestingly, McCord claimed that Aldridge never saw any of her serials when she made them. McCord: "Miss Aldridge had never seen any one of her serials until 1978 and, in fact, had never seen a serial of any kind and did not know what they were all about. 'I didn't understand the concept,' she said. 'I didn't know what a serial was when I made the serials.'"

However, an October 21, 1943 clipping found in Aldridge's scrapbook (publication unknown) proved McCord's claim is incorrect since it stated that Aldridge went to see *Perils of Nyoka* with a female journalist when it first ran in theaters. Aldridge is quoted as saying: " 'Oh is that really me,' when Nyoka appeared. She saw herself tumble down a precipice, she commented: 'No I shouldn't have done it that way.' At a climactic moment, she clutched her arm, saying 'Gee it almost scares me.' "

Carey: " 'Dancing in the Streets' is a flop, but Mary Martin finds another job for K.A. in a play by Ruth Gordon, 'Over Twenty-One.' Ruth Gordon (1896-1985) is a playwright and actress." The play is sometimes covered by the press as "Over 21," sometimes as "Over Twenty-One."

November 23, 1943: "Besides Jessie Busley, previously announced, performers set for Ruth Gordon's supporting cast in "Over 21," due here Jan. 4, [1944] are Harvey Stephens, Jack Durant, Carroll Ashburn, Katharine Wiman, E.G. Marshall, Tom Seidel, and Kay Aldridge." Although this is Aldridge's second Broadway appearance; it did not serve as an improvement over her Hollywood work, and again she is given a bit part just as with her movies.

More details regarding "Over Twenty-One" were offered on December 8, 1943 (*WP*), including that it is actress Ruth Gordon's first work as a dramatist, to be produced by Max Gordon, and directed by George S. Kaufman.

NYT, January 2, 1944: Aldridge was named among the residents that stayed at the Hollywood Studio Club, though she moved out recently. The cost is low, and actresses can stay for up to three years "to make good or/and move." The Studio Club has "One hundred girls at $8 a head (minimum) who get rooms, two meals a day, switchboard service, library, club rooms and USO dances for their money. They get mild house-mother supervision from a lady named Marjorie Williams, who's been there to handle things ever since the club started functioning."

WP, January 8, 1944: "K.A., the screen actress, plays a bit role – that of a secretary – in the final scene of "Over 21," the new hit which just opened. In that scene a movie producer orders her to record in shorthand all the conversation in the room. Miss Aldridge, a realistic actress, really recorded it all in Gregg. She was once a stenographer."

LAT, January 13, 1944: "Republic, which was endeavoring to secure K.A. for *Tiger Woman*, has decided not to wait. And so Linda Stirling, a model for Adrian, has been assigned. Miss Aldridge is footlighting in the East." Interestingly, Aldridge thought she made that serial according to McCord because she had a June 13, 1943 clipping from the *Philadelphia Inquirer* stating that she would appear in it after completion of *Daredevils of the West*. Also, she had some publicity photographs wearing a leopard outfit – however that was not the one worn in that serial.

LAT, January 24, 1944: "Heaviest bidder for 'Over 21,' the play in which Ruth Gordon is being starred in New York, and which was written by the actress herself, will likely be 20th Century-Fox. The play, which recently opened, has been referred to as a hit by the critics – a light, gay comedy, in which the star appears at her best..."

Carey: " 'Over Twenty-One' gets good reviews and runs for a respectable amount of time on Broadway."

Critic John Maynard says that Aldridge, among others in the cast of "Over Twenty-One," offers fine support. However, he then proceeds to single her out and reduce Aldridge's value to nothing more than eye candy. Maynard: "Miss Aldridge has little to do but happens pleasantly to be one of the most beautiful animate objects in this world."

CDT, January 30, 1944: Photos taken by *Tribune* readers, K.A. is remembered here pictured with her *Navy Blues* Sextette; Peggy Diggins, Lorraine Gettman, Georgia Carroll, Marguerite Chapman, Alice Talton.

The Brooklyn Daily Eagle offered "Kay Aldridge Poses for 50th Magazine Cover" on February 13, 1944. The paper reported: "Kay Aldridge, who is appearing in support of Ruth Gordon in "Over Twenty-one," the comedy at the Music Box, has set something of a record this week by posing for her 50th magazine cover, all of them national publications."

Life, February 14, 1944, pictured Aldridge appearing in the Broadway show "Over 21," with the following explanation: "Hollywood producer Joel I. Nixon (Philip Loeb), for whom Paula has done a script, arrives. He phones actor called 'Orson,' Nixon: 'Listen, Orson, yelling will get you no place. What? (Handing phone to secretary K.A.), Hang up on him!' "

NYT, April 6, 1944: "This afternoon Jane Sterling will enter "Over 21," succeeding Kay Aldridge, who is Hollywood bound."

Brooklyn Daily Eagle, April 6, 1944: "Miss Aldridge is returning to the Coast to resume her role in the movie serial *Perils of Nyoka*." Actually, she returned to do her third and final serial, *Haunted Harbor*, and then go to work at the Producers Releasing Corporation (PRC) Studios.

Aldridge's 22nd of 24 productions, *Haunted Harbor*, opened in theaters on August 26, 1944. Later it would be re-released as *Pirates' Harbor*. McCord: "Again Miss Aldridge played a dominant role in the serial and was involved in much of the action, including eight chapter endings (Chapters 1, 2, 4, 6, 7, 9, 12, 14)."

Alan Barbour noted: "Kay seemed to be knocked unconscious more than was required of the average serial heroine in this 15-chapter tale, but it was all appealing to matinee fans."

Carey: "K.A. appears in a photo story about frog hunting bordering on soft porn. It is one of the many images K.A. never showed her family, but nevertheless preserved. Letters by K.A. from this period show anxiety about her career and finances.

"The financial worries started as the limits of her acting abilities became glaringly apparent, and she could see her opportunities narrowing, 1943-44. This was around the time that she was going back and forth between New York and California, modeling in New York, being in 'Over Twenty One' for as long as she could and acting in serials in Hollywood, making ends meet."

After shooting was done for her first film for PRC, *The Man Who Walked Alone*, it was reported on January 3, 1945 (*LAT*) that: "Dave O'Brien [May 31, 1912 - November 8, 1969] and K.A.... will star again together in *The Phantom of 42nd Street* for P.R.C. This is from a novel by Milton Raison and Jack Harvey. Frank Jenks is in the support." Carey: "O'Brien is the star of the 1936 film that will become a cult classic, *Reefer Madness*."

NYT, January 4, 1945: "Producers Releasing Corporation.... Dave O'Brien, Kay Aldridge and Alan Mowbray will have the principal parts in the company's murder mystery, *Phantom of Forty-Second Street*..."

By now Aldridge had been connected to so many eligible bachelors and received so many marriage proposals that Hopper said the Hollywood circle had their doubts about Aldridge marrying an oil millionaire named Arthur Cameron.

WP, January 15, 1945, Hopper reports: "Betting around town is 7 to 4 against K.A. becoming Mrs. Arthur Cameron, even though he did take her to Phoenix, Ariz., over the holidays to meet his father, a preacher. I love Kay's description of him (Arthur, not his father): 'Sophisticated outside, old fashioned in.'"

K.A. received mention when she assisted her singer friend Helen Pender in getting a "break." *LAT*, January 20, 1945: "K.A., who has her own movie career to promote, proved that she could do a good deed for somebody else, and is receiving her share of plaudits for such unselfishness. A good friend of 22-year old Helen Pender, she drew this attractive brunette with singing voice to the attention of Producer Jerry Wald at Warners." K.A.'s effort paid off as the studio signed Pender.

The Man Who Walked Alone, Aldridge's 23rd film production opened on March 15, 1945. How far down the ladder Aldridge came from her start is indicated by this first of two PRC Productions. It played at the bottom of the bill opposite a Universal "B" film.

June Corby's "Screen" column in *The Brooklyn Daily Eagle*, April 10, 1945 reported: "*The Mummy's Curse*, newest in the series of horror adventures starring Lon Chaney, Peter Coe, Virginia Christine and Kay Harding will be shown for the first time in Brooklyn at the Strand Theater on Thursday. It tells the story of the return to life of the Egyptian mummies Kharis and Princess Ananka, who are unearthed by bulldozers during the draining of some bayou country. The co-feature will be *The Man Who Walked Alone*, a comedy of a GI Joe who is catapulted into a melee of ludicrous situations upon his return from the war. Featured are Dave O'Brien and Kay Aldridge."

Her 24th and final film production, *The Phantom of 42nd Street*, opened on May 2, 1945. Strangely the two low-budget PRC quickies offer the most value for Aldridge fans. In particular, *The Man Who Walked Alone* is a screwball comedy entry that gives Aldridge much to do as the co-star. It is in this low-budget quickie that Aldridge shines along with O'Brien.

Aldridge was reminded of the films made with O'Brien, who had also done serials including *Captain Midnight* and *The Black Coin*. Aldridge told Magers/Copeland: "I loved Dave O'Brien. He had the most marvelous personality. He wore a toupee. He had a great sense of humor about himself. He said, 'Kay, watch me.' He'd wait til he had an admiring group of girls visiting the set, whispering and looking at him. Then he'd very graciously tip his toupee to them. (Laughs) At night, when he'd go home, after people making a fuss over him at the studio, he told me, 'I was quite conceited and my wife noticed it. So, to take me down a peg or two she'd say—Will you take that toupee off and take out the garbage?' He was so much fun."

Years later Aldridge reflected quite correctly on her movie career. McCord: ". . . Miss Aldridge said she was given a lot of chances and had a lot of people pulling for her, but that she did not take advantage of the opportunities. She said, 'whereas the other girls under contract thought I was lucky, I said 'I only had two lines.' But now I realize I was lucky to get two lines. I was spoiled because I was the top in my field as a model, but I was certainly at the bottom there (at Fox). . . I think I was too immature or something. I didn't do my homework right. I was too frivolous about my career."

Aldridge explained why her movie career failed: "I just kept the attitude that this wasn't the right part. I didn't feel comfortable in the part, and I didn't have the director. I didn't really have any supervision. I think my looks made them treat me like I was a looker and emphasize my looks. I wish I had been more aware of my opportunities and had taken them more seriously. My movie opportunities were great. My career entrée through having been a famous model, and the doors that were opened for me were unusual for my experience. I wish I had had a serious director and a small role at first that was more correct casting and comprehending my talents.

"I wasn't happy with my films because I always wanted to do light romantic comedy. I was always, I felt, miscast as this superior Eastern society girl and haughty. Since I couldn't act and it (the role) wasn't natural in my personality, it was like casting across the grain. I didn't feel I was cast seriously. I think my career was handicapped by the overemphasis on how photogenic I was supposed to be."

Indeed, Aldridge's later assessment of her movie career showed she truly realized why her movie career never took off.

Chapter Seven:
"I Got to Get a Husband and Some Children!"

> "Katharine Aldridge: 'Romance is really a matter of geography.'
> - Jimmie Fidler: "Uh-huh, and in Hollywood it has lots of latitude."
> *Los Angeles Times*, March 4, 1941

New York Journal and American columnist Dorothy Kilgallen described Aldridge as "a honey-haired Southern honey with a *Gone with the Wind* accent." Aldridge made it clear to Kilgallen: "I do hope some man will marry me." This is just one of many times in press reports that Aldridge said that her main aspiration was to find a husband.

Kilgallen revealed: "She has been a pictorial 'bride' probably more times than any other model, and she loves to play the bride at a fashion show. 'I get right into the spirit of a wedding,' she says with zest. 'Do you know women cry at fashion shows when a bride walks in? If I play a bride and the audience doesn't cry, I feel I'm no good.' "

Carey: "K.A. takes part in a radio quiz show, pitting *Redbook* cover girls against deacons of a Brooklyn, New York Baptist Church. When asked on the air what her ambitions are, K.A. replies that she 'hopes some man will marry her' and she 'hopes he is listening in tonight.' This announcement, together with a December 20, 1938 *Look* magazine article entitled "Often a Bride But Never Wed" (a reference to her frequent bride poses) inspire a wave of fan letters."

The specific date of her appearance on the radio show, "True or False," is unknown, but it is confirmed by an article ("Our Covers Go On The Air") in the December 1938 issue of *Redbook* magazine. At this time, the long-running show was heard on Mutual.

The format of the show involved the host, Dr. Harry Hagen, asking a series of true-or-false questions. The contestants could win up to $500 if they answered correctly.

Redbook magazine: "Six *Redbook* cover girls were competing with six deacons of a Brooklyn, New York Baptist Church. . . . The deacons won, we regret to admit, but it was a hard, hard battle . . . . Miss Colby, who held her ground firmly and fought the deacons singlehandedly long after the other five members of her team had been disqualified for having given the wrong answers to Dr. Hagen's inquiries.

"Virginia Judd, Kitty Aldridge, Libby Harben, Betty Ribble, Peggy Farley, and Jane Charlton (substitute) watched Anita (their captain) breathlessly. They were hoping against hope." This is one of the few references to Aldridge as "Kitty Aldridge."

On the dating front, Crichton in *Collier's*, October 24, 1942, reported: "Her social career in Hollywood has been spectacular. Most of the eligible young men have escorted her about the dens of boredom in that sad village at one time or another, and many of them have had serious intentions.

" 'He's declared,' says Kay, showing the proper pride to the catch, with a hint that the young man had better not try to get out of it. At the moment she is trying to make up her mind. Her serial career is merely a money-maker. She admits it.

" 'I got to get a husband and some children,' she says. 'If they want to hang around a little movie money for six weeks a year, maybe we can all live on it.' " K.A. was referring to her brief work schedule doing serials

Aldridge was asked about her love life a week before her 26th birthday (though she claimed she was 3 years younger). In *Cue*, July 3, 1943, Aldridge revealed: "I'm beginning to worry about it. People call me the only virgin to come out of Hollywood and I'm 23. I used to dream I'd walk through the woods and find a man who'd broken his leg hunting and I'd take him to the hospital and he'd marry me. But I walked and walked and never found him. I'm always looking. When I find him I'll cabbage right onto him. If he were very poor, I'd go to California twice a year for the six weeks it takes to make a serial. The separation would keep our marriage spicy."

Carey acknowledged: "Articles and magazine covers provoke waves of marriage proposals." Her scrapbook revealed some of the leading contenders for marriage to Aldridge.

Carey: "K.A. is crazy about Sterling Hayden but the feeling does not seem to be mutual.... K.A., Sterling Hayden, William Holden and another actress go on a cruise covered by *Look* magazine.... Photographer John Swope is a major contender. On more than one occasion my mother said to me, 'Just think, you could have been Carey Swope...'"

A 1939 *WP* clip revealed: "In fact, an Army girl can average one proposal at each party, if she gives the army officers a chance. One lovely model, Kitty Aldridge, of New York, who came out here to pose for some pictures with leis and flowers in her hair, got seven proposals in one evening. So far as I know, that's a record; you've seen her on the magazine covers, so you'll understand. An average girl wouldn't do badly, either. Maybe the War Department should send out a regiment of girls."

From 1939 on, there are many gossip column references to Aldridge's dating, as the following clippings indicate:

June 9, 1939, *LAT*, Jimmie Fidler: "It's hearts and flowers for K.A. and Francis (Four Star) Hennessey, who's phoning daily from Mexico."

September 18, 1939, *CDT*, "Looking at Hollywood" by Ed Sullivan: "Ivan Lebedeff has succeeded Gregory Ratoff in the affections of Katherine Aldridge."

November 12, 1939, *LAT*, "In Palm Springs": "Desert Date-ing – Alfred Wright Jr. and K.A. sipping lemonade at the Doll House..."

January 22, 1940, *WP*, Louella O. Parsons: "John Swope flew in from New York and the reason is Katherine Aldridge..."

March 8, 1940, *CDT*, Ed Sullivan: "Lean and lanky Jimmy Stewart explaining to K.A. that he doesn't put on weight because he doesn't like food."

March 10, 1940, *LAT* ("A party at Ciro's given by Robert Kane honors Gracie Fields"): "Others at Ciro's that evening who enjoyed the impromptu entertainment of the Kane party were...Katharine Aldridge with Voldemar Vetleguin..."

March 30, 1940, *LAT*, Jimmie Fidler: "Add hearts-that-beat-as-one: K.A. and John (Jimmy Stewart's pal) Swope..."

March 30, 1940, *WP*, Louella O. Parsons: "Kay Aldridge, Twentieth Century-Fox beauty and the very polite Ivan Lebedeff, dining tete-a-tete at the Tropics."

April 7, 1940, *LAT*, "Spring Visitor Shares Honors": NY magazine editor Voldemar Vetleguin – "To say good-by to the friends he has made during his stay here...Among the guests were Bette Davis with Bon Taplinger... K.A. and John Swope."

January 30, 1941, *WP*, Photo piece entitled: "Film Stars Mobbed At Cocktail Party." " 'Magazine Cover Girl' - Kay Aldridge, who won the title 'the most beautiful girl in Hollywood' chats with Tony Muto, Fox Movietone cameraman."

March 20, 1941, *WP*, Louella O. Parsons: "Pat Morison, who is such a pretty girl now that she has taken off so much poundage, and K.A., one of the town's beauties, were at the same table with their escorts.

April 11, 1941, *WP*, Louella O. Parsons: "The biggest secret romance in town is that of Sterling Hayden and K.A...."

April 24, 1941, *WP*, Louella O. Parsons: "Sterling Hayden with his real heart, K.A., on a yachting trip with Bill Holden and Brenda Marshall..."

May 10, 1941, *LAT*, Jimmie Fidler: "K.A. and Writer-Captain Aeneas MacKenzie are altar-headed."

October 29, 1941, *LAT*, Jimmie Fidler: "K.A. isn't boasting when she tells about John McClain's great love for her."

December 19, 1942, *LAT*, Hopper: "K.A. went east to marry Lieut. Robert Combs of the Navy. But something happened? Wonder if that something was John Swope?... Is someone kidding?"

January 9, 1943, *WP*, Louella O. Parsons: "K.A. dining with Lt. Larry Rockefeller, a brother of Nelson, was a vision..."

February 16, 1943, *LAT*, Hopper: "When Johnny McClain, war hero, ran into Kay Francis in London, she said, 'If you reach Hollywood before I go, use my house.' He's using it. The town's giving him parties. The most envied girl in these parts is K.A., his constant companion. She takes off for New York Wednesday for 'Dancing in the Streets.'"

April 15, 1943, *LAT*, (also in *WP*, April 20, 1943), Hopper: "Bill tried to line up all the 'Claudia' girls for the picture, discovered there were seven, but only two are still working – Dorothy McGuire and Kay Aldridge. Other five have all married rich men."

June 19, 1943, *New York Post*: "Now I'm combining both careers [modeling and acting] while I wait for a certain soldier to come back from England." Irene Thirer explains: "Report has it that Lieut. John McClain, former newspaperman and scenario writer, is the soldier."

July 5, 1943, *CDT*, Hopper: "It's a tossup whether K.A. will come back and work for Metro or marry Johnny McClain."

September 29, 1943, *WP*, "Meet Professor Robinson": "K.A. tells me she and Johnny McCalin [misprint, McClain] definitely will marry on his next leave..."

The newspapers and dates are unknown for the following scrapbook clippings:

"Kay Aldridge, the starlet, and Lawrence Rockefeller, the lieutenant, are a heartillery barrage."

"Larry Rockefeller is making beauteous Kay Aldridge forget her long-time heart."

"*Vogues* beauty Katherine Aldridge is rumored altar-headed with San Francisco million-heir Jimmy Flood."

"Don't tell me Gregory Ratoff is romancing with Kay Aldridge. But I'll be darned if he didn't close the set after she came on it while doing a scene for *Intermezzo*."

"Up from Albuquerque, N. M., where he's learning to fly bombers, Lieutenant James Stewart spent one evening of his leave at the *Mrs. Miniver* premiere with Kay Aldridge and Margaret Sullavan. It's good to see Jim again, isn't it?"

Carey: "K.A. attends the premier ... with actor Jimmy Stewart and her talent agent Leland Hayward, and his wife, actress Margaret Sullavan."

"Loudest applause from onlookers outside theater was accorded Lt. Jimmy Stewart as he arrived with Kay Aldridge, Maggie Sullavan and her hubby Leland Hayward."

"R.E. 'Kay Aldridge and Jimmy Stewart terribly serious?' . . ." Carey: "How strongly Jimmy Stewart and K.A. feel about one another is never entirely elaborated on by K.A."

A headline asks: "Is Katherine Aldridge's Latest H --- Hughes ---? She Doesn't Deny It Strenuously, Say Reporters." The sub-title reads: "Rumors Fly that Famous Aviator Is 'That Way.'" Carey: "H.H. = Howard Hughes, aviation tycoon."

A newspaper offered a photo of "Miss Katharine Aldridge" with this engagement announcement: "Mrs. John Aldridge of 'Bladensfield,' near Richmond, Va., has announced the engagement of her daughter, Miss Katharine Grattan Aldridge, to Dr. Eugene McCauliff, son of Mrs. Eugene H. McCauliff of 1 Fairfield Road and the late Mr. McCauliff . . . He is a research chemist with the Hooker Electrochemical Company. Dr. McCauliff has won numerous tennis championships . . . " Of course, this engagement was broken.

"Kay Aldridge of the *Navy Blues* Sextet – Billy Rose called her the most beautiful girl in America – and John Swope are serious."

"How that fellow Cary Grant attracts the pretty girls! That's Olivia de Havilland next to him and 'the hat' is Kay Aldridge."

Ed Sullivan: "Kay Aldridge and Lt. John McClain an item. . . ."

With all her dating experiences, a magazine article appeared in Aldridge's scrapbook with her giving advice and tips on how to find a man. In "Big Game Hunting" by Jessie Henderson (publication and date unknown), Aldridge is pictured with the help of Robert Shaw acting out various taboos – of what not to do. The following tips are pictured:

"NEVER use his rear-view mirror for make-up is an excellent rule.

"DON'T be a tie straightener.

"DON'T read a good book . . . when he's there.

"DON'T get insulted – laughter's better.

"DON'T cry – you'll cry alone.

"NEVER get angry – he might laugh.

"DON'T turn half the lights out.

"DON'T give him that 'You're so brave and wonderful' stare when he is only telling you that the barometer says that a storm is coming.

"DON'T assume the 'I'm a pal, just treat me like a man' attitude, or you may find him taking your words literally. No fun when they believe you.

"DON'T settle down for a delightful long chat on the telephone with another man when he is calling on you. He won't be jealous, but just mad.

"DON'T ape the movies. He wants to see it.

"DON'T make scenes never! Never!

"DON'T kiss him good night, if you are at that stage, as if he were leaving for a dangerous journey into the heart of Africa.

"DON'T leave him branded with lipstick, especially if he has a small sister who asks a lot of questions.

"DON'T overdo the Little Homemaker business. Bake one cake if you want to, but don't hand feed it.

"DON'T be supercilious about his idea of a nice present even if you prefer orchids. He's trying and that's a lot."

Aldridge discusses more advice in the article for "serious husband hunters." She notes: "Romance is really a matter of geography. Girls love to think there's just one man, somewhere in the world – and I still believe it – but I guess it really isn't so. Where you live determines what you marry. And if you shut yourself in an ivory tower these days, you can stay there, for all anyone cares."

Aldridge is emphatic that Hollywood is not the place to find a husband.

Aldridge continued: "No, if you want to go get it. In a nice way, I mean. Mothers ought to bring their daughters up to be romantic. If a girl's romantic, she won't ever flit from man to man. You can't feel romantic about a lot of men.

After many suggestions, Aldridge acknowledges: "The problem of big game hunting has many points to be considered as a porcupine.... Looks like the only way you can be a success is to outthink and out guess a man ... be a little softer than he is, a little less affectionate, a little more calculating. If you can. And without letting him suspect it."

Henderson: "Then she laughed. 'With all this preachment, I'll probably end as a desperate old maid. Either that, or my mother'll engrave on the wedding cards: 'At long last, Miss Cornelia Ward Aldridge announces the marriage of her dau--.'

" '... Know what?' Katharine inquired, hazel eyes sparkling like zircons. 'You plod along, trying this method and that on that man and this. And you find a boy that nothing works on. And that's the one you marry.' "

Although Aldridge was serious about John Swope, she would eventually marry Arthur Cameron. It is interesting to see one particular clip, as Carey observed: "The gossip column from the *Philadelphia News* reports on K.A.'s romance with John McClain in the first paragraph and on Arthur Cameron's romance with Pat Stillman in the second paragraph."

May 13, 1943, *Philadelphia News*: "Have you seen Lieut. John McClain and starlet Kay Aldridge beautifying the pubs together? ... Is Arthur Cameron really going to marry starlet Pat Stillman when his Reno divorce from June Knight is final?"

Hopper expressed the confusion that some may have had about K.A.'s marriage status when it was announced she would marry Arthur Cameron. *LAT*, January 31, 1945: "The little squib in the paper that K.A. would become Mrs. Arthur Cameron brought this note from Fredericksburg, Va.: 'It couldn't be true. She's been married to Lt. Robert H. Combs, U.S. Air Corps, for approximately two years.' Which mixes me up completely."

Scrapbook clipping: "If Kay Aldridge marries Arthur Cameron, she'll quit Hollywood without regrets. 'I don't think it's such a grand *life* in the movies,' she said. 'The other night at a party a big star and I happened to powder our noses before the same mirror. She still was a beautiful woman but she had a haunted expression when she looked at herself. I don't want to ever be that way. If you are not in pictures, you don't have to compete with every new crop of faces. And I don't think the average Hollywood star even has as many beaus as a stenographer. The really good men seem to be afraid of them.' "

As Aldridge correctly predicted in her magazine piece "Big Game Hunting," the engagement card announced:

"Mrs. John Aldridge at long last announces with relief the marriage of her daughter Katharine Grattoan to Mr. Arthur Arden

Cameron, an unsuspecting country urchin, on Saint Valentine's Day, Nineteen Hundred and Forty-Five, Henderson, Kentucky."

In an article by Penelope Armstrong, "Thriller Girl Takes New Leap," it is revealed, among other things, that Cameron's third wife, June Knight: "in the suit for divorce, charged her husband [Arthur Cameron} with beating and choking her."

Carey underneath Armstrong's article wrote: "There are indications that Arthur Cameron may not turn out to be the prince of her dreams."

Hopper, *LAT*, February 15, 1945, "K.A. Married to Texas Oilman" incorrectly reported: "K.A. of the films and Arthur Arden Cameron, 44, Texas oil millionaire, pulled a fast one on their friends yesterday when, without fuss or feathers, they were married at Evansville [Indiana]. The marriage was performed by the bridegroom's father, Dr. Granville E. Cameron, retired minister. Kay's new husband is well known in Hollywood. In 1938 he had married the actress, June Knight, at Beverly Hills. She divorced him at Little Rock, Ark., in 1943." That article mistakenly stated that Knight was his first wife. Carey offered the correct information that Knight was Cameron's third of six wives.

Carey explained: "The February 15, 1945 article about her wedding is false. Her marriage ceremony was not performed in Evansville, Indiana, by Arthur Cameron's father, Baptist minister Granville Ewen Cameron. It was performed by a justice of the peace in Henderson, Kentucky. They were alone and grabbed some stranger to be the witness.

"K.A. becomes Arthur Cameron's 4th wife. Arthur is 18 years older than K.A." For the first few months married, Aldridge lived in the Evansville, Indiana mansion on a hill that Cameron built with his enormous wealth. The Cameron estate, now owned by a Church for visitors and missionaries, is located in the 400 block of Hebron Avenue facing Lincoln Avenue. "It sits 400 feet above sea level, the house sits on one of the highest points in the city and at one time could be seen from a mile in any direction." Jessica Levco in "The House on the Hill," *Evansville Living* Magazine, notes that today the hill is a delight to sledders.

Levco explained that Cameron, "according to local history accounts, bought some of the construction materials on the black market, due to shortages caused by the war effort. ...They [Cameron and his third wife Knight] built a swimming pool and a tennis court on the property and installed floor-to-ceiling picture windows on the back, known as 'Hollywood windows.'"

The July 8, 1945 issue of *The American Weekly*, offered an article entitled "The Girl Mr. Cameron Can't Forget," about the problems Cameron faced which were still unresolved after his marriage to Aldridge and were plaguing him for two years already.

The American Weekly: "Arthur started the parade of suits by filing for divorce in Houston, Tex. Then June sued him there for a divorce, a mint of alimony and counsel fees and half the property. That drove Arthur out of town. In Little Rock, Ark. he tried again – charging 30-year old June with: 'rudeness, unmerited reproach, contempt and studied neglect.'

"June followed and countersued and for a while Arthur stayed out of sight, if not out of mind. June's lawyers offered a $100 reward for him. But the oil man came out of hiding and the legal joust started.

"Arthur claimed June went out with an interior decorator and came home hours later 'fighting drunk and with her hair down over her face and her lipstick smeared.'

"June said she only had a nightcap in a bar and that when she got home Arthur threw cold water in her face, tore up her gown, and 'repeatedly choked me.'"

Besides the legal distraction, the newlyweds' time in Evansville was brief. The mansion was built for Knight, and when it was completed Knight wanted out of her 5-year marriage to Cameron. In September of 1943 Knight filed for divorce. Part of the two-year legal wrangling involved Knight suing Cameron for $100,000 worth of property which included the Evansville mansion she said he built for her as an anniversary present.

So the newlyweds Arthur and Kay decided to sell the 26-room house and move to Beverly Hills when Aldridge was six months pregnant.

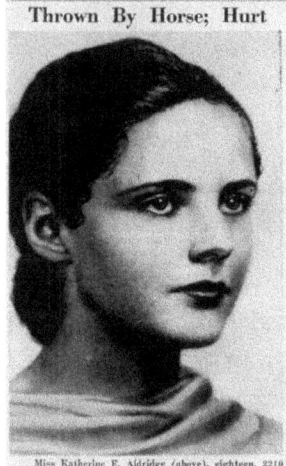

First print appearance of K.A.'s photo; The Baltimore News and The Baltimore Post. Photo courtesy Carey Cameron.

K.A. and her mother Cornelia. Photo courtesy Carey Cameron.

Bladensfield as it looked when K.A. lived there. Photo courtesy Carey Cameron.

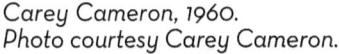
Carey Cameron, 1960.
Photo courtesy Carey Cameron.

Maizie, a.k.a. Alice Boyer.
Photo courtesy Carey Cameron.

Elsie and K.A.
Photo courtesy Carey Cameron.

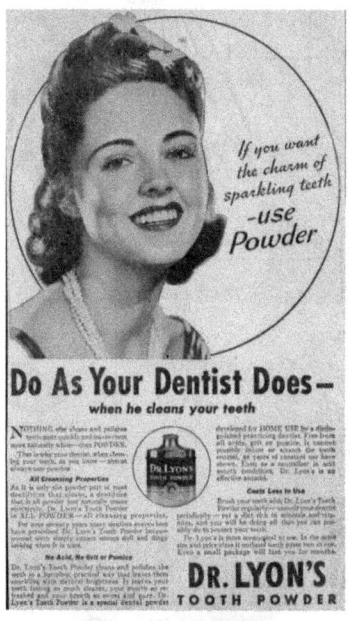

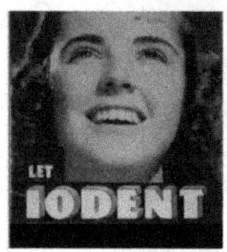

K.A. dental advertisements. Photo courtesy Carey Cameron.

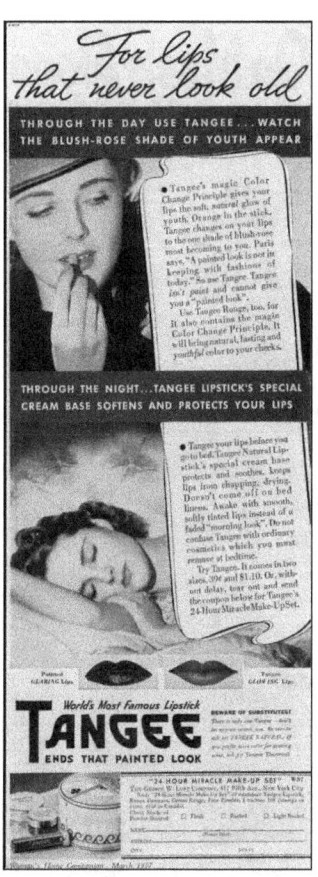
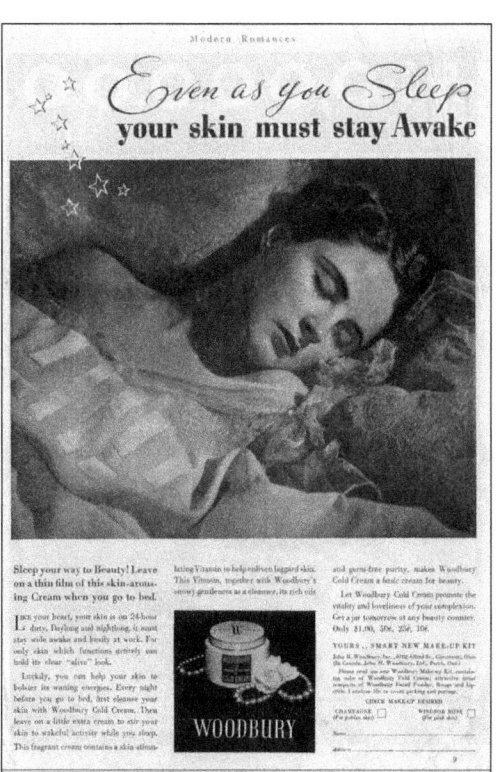

K.A. skincare advertisements. Photo courtesy Carey Cameron.

K.A. automobile advertisements. Photo courtesy Carey Cameron.

Sunday Evening
June 11th 1939

Dearests:

Tis Sunday evening and my first chance in a week to write you all the exciting things that have been happening to me too fast to give me time between to put them on paper to you.

Last Wednes'day Mrs. Zanuck, wife of the head of Fox, invited me to a private dinner party to meet the Marajaha of Capopouli of India (sp of course). She sent her car and chauffeur for me. I wore my accordian pleated blue chiffon with jacket and hair up. I was one of the first arrivals the only guest ahead of me was standing in the living room when I arrived. I walked right up to him and said: "Are you the Marajaha?" I knew he was much too attractive to be he and my remark had the desired effect. He grinned charmingly and said with an Austrian accent that melted my heart: "No but won't I do I'm Baron Hubert Puntz". I said: "Oh, Herbert Pants..what a sweet name...are you a phoney baron?" So with this start we were inseparable for the rest of the evening except for a little work Loretta Young put in on him. It turned out that he is a real baron not rich but dead attractive and one of the best winter sportsmen in his country over here doing something about establishing a winter resort like Sun Valley or sumpin. I was the only woman at the party who was not a star or wife of an executive. I sat at a table with Mrs. Gary Cooper who is herself very lovely and the one woman whose the right one for him it seems for he came over to the table and said something aside to her that just made you know that he really cares for her. They have a little girl now named Maria. Gary Cooper has the most marvelous smile I have ever seen on a man. Delores Del Rio looked beautiful as always and so did Loretta Young. Anabella was there with husband Tyrone Power. The Marajaha himself is dark but not negroid looking quite distingue but 65 is too old for me...he did sort of look at me with a gleam for both he and his son are great lady's men and they say he thinks nothing of bequeathing thousands of aches or a ruby or two to any pair of waiting arms but not for me those old boys. The baron took me home from the party via the Trocadero where we did some very fancy waltzing in true old Vienna style......he kissed my hand and now I know what hand kissing can be... terrific! I would like to have kissed him but demurred cause he is so attractive that I reckon they come easy to him and then I hardly know him though I always feel almost from the first that I know a person very well. He is leaving tonight for a trip to Arazona but will be back Tuesday....he called just now to say goodby. But I have two Austrians in my life now....the other is named Kurt Scharff and he runs a shoppe (very snooty) called Lanz of Austria...I met him as a customer myself and was later introduced to him socially and he is really the most wonderful dancer I have ever danced (with whom). He is fun too cause he says he has no heart. I warned him against myself being foreign and emotionaly I was afraid he would get serious about me so I explained to him that my friendly manner was really just me and that he must under no condition get serious about me but that I do enjoy dancing with him and he is fun to go out with. He just laughs at me and says you are very nice..pretty maybe...but me I have no heart.

The Marajaha invited me to a dinner party he gave last night at the Trocadero....called for me himself....and the funny part is I kept him waiting because I was being sewn into the dress I wore by the dressmaker who made it for me. Think of it "His Imperial Highness waithing for me". I made him late for his own party and instead of making up a false excuse told everybody the trutch and they all had a good laugh out of it.

June 11, 1939 letter from K.A. to her mother, Cornelia. Photo courtesy Carey Cameron.

This dress I wore is the loveliest dress I have ever owned. I saw a sketch of it in the original designs at this Lenz of Austria shoppe. This wonderful woman I know who sews beautifully took one look at the sketch and made it for me at half the price they would have charged. Kurt Scharff (who runs the shoppe) could not tell it from one of their own makes. It is made from starched white chiffon. It has a set in yoke neck tyrolian style, the yoke is outlined by a ruffle and the neck has a high ruffle around it. The bodice is sherred and the skirt has 17 yds around the bottem. The sleeves are enormous sort of bishop sleeves with tight wrist ruffles. It is called angle dress and that is what it looks like in this transparent material. Oh yes I have 7 crystal buttons down the front. I wore a gardeniain my hair as my only ornament and everyone remarked they had never seen me look as well. I wear it over a heavy satin slip the dress is so sheer. You'd just love it....I'm going to be photographed in it for you. Luckily it is not in style so it can never go out of style. The material I got a 20% off cause the dressmakers' daughter works at the store.

From the Marajaha's party I want to the phoney prince Michael Romanoff's party at the Clover Club. Everybody knows he is a phoney but he has such a wonderful sense of humor about himself that people like to have him around. He has made me the "Lady Katharine"....you would be so amused to hear his perfect oxford accent and he really is up on everything. People try to trip him all the time on the Russian aristoracy or Eaton or Oxford but he can even name his class mates. He has read everything. He even had nerve enough to say of the "Marjaha"...."that phoney...that pseudo visiting potentiate I'll throw him out". He said once to me: "You know what people call me don't.youth at dirty little bastard (with broad A) who thinks he's a prince". His party was too crowded to be fun so we went back to the Marajaha's.

About my carreer....I have been assigned a small part in "Falling Stars" with Don Ameche and Alice Faye in technicolor. I have two quite nice scenes in it.. I play an actress of the Theda Bara era. It is a story about the development of the moving picture industry. I wear an evening dress in one scene and in the other a very Queen of Sheba costume covered by ropes of pears and fancy headress. Odd part for me but gives them a chance to see me in technicolor. You see this star business is step by step. Tomorrow I'm going to make a fool of myself may be. I am going to ask David Selznick to test me for the part of Mrs. Max DeWinter in Rebecca. Folk say I couldn't look it but I can...the girls say I am too lively and self assured....that she was homely. But I say she wasn't really homely and they wouldn't have her so on the screen anyway. She was awkward..my newess to the screen makes me that anyway. I bet you think I couldn't too but I am going to try. The girl has to be an actress to depict all those feelings about Rebecca that can't be screened....I think it will make a wonderful movie and if I could get the part it would help me to live down what everybody is predisposed to think because I was a model....that I am a photogenic doll. I shall ask for the test even if he laughs at me and it. Pray for me. Even a great actress can not play a part to which she is physically unsuited....and if they feel that I am they won't even test me. We shall see. Today I met the most really lovely girl I have ever seen. Her name is Swedish and I can't pronounce it...she is brought here to play in the movie "Intermezz She is 5'8½"....sort of my coloring but with a complection so beautiful that she made mine look like a hide. The most winsome and exquisite face you can imagine. She is married and has an eight month old baby. Her husband is a doctor and likes her success.

I think it is thrilling that you are going to drive out to see me with Bernard. And of course, you are. It is the chance of a lifetime. Having lost your tegumental integrity some 25 years ago I think it is foolish to even care what folk think or say. I think it is the grandest idea I have ever heard. Perhaps I could drive back with you but I'll not be East to drive out here with you. I would want you to pay your own overnight expenses and some of your meals and can

certainly afford to give you this myself.

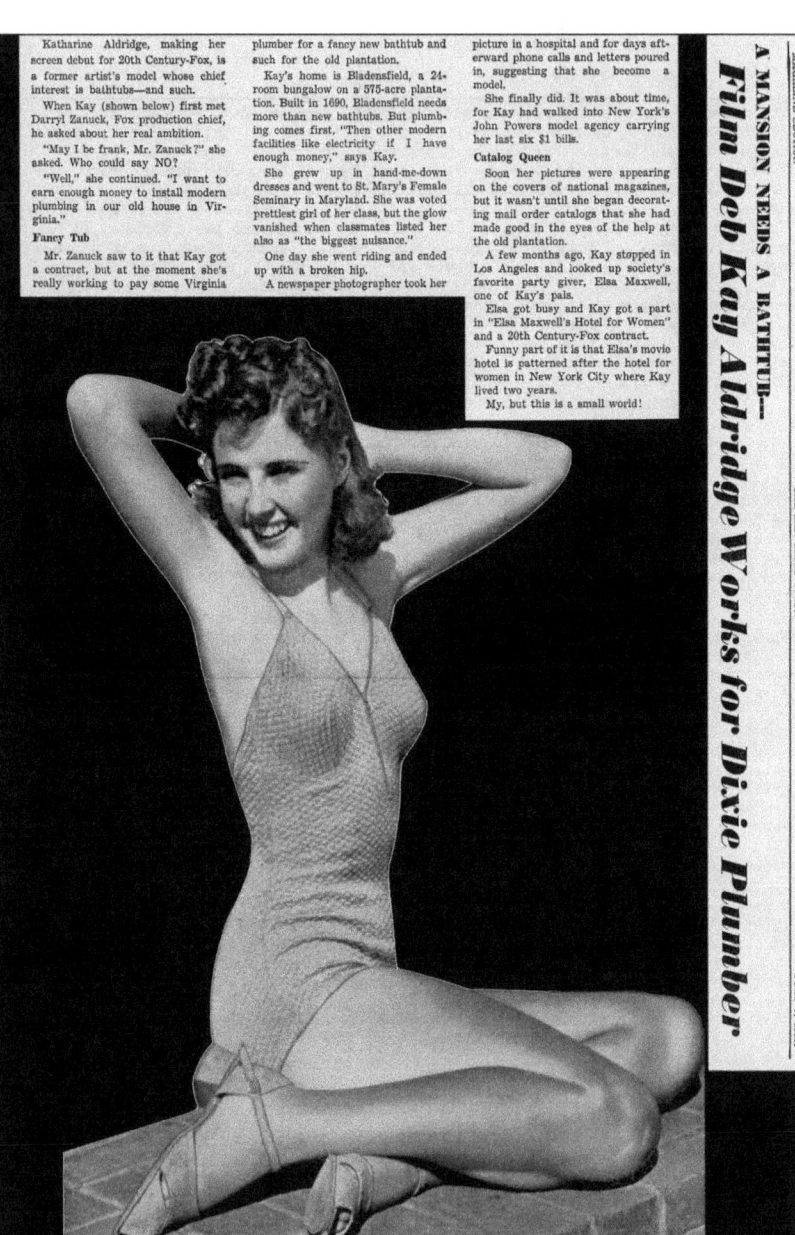

Newspaper article on K.A. Photo courtesy Carey Cameron.

September 10th, 1939

Dear Mrs. Aldridge:

Thank you for your letter. It came to me when I was taking my first vacation in the last five years. I tried for five years to get away for a least a few weeks but it could just never materialize. As I was on my vacation I did not want to answer your letter until I got back to Hollywood; now that I am back the war has broken out and with it our studio and the entire industry is facing so many drastic problems and changes that really before this moment I could not get myself together to write you a few lines.

I am sure that your daughter Katharine has on many occasions mentioned me to you and probably in her own way has given you quite a vivid characterization of her first director. I myself say that Katharine is quite an historical figure in my life as she is the first young girl who really has attracted me. I am in this country seventeen years; as a matter of fact on the 22nd of this month it will be exactly seventeen years since I first saw the skyscrapers of New York. I came here with my wife whom I married about one half a year before. Dispite the fact that all these seventeen years I have spent working in the theatre mostly in musicals and in pictures and have seen thousands of beautiful young girls I passed by them as I would the windows of some fifth avenue shops, knowing that they are very beautiful and attractive but I was just not interested. Then came the dawn!

My old friend, Voldemar Vetleguin, introduced me to your Katharine and I finally met my Waterloo. I fell desperately in love with her but found myself in the army of other unfortunates who met her and fell for her. The best thing about my attitude and relationship with Katharine is that I also happen to like her very much as a person. I think that she is without doubt the finest and nicest young lady I have ever met and her qualities and virtues are equal to her physical beauty. I will flatter myself by saying that it is very fortunate for Katharine to have met me as in my own field I will be as devoted and faithful to her as my friend Vetleguin was in New York. I perdict for Katharine a very big future in this town and in this industry. She may not get there as rapidly as for instance Linda Darnell, but there isn't a doubt in my mind that within a year or two Katharine will be playing very important roles and will be a name in this industry. I want you to believe me dear Mrs. Aldridge, that I am not saying all this to you just to make you happy and encouraged for when it comes to my business I am brutally and mercilessly frank and in this regard I could just as frankly told you that Katharine had'nt a chance. I am sure she will make the name of _Aldridge_ known to the motion picture fans all of the world.

Katharine is blessed with the faculty of captivating people the moment they see her. There were many who did not understand a first that she was not just a New York model out here to get herself a rich husband. These people today are all very fond of her and know that she is a simple sweet girl who has every quality you would wish her to possess.

I want you to know that as long as Katharine is here I will always remain her faithful and devoted friend and if, God forbid, anything should ever happen to her I will always be there to take care of her as I would my own sister.

I am hoping to hear from you often and I may accept Katharine's invitation to come and spend a few days with you at Christmas. My kindest regards and best wishes.

Sincerely,

Gregory Ratoff

September 10, 1939 letter from Gregory Ratoff to K.A.'s mother, Cornelia. Photo courtesy Carey Cameron.

K.A. on cover of Redbook, January 1937. Photo courtesy Carey Cameron.

K.A. on cover of Delineator, October 1938 Photo courtesy Carey Cameron.

K.A. on cover of Life, September 5, 1938. Photo courtesy Carey Cameron.

K.A. on cover of Life, March 27, 1939. Photo courtesy Carey Cameron.

K.A. on cover of Life, December 25, 1939. Photo courtesy Carey Cameron.

K.A. on cover of Sunday Mirror, November 26, 1939.. Photo courtesy Carey Cameron.

K.A. on cover of McCalls, March 1943. Photo courtesy Carey Cameron.

Kay Aldridge Becomes Highest Priced Model in United States

KAY ALDRIDGE receives $5000 check from Louis E. Golan for her services as "Lango Girl" at the fiesta during National Wine Week, October 12 to 19. She appears in several current films.

Kay Aldridge, named as America's "most photogenic girl" and hailed as one of the nation's most beautiful women, became the highest priced model in America today.

Because Miss Aldridge typified the California Sunshine Girl, she received a $5000 check from Louis E. Golan, industrialist and president of the company bearing his name, to represent his firm as the "Lango Girl" at the fiesta which will highlight the celebration of National Wine Week, October 12 to 19.

Miss Aldridge recently was featured in Paramount's "Louisiana Purchase" and also was a member of Warner Brothers' "Navy Blues Sextet."

Carey Cameron noted that this article contains another piece of information her mother never shared with her family. Photo courtesy Carey Cameron.

K.A. appears as bride on the cover of Ladies Home Journal, *June 1941. She is in her* Navy Blues *Sextette costume posing with the cover. Photo courtesy Carey Cameron.*

K.A. and first husband, Arthur Cameron. Photo courtesy Carey Cameron.

K.A. and second husband, Richard Tucker. Photo courtesy Carey Cameron.

K.A. and third husband, Harry Nasland. Photo courtesy Carey Cameron.

K.A. in pose from her 1943 serial, Daredevils of the West. It was "rediscovered" in 2008. Photo courtesy Carey Cameron.

K.A. with Zero Mostel in DuBarry Was A Lady. Photo courtesy Carey Cameron.

K.A. in pinup pose. Photo courtesy Carey Cameron.

Carey Cameron notes: "K.A. appears in a photo story on frog hunting bordering on soft porn. It is one of the many images K.A. never showed her family, but nevertheless preserved." Photo courtesy Carey Cameron.

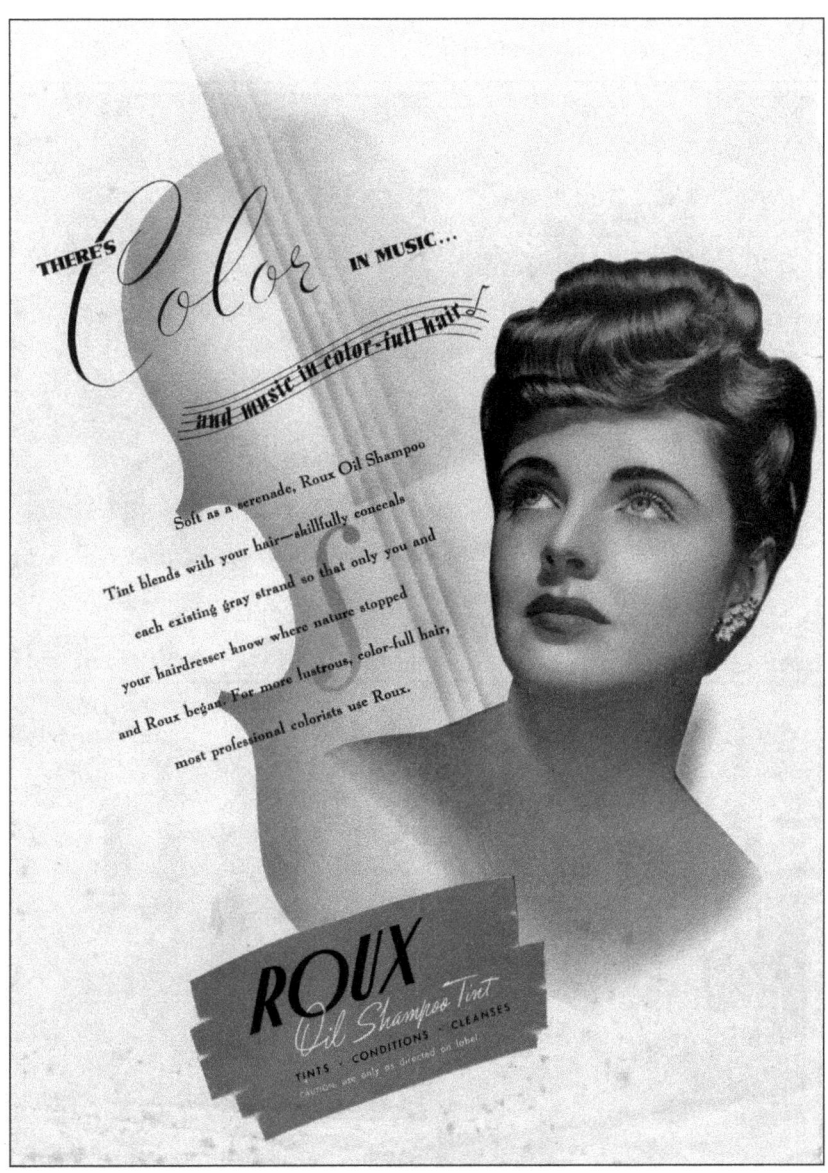

K.A. advertisement. Photo courtesy Carey Cameron.

K.A.'s last ad for cigarettes, 1944. Photo courtesy Carey Cameron.

One of K.A.'s last ads, April 1944. Photo courtesy Carey Cameron.

Re-release Lobby card for 1944 serial, Pirates Harbor (originally entitled, Haunted Harbor). Photo courtesy Carey Cameron.

THE THRILLS GONE BY: THE KAY ALDRIDGE STORY

Ma lei non è la donna Tarzan?

K.A.'s last appearance is at a jungle-girl-themed film festival in Italy, Rimini cinema 1989. Translation: "But you're not the lady Tarzan?" Photo courtesy Carey Cameron.

Page 4 • The Camden Herald • Jan. 19, 1995

Editorial

A Star And A Lady

Camden lost a fine lady last week with the passing of Kay Tucker. Her loss comes not so much from the fact that she was a movie star and one of the country's highest paid models of her day, but from the fact that she was a gracious, friendly lady who truly loved Camden and the many people she came to know here. Away from the bright lights of the movies or a photographer's studio, Kay glowed even more radiantly as a hostess and friend. Her generous hospitality was deeply rooted in her Southern upbringing and the strong traditions of her Virginia birthplace. She loved sharing her home and its magnificent view, and she took time to let her guests review the many books and photographs of her younger years. Her sharing of this life in the spotlight was never pretentious or done in a manner that ever hinted of superiority. She shared her present and past as an open book. She never tried to hide her famous past, yet she never flaunted it. The more you found out about her, the more you liked.

She was active in many worthwhile local projects. Yet, even with her lack of bashfulness for center stage, she did many great deeds that were known only to those who were touched by her kindness and thoughtfulness.

Many will miss this wonderful lady. Her star will now shine brighter than ever before.

K.E.B.

Anonymous notice printed in The Camden Herald following K.A.'s death.. Photo courtesy Carey Cameron.

JIM MANAGO

Following is a selection of images from Perils of Nyoka.
Photos courtesy Carey Cameron.

THE THRILLS GONE BY: THE KAY ALDRIDGE STORY

BURIED ALIVE and tortured by Arab spears, Kay is rescued in the nick of time. All this takes place in the Arabian desert, during a search for archaeological treasures

Kay Aldridge, the ex-New York model, now wrestles with a gorilla out in Hollywood. It is a real gorilla, she says, but tamer than any she ever encountered along Broadway.

TRAPPED AGAIN, Kay is about to be skewered on steel spikes, when "To be continued next week" flashes on the screen. And Kay lives to survive even greater dangers

A Hollywood lady getting her lumps: the lovely Kay Aldridge is booted over a cliff, part of her routine as Queen of the Serials

LIFE WAS NEVER LIKE THIS when Kay was a model. She's about to be boiled in a cauldron of oil — but it may be a steppingstone to a long screen career

Aldridge gave birth to her first child on November 9, 1945. In "K.A. Gives Birth to a Baby Girl," Hopper (*LAT*) reported the day later: "K.A., who once was a New York model and later a film actress, became a mother yesterday. The beautiful blond wife of Arthur Arden Cameron, Texas oil millionaire, gave birth to an eight-pound, one-ounce daughter at Cedars of Lebanon Hospital. The baby will be christened Melissa, Kay said."

Carey responded: "My mother was a blonde? She was utterly and profoundly brunette. [She] hated the idea of coloring her hair and (if the Jimmie Fidler article about her contract with Fox not being renewed serves) managed to avoid coloring her hair even when she was acting. She let her hair go grey naturally. She was also appalled by the idea of facelifts."

A year later, Hopper, *LAT*, November 5, 1946, questioned Aldridge concerning her braces: "Ran into Kay Aldridge Cameron at the Farmers Market, and asked why she was wearing braces on her teeth. 'Personal vanity – and for my husband,' was her reply. She has no intention of returning to pictures. Her one idea is building up a family. With her second child about to arrive, she ain't wastin' any time."

On December 27, 1946, Aldridge gave birth to her first of two sons. In *LAT*, December 28, 1946 ("Actress K.A. Gives Birth to Son"): "K.A., actress and former Powers model, and her husband, Arthur Cameron, became the parents of a son yesterday at St. John's Hospital, Santa Monica. Dr. Irving L. Ress said the baby weighed 8 pounds 13 ounces."

Press coverage gave Aldridge's sister Cornelia, known as Clelia, some attention. Clelia married a CIA agent, had 4 children, and lived many years in Latin America. *LAT*, August 13, 1947, Hopper: "K.A. introduced me to her beautiful sister, Cornelia Brady, from Washington. Maureen O'Hara and Susan Hayward were gracing the same table. I heard a guest say, 'That's unfair to the rest of us.'"

Her brother John had 2 children, but his health was a major distraction during the filming of *Haunted Harbor*, as he died at the age of 36 of multiple sclerosis. Bill, her second brother, married twice, had no children, and had various jobs over the years.

Her brother Ran caused Aldridge the most distress and embarrassment. Fortunately, the press did not report on his never-ending problems.

Carey: "K.A.'s brother, Randolf (Ran), a career criminal, is a constant source of pain. A dyslexic, his first criminal act is steal the technical equipment from the biology lab of his boarding school and hawk it on the streets of Baltimore. Imprisoned for manslaughter in Hawaii, he is released after a few years and joins K.A. in Los Angeles. K.A. sets him up in a tree surgery business: he absconds with the funds. He resurfaces in Minnesota where he is paralyzed from the waist down in a car accident while trying to outrun the police. Well-wishers set him up in a radio repair business in Minneapolis: once again he absconds with the funds. Ran dies in prison in Alabama at the age of 47."

There is a mystery concerning Aldridge: what Carey calls "The Dear John Mystery." This refers to a letter sent to *New York Sun* drama critic/columnist John McClain. "He is a member of the Algonquin Round Table, a group of notable, humorous New York writers who met regularly in the dining room of the Algonquin Hotel."

Apparently, McClain's column published a letter sent to him written by a regretful man. In his column, "Man About Manhattan," McClain offered the following letter:

"Dear John – People are saying, 'How come you aren't married?' There are two ways of delivering the query, depending upon the inflection. If the accent is placed on the 'you' the implication seems to be, 'How come YOU escaped this fearful fate!' But if the word 'married' is stressed the insinuation is that there must be some secret and sinister deficiency that has rendered me unacceptable through the years.

"My answer is ever adequate. For a time I cried saying. 'I haven't had any offers,' but that is evasive and slightly conceited and doesn't fool anybody. Lately I have been saying, 'Well I've had some near misses – if you'll pardon the pun.' That gets me off the hook but, of course, it by no means answers the question.

"So I might as well come clean and tell the truth.

"Just before the war I WAS going to get married. I was in love with this girl and she gave every indication of being in love with me. She was beautiful and exciting and great fun. It was only a matter of time until we tied it on.

"But then somebody blew a bugle and the first thing I know I was in the Navy. In a matter of months I was abroad and the romance continued by mail. I had all the equipment – the picture in the wallet, the inscribed St. Christopher's medal, and the poignant lock of hair.

"At the end of a year there was a joyous reunion when I came home on leave. At one point, in a moment of exuberance, we almost decided to run away from some place and get a justice of peace to do the job. But the end of the war seemed a long way off and we both agreed that if the thing was any good it would wait.

"A year or so later I found myself stationed on a small section of mud and sand in the Pacific answering to the name of Guam. This was the headquarters of Admiral Nimitz, the Commander in Chief of the Pacific Fleet, and his staff was comprised of several hundred officers, many of them, like myself, reconverted civilians. In the particular section of the island where I was quartered, a group of the staff personnel who had not been home for more than a year founded their own informal organization.

"It was called the Brush-Off Club and to qualify for membership one was required to produce a certain type of letter that was arriving with increasing regularity. The letters usually began: 'Dear Harry-You will always remain in my memory as the most kindly and decent and attractive man in the world, BUT . . . '

"After the letter had been read by all the members it was posted on a bulletin board and in due course the neophyte was permitted to stand a round of drinks for the members, take the oath of allegiance and become a brother in full standing.

"I must say in all honesty that my attitude toward this organization was confused. I would have liked to become a member, but I was also enjoying a certain smugness in the knowledge that it couldn't happen to me.

"Well, I guess even from here you can see the pay-off. I got the letter. The girl is now the mother of two, very happily married to a nice guy, but I can still quote verbatim the opening of my particular letter. It began: 'Dear John – This is being written on the train that is taking me to be married' . . .

"With all due modesty I must report that after my letter was posted and I was made a member they changed the name of the club.

"They decided to call it the Dear John Club."

(John McClain's column appears Monday, Wednesday, and Friday.)

Carey: "Is K.A. the author of the original 'Dear John' letter? If so, it, like the Varga mystery, is another piece of her past K.A. never claimed. The letter no longer exists, it is gone, along with John McClain. The McClain column, together with the fact that K.A. preserved it, and the existence of a humorous telegram K.A. sent to McClain in the early 1950s after the column appeared, tends to point to McClain as the recipient of the original 'Dear John' letter, and to K.A. as its author."

Aldridge made her television debut when the TV listing for *LAT*, July 9, 1952, pictured Aldridge with the caption "Cool and Collected. K.A. faces the masculine fire of "Bachelor Haven" on KNXT (2) tomorrow at 10 p.m."

The following week, *LAT*, July 16, 1952 noted: " 'Bachelors' Paul Coates and Tom Conway aim their barbs at sultry Hazel Brooks and K.A. tonight at 8, KTSL (2), on another session of *Bachelor's Haven*. The fellows, both married, are trying to prove bachelorhood is superior to marriage or something. Miss Brooks is replacing ZsaZsa Gabor for tonight's show. Johnny Jacobs attempts to act as peacemaker and moderator."

WP, July 27, 1952, Winchell: "K.A., who married oilionnaire Arthur Cameron, has her own coast teevy show '*Bachelor's Haven*,' too. One of the top-flighters out there, we hear."

Carey: "K.A. retires from acting and modeling following her marriage. K.A.'s subsequent appearances are (in large part) only for charity events. In 1952, however, K.A. appears on television in a live panel show with ZsaZsa Gabor. [Her husband] Arthur is so upset by K.A.'s risqué comments that he obliges K.A. to withdraw from the show."

As the following clippings indicate, Aldridge kept socially active during the 1950's, with many of the functions being charitable or related to her social connections both from her career and her marriage to Arthur Cameron.

LAT, August 12, 1951: Aldridge was pictured appearing at the Biltmore in Los Angeles: "Preview – Kay Aldridge models gems for third Jewelry and Silverware Show.... 65 exhibitors, including California and eastern manufacturers, displayed the latest models."

Hopper, *LAT*, December 25, 1952: "The name of Marion Davies calls up a fabulous era in Hollywood. 'Having finished her contract at Warners,' I noted, 'Marion is again moving that famous bungalow through which practically every celebrity in the world has sometimes walked. It was moved from the Metro lot in Culver City to Warners in five sections. Now it's to be lifted from Burbank to Beverly Hills. Marion will add a swimming pool and tennis court.' Now that house is occupied by Kay Aldridge Cameron and their four children, and Marion is their fairy godmother-landlady."

LAT, May 4, 1953, Hopper: "New Tenants K.A. and Arthur Cameron have bought Marion Davies' Benedict Canyon home. This was Marion's bungalow when she was making pictures. It was moved from the MGM lot to Warner Studio; then to Beverly Hills. Cameron bought the lot next door so their four children can have more room. A bridle path is being built for the kids' ponies, and the parents can keep a watchful eye on the tots from practically every window in the house. The only fly in the Cameron ointment is that Arthur has to spend so much time in Midland, Tex., where the oil flows – not like molasses but maple sugar. With most people cutting down on expenses, the Camerons have spread out over six-and-a-half acres in the choicest part of Beverly Hills."

LAT, March 4, 1954: "The Bonner School Parent Group of Brentwood staged its annual spring benefit luncheon and fashion show yesterday in the Garden Room of the Miramax Hotel.... The group's tradition of giving aid to a young children's organization is donation of this season's proceeds to the John Tracy Clinic. A Beverly Hills shop presented the fashions and Mrs. Arthur Cameron (K.A.), a member of the group commentated the showing."

LAT, November 1, 1954: Pictured: "Reunion: John Robert Powers, New York modeling agency head, has reunion in Hollywood with former alumnae at party for Ruth Hussey. From left, top row, Kay Aldridge Cameron, Dusty Anderson Negulesco, Bertha Mathews Schleussner; bottom row, Powers, Elyse Knox Harmon, Ruth Hussey Longnecker."

LAT, November 11, 1954: "Los Angeles alumnae will gather at the Terrace Room of the Santa Ynez Inn Saturday for a luncheon and fashion show to benefit the John Tracy Clinic and the Save the Children Foundation. Kay Aldridge Cameron will commentate and Nadine McNulty will co-ordinate the style parade from Santa Monica-Pacific Palisade shops."

An ad for Pasadena Home Show in *LAT*, September 25, 1955 read: "'Glamour Hunt!' a search for the most promising amateur model of the year." The hunt first prize offered a 6-8 month scholarship for Professional Finishing Course at the John Robert Powers School. The famous judges included former Powers model and actress, K.A.

LAT, November 15, 1955, "Catholic Women Will View Styles": "Mrs. John J. Tully, president of St. Martin of Tours Council of Catholic Women, announces a luncheon and fashion show at noon today in St. Martin's School Hall, 11955 Sunset Blvd., Brentwood. Fashions from a Brentwood shop will be commentated by K.A. . . ."

LAT, June 3, 1956, Pictured: Book of Famous Faces and Names, all former residents of Hollywood Studio Club, recalls memories for Actress Kay Aldridge Cameron, left, a club alumna, and Mmes. Thomas Workman and Jason S. Joy of the club management committee who are planning 40th anniversary luncheon Thursday at residence club for young women.

Then on June 5, 1956, the news reports changed dramatically from society articles to talk of divorce, though the latter was in the air for two years by then.

LAT: "Oilman Asks for Custody of Four Children": "Arthur A. Cameron, 54, multimillionaire Beverly Hills oilman, charged yesterday in Santa Monica that his wife, the former actress K.A., 38, is not a fit mother to have custody of their four children. In a Superior Court action, Cameron seeks modification of a previous order which granted Mrs. Cameron $3500 temporary monthly support and custody of the minor children pending a divorce hearing set for June 11.

"The wealthy oilman charges that since Mrs. Cameron was awarded the children last March 22, she has become an unfit mother. The document also asks that the support payments be reduced and that he now be granted custody of the children, aged 4 to 10. Judge Orlando H. Rhodes set the matter for hearing next Monday. In support of his modification request, Cameron alleges that his estranged wife has been 'openly and notoriously engaging in adulterous relationships with one Henry W. Doyle.'

"Cameron was sued for divorce two years ago by the former Powers model. He subsequently filed a cross-complaint and the divorce hearing is also scheduled for next Monday." Of course, Cameron then abandoned his complaint in which he sought divorce.

LAT, June 16, 1956 ("K.A. Granted Divorce From Oilman"): Pictured "Divorce Uncontested – Mrs. Katharine Cameron right, former Actress K.A., leaves court after winning uncontested divorce from millionaire Arthur Cameron, 56. . ."

The article read: "K.A., actress, was awarded an uncontested divorce yesterday from her husband, Arthur Cameron, 56, millionaire oilman. Her husband was ordered to pay $3000 a month support plus $1200 monthly for their four children. Miss Aldridge, 38, testified in the Santa Monica court that her husband criticized her continually during their nine-year marriage. Her corroborating witness was Mrs. Margaret Haberman, a nurse in the Cameron home for six years.

"The court found both parents fit to have custody of the children. However, it was specified that Miss Aldridge was to have them in her custody during the school year. Her attorneys said they would return to court Monday in an effort to collect an additional $60,000 in fees from the oilman."

LAT, December 26, 1956 ("Hollywood Sets Normal Record in Divorce Courts: 1956 Was Not Happy for Many in Film Colony"), reports divorces, including Ruth Roman, Joan Collins, Jeanne Crain, Edward G. Robinson, Edmund Purdom, Lurene Tuttle, Leo Gorcey. "K.A. received a decree from Arthur Cameron, oilman, after complaining: 'He criticized me continually.'"

Carey: "K.A. and Arthur will stay married for 9 years. Arthur will marry twice more and will die single, in 1967, at the age of 66."

After a failed first marriage, Aldridge married painter Richard Tucker later in 1956. His summer home in Camden, Maine influences the rest of Aldridge's life as she spends many years, including her final ones, in the picturesque coastal city. At first she spends the summers there with Richard and her 4 children by Arthur Cameron. By the late 1960s, they were living in Maine year-round.

Columnist Parke Rouse explained it best, as Tucker " . . . became the great love of her life. At his studio and house in Maine she found her spiritual home, in a community of conventional New Englanders who are charmed by her wit and spontaneity."

Interestingly, K.A. moved up to the northernmost state of Maine to share her very Southern style of warmth and love with the community for the next 38 years until her death.

After the Aldridge-Cameron divorce settlement, the coverage returns to Aldridge's community work and social life.

LAT, May 21, 1957: "The coral and white lanai at Mrs. John Stillman's home promises a delightful setting for the tea June 5 at which she will fete Kay Aldridge Cameron. Mrs. Stillman has invited many of Kay's friends to the party."

LAT, February 7, 1960: "The show co-ordinator is Joan Fotre and commentator will be K.A." This Valentine luncheon for 500 couples was staged by the Fashionettes to raise funds for Cobalt 60 equipment to bombard cancer cells at the cancer clinic of the Hollywood Presbyterian Hospital.

LAT, February 19, 1962: "The California Cliffdwellers' party the same evening was worthy of note, too. It was their semi-annual party and divertimento, a dinner in the home of Mr. and Mrs. Richard Tucker (K.A.) of Pacific Palisades.

"The original Cliffdwellers Club is in Chicago, and is so named because it is on top of Orchestra Hall. Membership is limited to men affiliated with the arts. The California branch meets monthly for lunch and conversation; there are no dues; there's a strict taboo covering conversation about money and politics.

Entertainment at Saturday's event was provided by members and guest artists.... Mrs. Tucker invites... etc."

A follow-up to Arthur Cameron's many marital woes appeared in *CDT*, April 5, 1962 ("Actress Sues Husband For 7.15 Millions: Marriage Fraudulent, Ann Miller Claims" by Seymour Korman). The article reported that Cameron misrepresented to Ann Miller that "he was divorced from his third wife Jean Lawrence, a Texas model, and was free to remarry." However, this article misstated that Lawrence was his third wife. Actually Cameron divorced his third wife June Knight (1943), divorced his fourth wife K.A. (1956), separated from his fifth wife Jean Lawrence (3/1/61), and after seven months of marriage fraudulently 'married' his supposed sixth wife, Ann Miller (5/25/61).

CDT, August 4, 1962, Hopper: "Arthur Cameron is off for a month in Honolulu with his four children by K.A. The children are not only photogenic, but have been beautifully brought up. This is a yearly pilgrimage with father."

LAT, February 21, 1963: "Sophie outdid herself with the gowns shown at Saks Academy Award fashion show in Ray Burr's art gallery. Her gowns and all the others got cheers from the ladies and feet-stamping from the men. The models were beautiful, and George Masters' hairdos extraordinary. Sat with K.A. and her husband Richard Tucker. Kay had some wonderful news. As a present for her oldest daughter, Melissa, who graduates from St. Catharine's School in Richmond, Va., former husband Arthur Cameron is sending Kay and their four children on the grand tour of Europe. They sail on the France, June 13."

LAT, November 27, 1963: "Art in Action: Understand actor Lloyd Bridges never worked as hard as father Lloyd Bridges when he was volunteer auctioneer at Westlake School for Girls' art auction. Not only did he carry on the auctioneer's chant, but watched his daughter Kathy spend her allowance and even authorized more for the purchase of pictures. Aiding him was Kay Aldridge Tucker (Mrs. Richard) whose daughter Carey Cameron also attends Westlake. Art ranged from the 7th graders Christmas 'primitives' (at 25 cents) to 11th grader Sandy Dunbar's (one of hers bought $150!) and Nancy Urist's really breathtaking canvases."

NYT, March 29, 1964: "William K. Everson offered scenes from 12 serials, noting: *"Perils of Nyoka* – Zam! Pow! S-e-x! Evil Vultura orders her gorilla to do away with Kay Aldridge (1942). The beast fails in his mission – with tremendous suspense."

A TV listing from *LAT*, December 4, 1966, 2:30 (11) offered the feature version of her most famous serial: "Movie - Drama *Nyoka and the Lost Secrets of Hippocrates*. Kay Aldridge, Clayton Moore. The following week, the feature was repeated. New York viewers saw the film on January 29, 1967.

The headline in the *NYT*, March 3, 1967, read: "Arthur Cameron, 66, an Oil Man, Is Dead." *CDT* reported "Cameron, Oil Millionaire, Is Found Dead." It noted: "Arthur Cameron, 66, multimillionaire oil man, whose wives included Ann Miller, June Knight, and K.A., actresses, was found dead in bed in his mansion here.

"Cameron, whose wealth once was estimated at 10 million dollars, had extensive oil interests in Oklahoma and California. He was the brother of George Cameron, owner of the Desert Sun newspaper and radio station KDES and KBLA, Burbank. Cameron also had been married to a former Conover model, Jean Lawrence. He is survived by three sons and a daughter, by his marriage to Miss Aldridge, and his brother."

Carey: "I remember at the time of my father's death that an article stated that my father had a daughter and 3 sons. That was news to my sister and me. He had 2 sons and 2 daughters, all by K.A. and not by any of the other women he was married to (self preservation on the part of the other women, I presume)."

LAT, March 3, 1967: "Multimillionaire Arthur A. Cameron, 66, was found dead Thursday in his palatial Beverly Hills home. Police said death was apparently due to natural causes but an autopsy will be performed because no physician was in attention. Cameron's body, clad in pajamas, was found in his bed in the mansion at 920 Benedict Canyon Drive by his housekeeper Therese Kozak. He had lived there alone since annulment of his marriage to dancer Ann Miller in 1962.

"The housekeeper called Cameron's physician, Dr. Arthur D. Brody, who in turn called police. Beverly Hills Police Chief Anderson described the death as 'nothing unusual.' There were sleeping pills in an adjacent bathroom, said Anderson, but no indication that Cameron had taken any of them."

The next mention of Aldridge occurred nearly 3 years later related to a TV listing for the feature version of the *Nyoka* serial in *LAT*, October 5, 1969: "11 Movie – Adventure (1966) *Nyoka and the Lost Secrets of Hippocrates*, K.A. (2hrs)." Later when the television stations brought back chapters of *Perils of Nyoka* serials, they tended not to show all of the 15 chapters, but played several sporadically over several months.

Chapter Eight:
The Fans Rekindle the Thrills

"Some of the fans are a little strange, and they like to see women tied up, and send me very passionate letters about that."
- Kay Aldridge as told to Roy Kinnard

Aldridge told Kinnard: "I feel very happy at this time in my life – I look out of my windows and see the lighthouse and islands, and boats sailing. Penobscot Bay is right outside my house, and there are mountains running down to the sea."

Carey: "Apart from divorce, marriages, and children, life is relatively quiet for K.A. until 1977, when a serial fan writes to a Maryland paper, trying to find her."

The June 13, 1977 piece entitled "Historian Looks for Actress," by Dr. George A. Schaeffer (Blue Ridge Summit, PA) said: "I am writing to find out if any information can be found on a Kay Aldridge. The only information I have is that she was born in Westminster, Md. Kay was a star in the B-westerns and serials made in California during the 40s. During the course we took on B-movies and Westerns we were able to see some of Kay's serials especially the *Perils of Nyoka* serial.

"If Kay is living back in Carroll County or if anyone has information concerning her I would appreciate having them let me know. Those of us who remember her would like to see her again, if she is still around the area."

The first gathering of fans, many waiting 25 years to meet Aldridge, took place in Washington, D.C. in May 1978. McCord organized the sold-out event, which exhibited some excerpts of her serials. McCord utilized a private screening room at the American Film Institute in the Kennedy Center for Performing Arts. Aldridge, at the time 60 years old, observed: "I was quite overwhelmed by the total sense of identity with me that I felt from the audience."

Washington Star, May 9, 1978, John Sherwood revealed: "She is wonderfully scatter-brained and disorganized, in a refined Southern belle sort of way, and her mind darts as quickly from one thing to another, as her body in *Nyoka*.

"She also stopped by the newspaper with McCord who packed his sound projector and his collection of Kay Aldridge serials. She, in turn, brought along a suitcase full of old cover-girl portraits, scattering them helter-skelter on a desk as she rambled on, ducking back and forth to the ladies room to comb her hair. McCord showed some of the chapters that Aldridge herself had never seen.

"'I can hardly remember it, looking back,' she says. 'I did it sort of tongue-in-cheek, and I needed the money. I was paid $1,000 a week. I never did understand the plot – not even to this day. It was filmed in California and it supposed to be the desert of North Africa, I think. I never was really too sure about that. The director told me to run here, run there, jump on a horse and jump off, hit this guy and shoot this one.'"

"She remembers an assistant director telling her, 'Now, this afternoon, there's a gorilla, and the gorilla chases you. You fight like hell, then come out of the clinch when the pillar gives way and the roof falls on you. Got that?'

"She looked at Bill O'Sullivan, her producer: 'A gorilla, he says.'

'Yeah.'

'Is it all right?'

'Sure. The gorilla's only Emil Van Horn in the most ridiculous gorilla suit imaginable.'

'Is Emil all right?'

'You got me, darling,' said O'Sullivan.

"Asked if she did the stunts herself, she lied in the sweetest, most sincere Southern belle manner and said that she did. She did not want to 'destroy the illusion,' she confessed. " As McCord noted, serial buffs knew all the tricks anyway and that was the charm of them.

McCord: "The fans were taken by her friendliness, her straightforwardness, and her eagerness to mingle with them and answer their many questions. Despite personal tragedies and the disappointment over her film career, she retained a keen sense of humor and a bubbling personality. Her weight (123 pounds) is the same as when she appeared in films. And she still has striking beauty. And the mannerisms embedded in her by the genteel upbringing still come through.

Carey: "K.A. channels her 're-discovery' to go on a book tour to promote the tale of a posthumously published memoir by her great-aunt, Evelyn Ward.... The proceeds of the book sales go to a fund to restore Bladensfield. Following K.A.'s tour, Bladensfield is named a state landmark.... Indoor plumbing has been enjoyed at Bladensfield since the early 1960's."

The Camden Herald, June 8, 1978 ("Kay Tucker Leads Wild Night at the Opera"): reported Aldridge's comeback evening on June 2, 1978 at a benefit for the Rockport Opera House in Rockport, Maine for the Penobscot Bay Medical Center. The event featured the screening of six episodes from her three serials. Aldridge appeared in order to thank the facility for taking good care of her husband, Richard Tucker.

Between the serial episodes shown, the event had the costumed Aldridge and others reenact and spoof bits from *Perils of Nyoka*, including grappling with Vultura. Afterwards, Aldridge said: "Richard and I are still glowing from the warmth of feelings we shared with the standing room audience.

"Everyone who went along with Nyoka's adventures on stage were wonderful sports for our live action bits were mostly unrehearsed. Obviously Vultura (spoofed by Dorothy Seits) and Nyoka had not planned to have the former's glorious posterior overexposed. Some local cats have even remarked that they hoped the photographer was using a wide-angle lens.

"When I came on stage at the end of the evening of such excitement and violence I intended to thank everyone who had taken part in the whole event but it was difficult for me to think straight after all I had gone through and I was somewhat overcome with the emotions of the whole nostalgic evening."

Even her grandson Jeremy Tucker participated. The *Camden Herald* reported: "It was the histrionic talents of Jeremy Tucker that made him attack his Grandmother Nyoka with such abandon that her knees and legs are still black and blue, just like old times."

Carey: Jeremy Tucker was a step-grandson, grandson of Richard Tucker. Richard Tucker was a widower with 3 children (much older than me and my siblings) when he married K.A. His children had children, hence Jeremy and many others.

Aldridge's second husband, Richard Derby Tucker, died the following year in 1979.

Three years later, Aldridge married for a third time. She first met building contractor Harry Nasland back in 1940 at the Kemper Campbell Ranch. Interestingly, the wedding invitations pictured the couple in Los Angeles when he was her beau some 42 years earlier. It read: "Katharine Aldridge Tucker and Harry Nasland announce their elopement May 5, 1982." They were married on May 10th. . . . Although he owned a motel in California, the couple moved to Maine.

This marriage would end quickly - just eight months later. Nasland, eighteen years her senior, suffered a fatal heart attack.

Harry was part owner of the Green Spot Motel (C Street just off Seventh Street) along Route 66 in Victorville, California. The plaque at the entrance to the motel read "Nyoka's Hideaway," but this meant little to the people residing in this neighborhood. After Harry's death, Aldridge inherited the motel, and so she returned with a mission.

Victorville Daily Press, July 29, 2012, explained: "By that time, the once popular motel was in disrepair and had more than its share of alcoholics, prostitutes, and drug users. That's when Aldridge decided to clean up the place and the people who lived there. . . .Her real-life attempt would end up rivaling her fictional cinema roles."

Carey: "She was a very trusting person. She believed everyone could improve. She tried to make it respectable, but she had never before been in contact with the rougher side of life."

Aldridge's public appearances included being a guest at the Western Film Fair in 1978, the St. Louis Western Film Festival in 1979 and the first Knoxville, Tennessee Film Convention in 1986.

Carey remembered that her mother made her final appearance to fans at "Rimini Cinema 1989." The film festival in Italy celebrated jungle-girl films. An Italian newspaper photo of the smiling Aldridge in between two male attendees asks, "Ma lei non e la donna Tarzan?" (Translated: "But you're not the lady Tarzan?")

Aldridge was scheduled to appear at the 1994 Knoxville Western Film Caravan, though she never did. In addition, some references to the Lone Pine Film Festival list Aldridge as attending their 1994 convention.

However, Aldridge apparently stopped making appearances after Rimini. Carey: "K.A.'s last appearance was at Rimini. She would not have appeared at anything later, especially in 1994, because my sister was very ill. My sister was in fact dying, and my mother only traveled to New York to be with my sister."

Aldridge told Kinnard: "Tom Steele, the famous stuntman, told me at a convention in New York that he was married just before we made *The Perils of Nyoka*, and he said, 'I've been happily married and have stayed married, but I have to tell you, when I first met you... if I hadn't been married I certainly would've tried to get you!' He was cute about it. He was really a lovely fellow, more of a gentleman than most men in the movies, really a marvelous gentleman. He just died recently, and I felt so badly because we had such a nice reunion.

"I do nostalgia conventions. People are so nice to me, but it's exhausting, because you give out a lot and because you don't want to hurt anyone's feelings or be a disappointment. I find the fans are very, very loving, and nice people, and they care about you. They're much more loyal, I'm sure, than the present day fans of modern movie stars... I have baskets of really kind letters that people have sent to me, and it worries me because I just can't take care of it all. I'm so involved with my family and in raising funds for this cause and that. My past was fun, but it's something else.

"In the *NYT* recently, they ran a serious article on entertainment with a writer revealing all of the movies that impressed him when he was growing up, and he said, 'I'll never forget the bosom bursting charm of Nyoka!' So Nyoka's feeling very well and she's happy that she's remembered, and when her grandchildren saw

The Perils of Nyoka they say, 'You sure do fight good, Grandma!' I have a very good life, I have four children – two daughters and two sons, and dozens of grandchildren – and I'm not sad!"

Columnist Mike Newton, ("White Hats and Black Hats," *Classic Images*, No. 223, January 1994) noted: "When her young grandson first saw her in the *Nyoka* serial, doing the fight scene with Adrian Booth [AKA Lorna Gray who played Vultura], his comment was 'You sure could fight good, Grandma. That lady was chicken, she didn't fight fair.'"

Chapter Nine:
Good Night, Good Looking!

> "Beautiful, charming, ribald, lively, disorganized, humorous, affectionate, perceptive, inquisitive, exuberant, talkative, nosy, flirtatious, playful, forgetful, generous, spontaneous, incautious, hospitable, gregarious – that was Katharine and more."
> - Carey Cameron, in booklet distributed at K.A.'s funeral

Aldridge had been residing in Camden, Maine, when she needed serious medical attention. While receiving care at Penobscot Bay Medical Center in Rockport, Maine, her aorta ruptured. It happened when she was on the phone talking long-distance to Carey's husband. Her friend Lester Glassner reported her untimely death.

Carey: "K.A. dies of an aneurysm of the aorta on January 12, 1995 – my 43rd birthday. She is 77 years old. K.A. dies three months after her oldest daughter, Melissa, 48, [who] dies of adrenal cancer."

It had been incorrectly reported that the funeral at St. Thomas Episcopal Church in Camden had buses bring people to pay their respects. Carey: "Though the church was indeed full, buses did not bring people to the funeral. People simply drove to the funeral and parked in the ample church parking lot. There was a reception afterwards at the house, and as parking at the house was limited, buses were employed to ferry people from the church to the house and back to the church for their cars.

"The burial of her ashes occurred later, on her 78th birthday, July 9, 1995. Buses were employed at that time as well to ferry people from the cemetery to the house for another reception and back to the cemetery for their cars. The burial followed a small film festival organized at the local movie theatre, featuring *Nyoka* and *The Man Who Walked Alone*. Vultura, AKA Adrian

Booth, attended and also a film expert whose name escapes me at the moment but who was based in Chicago. Vultura and the man from Chicago gave some small talks."

Rouse offered a reflective article "Peninsula Beauty Never Forgot Her Home" (March 5, 1995), with quotes from Carey and her childhood friend Elsie West Duval. Rouse's memories of Kay started with the fact that "she never lost touch with her family in Tidewater or her school friends in Newport News. But despite her celebrity-hood and wealth, she never ceased to be the warm and upbeat comedian we, as students in Stonewall Jackson School, found her to be... We called the lanky girl 'The Village Halfwit,' shortened to 'Village.'"

Elsie had spent four days with Aldridge in Maine a few months earlier. Elsie: "She was still beautiful, spontaneous and full of vinegar as when I met her at 8 in Newport News. I remember clearly the childish tricks she was playing then, and at 78 she was still playing them. I doubt anyone alive will miss her more than I do, yet I do draw comfort in knowing that she went out with all her faculties intact. And when the final curtain fell, she was well aware of the mark she had left on the world."

Carey offered a correction: "Elsie met K.A, when she was 10, not 8."

The *NYT* obituary recalled that she was "... an actress and model who was one of the most photographed women in the country in the 1930's."

The *Camden Herald* offered an editorial entitled "A Star and A Lady," January 19, 1995:

"Camden lost a fine lady last week with the passing of Kay Tucker. Her loss comes not so much from the fact that she was a movie star and one of the country's highest paid models of her day, but from the fact that she was a gracious, friendly lady who truly loved Camden and the many people she came to know here. Away from the bright lights of the movies or the photographer's studio, Kay glowed even more radiantly as a hostess and friend. Her generous hospitality was deeply rooted in her Southern upbringing and the strong traditions of her Virginia birthplace.

"She loved sharing her home and its magnificent view, and she took time to let her guests review the many books and photographs of her younger years. Her sharing of this life in the spotlight was never pretentious or done in a manner that ever hinted at superiority. She shared her present and past as an open book. She never tried to hide her famous past, yet she never flaunted it. The more you found out about her, the more you liked.

"She was active in many worthwhile local projects. Yet, even with her lack of bashfulness for center stage, she did many great deeds that were known only to those who were touched by her kindness and thoughtfulness.

"Many will miss this wonderful lady. Her star will now shine brighter than ever before. K.E.B."

Again, the press erred. K.A. was born in Florida, not Virginia.

Her serial director Bill Witney told Magers/Copeland: "Kay was a sweet, pretty and thoughtful person. She never met a stranger in her life and the crew loved her. One couldn't help but like Kay. She bore the bumps, bruises, skinned knees and elbows that go with being a serial leading lady without a complaint. She stuck around the set looking over my shoulder long after she was dismissed for the day. She was one helluva gal. I'm sure there is a place in heaven for a beautiful, gutsy, fun loving, caring person like Kay."

Magers/Copeland acknowledged Aldridge was: "The beautiful and gracious star of three of Republic's absolute best cliffhangers... Kay was a delightful and charming performer, wore a constant smile, and enjoyed answering questions and attending film festivals."

Carey: "Nine months after K.A. dies, Bladensfield burns to the ground. Though the fire was deemed suspicious at the time, and probable arsonist individuated, no suspect has ever been prosecuted."

The *Fairfax Journal*, November 1996, "Fire claims historic Northern Neck mansion," reported: "Warsaw (A) - A fire has claimed one of the oldest houses on the Northern Neck and a state and federally recognized landmark. The fire at the Bladensfield mansion was first reported to the Richmond County Volunteer Fire

Department at about 9:50 a.m. Wednesday. When the first firefighters arrived five minutes later, 'she was gone completely,' said Assistant Chief Dennis Hanks.

" 'This is a nightmare,' said part owner Evelyn W. Overton as she watched the smoke rise from the rubble surrounding the huge brick chimney stacks that were the only part of the house left standing.

"Bladensfield was a three-story frame house that served as a girls' boarding school during the 1840s. It contained 20 rooms and was a trove of antiques, old family portraits and memorabilia, said Mrs. Overton. Overton, who lives next door to the property, said she left at 6:30 a.m. Wednesday to take her cousin, who lives in Bladensfield, to the hospital for knee surgery. 'He said the heat was off and he had unplugged everything because he knew he'd be gone for a week,' said Overton.

"She said at least two neighbors noticed smoke coming from the general area of the Colonial mansion, but assumed it was a controlled burn by foresters who had been working in a nearby timberland. State and local investigators were looking for clues. 'It's not suspicious, but we're looking for what caused it' said Richmond County Sheriff Gene Snyder.' "

Indeed, it had been a quick and sad ending to the mansion that stood for over 300 years. Aldridge spent her early life there, and that experience motivated her to pursue a career that could offer her the means of upgrading it, so it eventually would have modern necessities; such as running water, electricity, and heat.

The photogenic Kay Aldridge is gone, and the historic Bladensfield is gone. The story does not end here. It continues as long as memories are kept alive by you and me.

In her mother's scrapbook, Carey offered this conclusion: "In 2008: the serial, *Daredevils of the West*, lost for 65 years and believed missing, is found in the film archives of Brigham Young University. Some members of K.A.'s family attend a screening in 2009 in Lone Pine, California, where the serial was originally filmed.

"K.A.'s star is a very little star, but it keeps on twinkling, here and there, when you least expect it, in keeping with K.A.'s personal disregard for boundaries and love of surprise. If you keep your eyes open and know what to look for . . . K.A.'s star will twinkle for you, too."

Carey: "I wrote the following tribute for a booklet distributed at her funeral service in January. The booklet was basically the order of the service. I was asked to write about her life. It was put on the inside front cover of the booklet, and had to fit there." The *Camden Herald* published it:

"Katharine Aldridge Tucker was born July 9, 1917, in Tallahassee, Fla., the fourth of five children. The death of her father in 1922 caused her widowed mother to return to 'Bladensfield,' her family home in Virginia where Katharine lived on and off until she was 16. At 16 she went to work as a secretary in Baltimore, first for the Production Credit Corp., and then for the Army's 3rd Corps Area Headquarters. A bold visit at 18 to John Robert Powers Modeling Agency propelled her to fame – first as a model and cover girl and then as an actress in many Hollywood films and star of serials, among them the *Perils of Nyoka*. She retired from acting professionally in 1945 upon marrying Arthur Cameron, with whom she had four children – Melissa, Arthur, Scott, and Carey. The couple were separated in 1954.

"In 1956, in a living room on Fishers Island in Connecticut, Katharine met Richard Tucker, who upon seeing her said to himself, 'That's the woman I'm going to marry.' Katharine and Richard were married in 1957 and it was 1957 that Katharine found her spiritual home, in Richard's house in Camden, Maine. It was there that Katharine lived for the next 38 years, involving her so much in the community that she became a part of the landscape, as much as Mt. Battie or the belted Galloways, only a thousand times more animated.

"Though her professional acting career ended in 1945, Katharine in a sense remained on stage throughout her life. Beautiful, charming, ribald, lively, disorganized, humorous, affectionate, perceptive, inquisitive, exuberant, talkative, nosy, flirtatious, playful, forgetful, generous, spontaneous, incautious, hospitable, gregarious – that was Katharine and more. But it was not these qualities alone that made Katharine unique. It was her ability to use her resources to ignite the light within quieter souls, to bring forth in them qualities which they often never realized themselves. Hers was a soul that which lit up Camden and a good part of the Maine coast as well. Playful to the end, Katharine died while telling a joke on the phone to her son-in-law."

Carey: "I started to write about her life, and should have continued in that vein, giving the facts, but I veered off into a description of her character—not necessary, for Father Henderson's eulogy, which I unfortunately do not have, did a better job. I can only remember his words at the end. Father Henderson was referring to the phrase "Good night, sweet prince." (Shakespeare? John Barrymore?) Father Henderson paraphrased it: "Good night, sweet princess—for just a little while."

A notice printed anonymously in the local paper, *The Camden Herald*, following Aldridge's death reads:

GOOD
NIGHT
Good Looking
Katharine Aldridge Tucker
Lived well.
July 9, 1917 – Jan. 12, 1995
Thanks for the memories
of kindness and courage.

Part Two: The Serial Thrills

Chapter Ten:
Perils of Nyoka (1942)

"Let's see, I was boiled in oil, I went over a cliff in a chariot, I was buried alive, engulfed by flames, and caught on a rope bridge that crashed into a gorge. I was never tied up on a railroad track" (she said sadly). "But I was tied up on a rack and stretched!"

- Kay Aldridge, *New York Times*, April 19, 1989.

The studios that made serials during the sound era (primarily Republic, Universal, and Columbia) produced them to offer Saturday matinee thrills for youngsters. As such, they were action-packed, male-dominated adventures designed to bring fans back week after week to see another "cliffhanger."

At first, the viewer must acknowledge the basic juvenile adventure nature of serials as they are full of nefarious characters doing some very violent actions. Nevertheless, all the scenes have a stylized violence which shows no realism as far as pain, blood, or grief. We see none of the latter realities in the world of serials.

There were other Serial Queens before Aldridge got the title. But when those Queens reigned, serials were geared to the adults – and they were equally if not more important as the features they accompanied. The females that reigned were all part of the silent film era: women such as Pearl White, Helen Holmes, Ruth Roland, Kathlyn Williams, and others.

After her Fox contract is not renewed, Aldridge found work in 1942 as the "Queen of the Serials" at Republic Studios. Of all of the serial female stars, only a few stand out. Thanks to Republic Studios, Aldridge's Nyoka was a one-time effort to recapture the glory days of silent serials.

There have been a few self-assured and independent women in the serials in the sound era prior to Nyoka. One that best comes to mind is Priscilla Lawson. In just one role over at Universal Studios, Lawson excelled as the strong-willed, raven-haired and feisty Princess Aura in the first Flash Gordon serial in 1936. Although she played a woman who got what she wanted by letting no man stand in her way, she was not a heroine and could not be considered a Serial Queen as she acted in a selfish and manipulative manner.

Republic offered the skimpily-clad Francis Gifford as the first real heroine in the sound serials as she played the earlier character named Nyoka in *Jungle Girl* in 1938.

Despite this, it is Aldridge's follow-up role as Nyoka that stands out above all others. But after just three serials, Aldridge retired from acting.

Republic turned to Linda Stirling to fill the part of serial heroine again. Although Stirling offered some fine moments in the memorable serial from 1946, *The Crimson Ghost*, her best accomplishment came with her Serial Queen presence in the first seven chapters of 1944's *Zorro's Black Whip*. Strangely, that part of the serial seems clearly feminist-centered on Stirling, but then the balance of the chapters shift to the conventional male-centered storyline, and Stirling's character quickly falls into the background.

It is only the character of Nyoka in Aldridge's first serial that the question of her value as a feminist role model to young girls is relevant. Nyoka is a strong, independent woman who cares about others. She controls her own destiny without needing a man to assist, although she takes full advantage of any support (male or female) that she can get.

More importantly, she adopted a look that de-emphasized and downplayed her sensuousness. That is, Republic did not promote the glamour puss look as done by Fox and Warners. Or offer the eye candy appeal of Gifford's *Jungle Girl*. Here at Republic, Aldridge did not pander to male desire as an eye candy model or starlet. It seems that if she did do so, it would be inconsistent with the prevailing tone of the action serial.

Though it is not always the case with the cliffhangers when she needs rescue from a perilous situation, the fact remains that there is some very precious moments of Aldridge offering a superb feminist role model scattered throughout the chapters.

Carey: "K.A. views her acting in serials as a comedown, but the serials are the works of K.A. that turn out to have the most staying power, continuing to generate fans, even to this day, and inspiring directors such as Steven Spielberg in the making of 'Indiana Jones.'"

Perils of Nyoka came about because Republic wanted a sequel to profit from the success of *Jungle Girl*. But *Jungle Girl*'s connection to the estate of Tarzan creator Edgar Rice Burroughs meant Republic needed some distance from that production to avoid legal problems. They only kept the first name of "Nyoka" taken from it. The heroine was now "Nyoka Gordon." It has been said that Francis Gifford, on loan to Republic, was supposed to do the sequel, but when she became unavailable, in stepped Aldridge. The storyline was changed as much as possible to avoid resembling the Burroughs property.

McCord: "According to [director William] Witney, about 50 girls, including Yvonne de Carlo, were tested for the Nyoka role. Witney described Miss Aldridge as pretty and lovely but uncoordinated. 'I liked her,' he said. 'You couldn't help but like her. She was charming.'"

Edith Lindeman in "Virginia Tomboy Becomes Serial Queen" (*The Times-Dispatch*, Richmond, Va.) claimed a much higher number of girls were tested for the part, and that Aldridge was among those tested. Lindeman: "When Republic tested 200 girls for the role, Kay was one of the leading contenders. But there were some that argued: 'She won't do. She's used to posing and walking with a graceful glide. She hasn't enough bounce and energy for a Serial Queen.'"

When the group was narrowed down, the ultimate test was to see how well each climbed a tree. Aldridge proved to do the best. Lindeman said that Aldridge refused to have a double because she said that serial work was "too much fun." Nevertheless, in actuality she did have a double, stuntman Dave Sharpe.

At a 1989 retrospective, "In the Nick of Time: Thrills on the Installment Plan," the American Museum of the Moving Image in Queens, New York, screened 25 serials. The museum offered a panel discussion in which Aldridge spoke along with other serials actors—Kirk Alyn, Henry Brandon and Tom Steele—and serial director William Witney.

Aldridge told Glenn Collins ("Chills! Thrills! Cliffhangers!" *NYT*, April 19, 1989): "And they are reading sociological significance into my performances. . . .I was a brave, independent woman in the forest, frisking around." She noted that she had been asked by colleges to talk about feminism in film. Aldridge: "Of course, I was blithely unaware that I was a social statement. I was just a hungry actress."

Aldridge said that her eight grandchildren ask: 'Is that really you doing all that, Grandma?' And then they watch the videos over and over again. It's nice to think they still have an audience."

As regards the technical production aspect of serials, Collins explained: "In the 1930's, serials were shot for $175,000 to $225,000 or more, and many were produced in a month or less. Mr. Witney recalled that it took only 15 to 18 days to shoot an entire serial of 12 to 15 episodes. Generally, the first episode was 27 to 30 minutes long, and later episodes lasted from 12 to 15 minutes, each ending in a cliffhanging situation that impelled moviegoers to return. But even without retakes, the only way scenes could be shot so rapidly, Mr. Witney recalled, was that most serials 'had two directors so you could shoot one day, and then plan the next day.'"

Newton: "To little boys, the heroines at times seemed to be a bothersome hindrance to the heroes. Instead of following orders and remaining behind out of harm's way, these over-confident females decided to take matters into their own hands and wound up getting captured by the villains.

"To the little girls in the Saturday matinee audience, the heroines were seen in a different light. Serial heroines could be role models who showed girl's how they could beat their opponents by using brains instead of brawn. In any case, it is hard to imagine the serials of yesteryear without the strong, smart and attractive women who did such a beautiful job of bringing audiences back to the theater week after week."

With the Hays Office Production Code you could show women tied up but couldn't show it being done. Newton: "Usually, a cut was made just as the woman was about to be bound, and we would see the smile on a henchman's face as he or another villain cruelly tied knots around their lovely victim. The heroine's attire could not be shown in any disarray so as to expose any cleavage or undergarments" ("Past Issues: Jean Rogers, Linda Stirling, Frances Gifford, et al: Perils of the Serial Heroine," by Mike Newton).

Once one of the technicians played a practical joke on Aldridge while location shooting. It backfired. She was told to set her alarm for 3 a.m. for the next day's shoot. When she awoke, she thought everyone else overslept, so she "banged on doors and rang bells until everyone was awake," according to Lindeman.

In addition, the latter reported: "She ate off a mantel for a couple of days after a scene in which the script called for her to roll down the side of a hill. She slid instead of rolling 'But I'll bet it looked better the way I did it,' said Kay between applications of liniment."

Her co-star, Lorna Gray, later known as Adrian Booth, once recalled her friendship with her on-screen adversary and how Kay stood on a ladder until just before the camera rolled. When the crew pulled the ladder away, leaving her hanging, Kay looked heavenward and cried out, "Oh, Lord, send me a man, and make it now!"

Aldridge told Kinnard: "Lorna Gray (who played Vultura) was exactly the same off screen as she was in the movie, not villainous, but like a lot of movie girls, more like girls are today, more 'liberated' – or whatever you want to call it. I thought, though, that she was a better actress, a much better actress than I was."

Aldridge has not been without her detractors. For instance, serial authority Alan G. Barbour, (*Saturday Afternoon at the Movies: 3 Volumes in 1*) complained: "K.A. had an accent you could cut with a knife, looked terrible in a poorly designed costume (whereas Gifford's outfit was ideal), and couldn't act well enough to deliver more than an adequate performance."

Nevertheless, even Barbour recognized her unique place in film history. Barbour quickly added: "Yet she became one of Republic's best-exploited and most liked serial heroines, appearing in three of their best serials . . . . True to the standard heroine's role, Kay received her full share of blows on the head and holds the dubious distinction of being knocked unconscious twice in a single episode of *Haunted Harbor*."

Aldridge: "At the time, perhaps all of these gals seemed more than a hindrance than a help to the serials' action, but it was still nice to have them around."

Aldridge told Kinnard: "In the *Perils of Nyoka* there is only implied romance. Do you get any feeling that Larry (Clayton Moore) and I were in love? It's more like we're equals, and I'm as brave as he is. Maybe I was ahead of my time."

As regards to her favorite co-star Clayton Moore, Aldridge told Magers/Copeland: "Clayton had a lot on the ball. He had classical good looks, and he wasn't conceited." On Bill Witney, Aldridge added: "He didn't seem like a director. He was an action man. Action directors are entirely different from other directors. He was good to work with, and he and his wife (former actress Maxine Doyle) used to have me over for dinner. He was personally nice with me. *Perils of Nyoka* inspired *Raiders of the Lost Ark*. We may not have made as much money, but we've lived a lot longer."

Aldridge continued, remembering Chapter 6's cliffhanger when she was "suspended over a blazing abyss." She explained: "I was tied up but the tension was taken off under my feet so I wouldn't just be hanging there except for a little while... but it was scary. I have a freezer burn because they used dry ice to make that smoke. It took some meat off of one leg a little bit. They tried to be thoughtful of us and not draw and quarter us but it was rough. Actually, the serial sort of drove me into matrimony. It was such a beating and I was being pressured by a gentleman to marry him, so it just seemed less dangerous. (Laughs) But I made another serial, *Daredevils of the West*, with Allan Lane."

McCord: "The burn is quite visible at the end of Chapter 7 when Satan, the gorilla, pulls her back up a cliff on a rope. She was truly frightened by the Chapter 6 cliffhanger in which she had to hang over a fiery pit."

A brief but closer examination of the fifteen chapters of *Perils of Nyoka* clearly identifies Aldridge as the quintessential serial heroine. Each chapter, except the final one, ends with a cliffhanger with the heroine Nyoka put in peril for her life. Of course each chapter, except the first, resolves the previous chapter's cliffhanger. As is the case with cliffhangers, audiences enjoyed finding that they were misled as they were cheated from seeing the footage showing that the hero/heroine really did not die in the perilous finale of the previous chapter.

Of course *Perils* has its share of mistakes. John Sherwood observed that when "... a crew member walks out from behind a tree, is filmed, and then ducks backs again only to pop out again, and then – incredibly – ducks back a second time. All this stayed in the final version.

"Hollywood's idea of the native dialect is a huge joke – 'Verily, Fang (Nyoka's dog) leads us on a true trail' – but Nyoka's cultured, refined ... southern accent was equally puzzling. Her jungle suit was a horribly ill fitting pair of culottes that she hated. She said her lines could be understood, but that was about it" (The *Washington Star*, May 9, 1978). Apparently she felt that the shorts were too long.

Newton: "Nyoka, the Jungle Girl, as she became known, was popular enough to have her own comic book with photos of Kay Aldridge in costume on the cover. In 1952, the serial was reissued as *Nyoka and the Tigermen* and later featured in a 100-minute condensation for television in the late Sixties."

Though the best enjoyment always comes from watching a serial, and not reading a breakdown of every scene, what follows is a brief examination of each chapter (here and in the following two chapters) just to help readers better understand Aldridge's roles. However, the complexity of the plot details will not be discussed here as the fun comes from watching for the ridiculous limitations given to the characters, especially Aldridge's heroines.

The plot of this serial is simply put that Nyoka Gordon is searching for her lost father in North Africa. An archaeologist named Dr. Larry Grayson (Clayton Moore) finds a papyrus, which tells of a treasure and the Golden Tablets of Hippocrates with secret medical knowledge. Nyoka is able to decipher the message of the papyrus so they could find the Tablets. This entails fighting the evil Queen Vultura and her cohorts, particularly Cassib (Charles Middleton).

Overall, *Perils of Nyoka* is Aldridge's best of her three serials. Aldridge's role is prominent and she indeed deserves the title of "Serial Queen" as billed in the trailer. She plays a role in the action sequences equal to that of the male co-star, Clayton Moore. Nevertheless, Aldridge's limitations as an actress become obvious, particularly as her Southern accent seems unavoidable.

For every chapter of Aldridge's three serials, it will be noted whether she is in peril at the chapter's cliffhanger. Only here, in *Perils of Nyoka*, is Aldridge featured in every one of the possible fourteen chapter cliffhangers.

Chapter One: Desert Intrigue

The first chapter opens on a screen title card that reads a location called Wadi Bartha. When Nyoka Gordon meets her nemesis, the sultry Vultura (Lorna Gray), she engages in hand-to-hand combat with her. A gorilla named Satan helps Vultura.

Nyoka is captured and tied up. Her German Shepherd named Fang finds her and even helps to untie her bound hands.

Her male associate, physician Dr. Larry Grayson (Clayton Moore) and Red (William Benedict) engage in a gunfight. Nyoka and Larry go to Vultura's palace to get the most sought-after papyrus, whereupon they find themselves engaging in a fight. An object thrown by a servant girl hits Nyoka. This is already the second time in this chapter that this has happened. She is disoriented and so easy to be grabbed and tied to a palace stone column by Vultura.

This is an example of how females and males are treated so differently in serial storylines. The males always duck to avoid objects, but the females do not. In all three of Aldridge's serials she is constantly being easily knocked out by hitting her head on something or having objects hit her. This is an example of a repetitive and overused plot device wherein woman's reflexes are poor enough that they do not duck. Even here, in the supposed most feminist-positive *Perils of Nyoka*, women are not treated any better than anywhere else, especially as compared to other serials.

While on the subject of females being knocked-out, Aldridge's repetitive falls and knock-outs in all of her serials often appear fake and unconvincing. Here while Satan is fighting with Larry, she seems to get somehow knocked out. Then she awakes and the dislodged columns cause the ceiling to fall upon her. Indeed, our feminist icon and heroine Nyoka is not a super-hero for she is not above the ordinary or safe from the dangers of the world.

In the final moments of the chapter, Nyoka starts to scream, and she puts her hands up over her face as the stone ceiling starts to fall down on her!

K.A. Cliffhanger: Yes.

Chapter Two: Death's Chariot

Screen title card reads: "LARRY - Is attacked by a gorilla in Vultura's Temple while trying to rescue Nyoka."

This chapter opens with Nyoka just waking up as the palace columns come falling down. As stones fall on her and she screams, Larry helps free her. A papyrus to decipher the message on the stone is offered by Cassib's men for $1,000. Nyoka accompanies an Italian Count, named Torrini (Tristram Coffin), to check their claim. Torrini works with Nyoka, although we know that he actually introduced himself to a villager as a friend of Vultura (in Chapter One). They are ambushed, and Nyoka is chased and captured.

Vultura wants Nyoka to translate the ancient papyrus that describes the hiding place of the Golden Tablets of Hippocrates and the treasures buried with them. This proves that Vultura acknowledges that certain women are smarter and could know more than her. However, this is a trick of Vultura.

Nyoka is stretched out and tied to a torture rack. It is increasingly tightened until she relents. She is then released. However Nyoka and Vultura battle again. Indeed it is a cherished moment as it is rare in sound serials to see two females in combat.

The two women wrestle, and then Nyoka punches down on Vultura. Nyoka takes off in Vultura's chariot. She lets go of the chariot's reins after Torrini hits her with something. The chapter ends as Nyoka is knocked out and falls down in the chariot. Then it goes over a cliff apparently with the unconscious Nyoka inside it!

K.A. Cliffhanger: Yes.

Chapter Three: Devil's Crucible

Screen title card reads: "NYOKA –Attempting to escape in a chariot is overtaken by Cassib's Warriors."

We see what we did not see in the last chapter as Nyoka apparently awoke inside the chariot and she jumped out just in the nick of time. Nyoka has the papyrus. She deciphers the stone to learn where the Golden Tablets of Hippocrates are located. Their mission is to go to the Lair of the Eagles. There they will find the Tunnel of Bubbling Death. Then they will reach the ancient valley of the Tuaregs. The latter are cave dwellers. The inscription there will point to the Tablets.

Cassib's men attack Nyoka and her friends. Cassib's men are cutting down a rope footbridge. Nyoka is still walking on it as it falls. She falls against the rocks and climbs back up. Nyoka acknowledges, "Thanks Larry," as he lifts her up the peak.

Nyoka and Larry follow Cassib's men after they enter the Tunnel of Bubbling Death. A fight ensues between Cassib's men and Nyoka and Larry. Nyoka is hit with an object thrown in her direction. She screams as she seemingly falls into the fiery pool of bubbling lava!

K.A. Cliffhanger: Yes.

Chapter Four: Ascending Doom

Screen title card reads: "NYOKA and LARRY - Are trapped by Cassib in the Tunnel of Bubbling Death."

Again we were fooled in the last chapter's cliffhanger as Nyoka only fell down on the edge, and not into the bubbling lava.

Vultura uses the Sun Goddess to intimidate the Tuareg people. She convinces them that Nyoka and friends are infidels determined to drive them out of their valley. The Tuaregs take them as hostages, and they think Vultura is their Sun Goddess. Vultura riles up the Tuaregs by saying that the infidels must die. A fight ensues. Nyoka enters the cave to rescue Larry. A trapdoor in the floor is opened and Nyoka and Professor Campbell fall into a pit. Their fate seems sealed as spikes in the pit's ceiling move toward them!

K.A. Cliffhanger: Yes.

Chapter Five: Fatal Second

Screen title card reads: "VULTURA - Posing as the Sun Goddess, denounces Larry and Professor Campbell to the Tuareg Chief."

Actually a rock thrown by a Tuareg stops the lever and reverses the approaching ceiling spikes. Larry opens the trapdoor and rescues them. Nyoka, Larry and Professor Campbell run away in order to escape the Tuaregs.

The Tuareg Chief is not convinced Vultura is the Sun Goddess. Vultura locks the Chief up and continues her pose to fool the Tuaregs. With an attack by the Tuaregs, Nyoka goes back to find the cave inscription as she feels it may lead to her missing father. Professor Campbell says that her plan is too dangerous.

Larry goes after Nyoka. The latter is shown jumping one of the Tuaregs to the ground. She tries to fire a pistol and it fails, so she throws a spear that knocks him down.

Vultura comes upon Nyoka in the cave. Nyoka screams as Cassib's men grab her. Larry arrives and fires his pistol as Nyoka tries to read the inscription. As she pushed open the doors in the chamber with the inscription, she inadvertently ignited a fuse. As Nyoka dusts off the Tablet, the fuse explodes!

K.A. Cliffhanger: Yes.

Chapter Six: Human Sacrifice

Screen title card reads: "NYOKA and LARRY – Are ambushed by Vultura and Cassib while searching for the Tablets of Hippocrates."

We learn Nyoka was not in the room as Cassib's men apparently grabbed her right before the explosion. Red gets the monkey named Jitters to take a message. Nyoka and Larry smile when they see Jitters with a message.

A fight ensues between the Tuaregs and Nyoka and Larry in the cave. Nyoka's hands are tied over her head and she is suspended over a fire. The Tuareg Chief says, "Woman of white infidel, you have profaned the Sacred Temple of the Tuaregs, attempted to steal the Tablets, you must die in the fiery pit!"

Just then Nyoka recognizes that the Tuareg Chief is really her father. She sees his initials on his ring ("H.G."). The Chief denies it; however, he seems to be bothered by the initials. Chief: "That's strange."

The chapter ends as the rope suspending Nyoka is burned away by the rays of the Sun Goddess! An extreme close-up of Vultura's eyes reveals her as a most appealing villainess.

K.A. Cliffhanger: Yes.

Chapter Seven: Monster's Clutch

Screen title card reads: "NYOKA - Is condemned to die in the Pit of Fire by her father, Chief of the Tuaregs."

Nyoka is rescued just in time before she falls totally into the Pit of Fire. Larry throws a rope down to her from a hole in the rocks above her. Red and Professor Campbell pull her up. Nyoka is intent on going back to try to make her father remember her.

A fight ensues between the Tuaregs and Nyoka and Larry. Nyoka knocks a spear into one of them, which forces him into the Pit. Nyoka and Larry go to Cassib's camp, and they plan to enter Vultura's palace from the rear. Vultura learns of their plan. Nyoka and Larry enter with their guns drawn. Satan grabs Larry. As Nyoka and Vultura wrestle, Nyoka punches Vultura, and knocks her out. Nyoka runs from Satan.

When she lowers herself down the mountainside, Satan uses the rope to pull her back up. When he grabs her hair (actually Aldridge's double), her wig comes off unintentionally. The chapter ends as Nyoka apparently falls down the side of the mountain!

K.A. Cliffhanger: Yes.

Chapter Eight: Tuareg Vengeance

Screen title card reads: "NYOKA and LARRY - Are attacked by a Gorilla while trying to rescue Nyoka's father from Vultura's Temple."

We see that Nyoka was not crushed as she survived the fall from the cliff by landing in the water. Nyoka and her friends escape by horseback from the temple. Vultura thinks Nyoka is dead. Nyoka and Larry go to the Devil's Gorge to rescue her father. They seem doomed as a rock landslide comes down on top of them after the Tuaregs cause the disaster!

K.A. Cliffhanger: Yes.

Chapter Nine: Burned Alive

Screen title card reads: "NYOKA and LARRY - Try to rescue her father from Vultura and Cassib at Devil's Gorge."

The rocks did not fall on Nyoka and Larry as they apparently took cover to avoid being bombarded by the landslide. Nyoka:

"Larry, they captured father." Larry: "We got to help him. Let's get to our horses." When the Tuaregs grab Nyoka and Larry, a fight ensues. Nyoka is knocked off her horse, and she plays dead and trips one of the Tuaregs. One of the dialogue errors is here when Nyoka says, "get out of here before the Tuaregs come here too."

Vultura and Cassib try to get information from the Tuareg Chief. Nyoka goes to Cassib's village disguised to look like one of their women using a burkha and a robe. She sends Fang who alerts Larry and the others that Nyoka is in trouble. She is to be burned at the stake. She is tied to her father on a pole inside a tent as a fire is started and spreads. Vultura and Cassib run off. Nyoka repeatedly screams for help as Larry and the others arrive at the camp. Nyoka: "Larry! Larry! Help!"

K.A. Cliffhanger: Yes.

Chapter Ten: Treacherous Trail

Screen title card reads: "LARRY – And the other members of the Expedition raid Cassib's Camp to rescue Nyoka."

Larry extinguishes the huge flames of the fire by simply pulling down the tents. Amazingly, Nyoka and her father survive the devastating fire unsinged.

Larry examines her father and says that bone pressure on his brain has caused his loss of memory. Nyoka's father tells Torrini that the Tablets must be saved. Torrini secretly injects him. Her father says that they are located in the Tomb of the Moon God. Jitters the chimpanzee discovers Torrini's cigarette butt left near the father, and brings it to Red's attention. As such, Torrini is exposed as a traitor. He runs off, and he is pursued.

Torrini knocks Nyoka off her horse, and she is unconscious. He captures Nyoka and Larry, and he brings them back to the Temple. Vultura and Cassib have the ground mined around the Temple to protect it. With Nyoka and Larry his prisoners, Torrini drives his car over a mined section of road and it explodes, apparently killing them all!

K.A. Cliffhanger: Yes.

Chapter Eleven: Unknown Peril

Screen title card reads: "TORRINI - Fleeing with the secret of the Golden Tablets, captures Nyoka and Larry."

As you may has suspected, Nyoka and Larry jumped out of the car just in time before the explosion kills Torrini.

Nyoka's father tells Nyoka and Larry of how he discovered the Tablets, fell and hit his head. The Tauregs took care of him.

Nyoka and Larry go to the tomb that leads to a narrow gorge called Needles Eye. They get into a fight, and Nyoka fights the warriors. She is knocked out and placed on an altar that rises up toward a swinging pendulum blade that inches closer overhead as it was accidentally turned on (reminiscent of Edgar Allen Poe's "Pit and the Pendulum")! Once again, Nyoka's situation seems hopeless.

K.A. Cliffhanger: Yes.

Chapter Twelve: Underground Tornado

Screen title card reads: "NYOKA AND LARRY - Are attacked by Cassib's warriors in the Temple of the Moon God."

Nyoka is saved as Fang draws the attention of Red and the others to the cave. Fang helps Larry so he can stop the swinging pendulum by moving a lever.

It is demonstrated that no force can challenge the Taureg wind god where the Tablets were hidden. Larry tells Lobar, now the new Tuareg Chief, how the Tablets have secrets that belong to all of mankind. Larry, with an object thrown at him, overpowers the guards so that Nyoka and her father Professor Gordon can get the Tablets. However, the wind tunnel release is activated, pushing Nyoka out of the tunnel into the mountainside!

K.A. Cliffhanger: Yes.

Chapter Thirteen: Thundering Death

Screen title card reads: "NYOKA AND LARRY - Attempt to obtain the Tablets of Hippocrates from Lobar, new Chief of the Tauregs."

Larry threw a rope out as Nyoka flies out from wind currents, but the edge of the tunnel stops Nyoka's fall. She gets the Tablets, and says the inscription on their back tells of the hidden treasure, and that it can be found at the Shrine of the Evil Bird.

Cassib's men fight Nyoka and Larry. Larry is grazed in the head by a gunshot. Nyoka runs off with the chest containing the Tablets. One of Vultura's men bends down on his horse to grab the chest. The chapter ends as Nyoka screams when the horses apparently gallop over her!

K.A. Cliffhanger: Yes.

Chapter Fourteen: Blazing Barrier

Screen title card reads: "VULTURA - Ambushes the Expedition as they are escaping with the Golden Tablets."

Of course the horses did not gallop over Nyoka.

Vultura: "Stop that girl!" Vultura finally gets the chest with the Tablets. Now she needs to get them translated so Larry and others pursue them at Wadi Bartha. Larry and Red disguise themselves wearing robes to slip into town to find the Tablets.

Jitters throws flowers out of the room leading Vultura's men to find them. A fight ensues. Larry and Red are captured and tied up. An interpreter deciphers the Tablets for Vultura and Cassib.

Jitters leads Nyoka to a building fire. The chapter ends as Nyoka seemingly falls into the fire as she catapults on a chandelier to rescue Larry and Red trapped inside.

K.A. Cliffhanger: Yes.

Chapter Fifteen: Last Chapter - Satan's Fury

Screen title card reads: "Nyoka rides to Wadi Bartha to prevent Vultura from learning the secret of the Golden Tablets."

We learn that Nyoka did not fall into the fire, but just passed it. Yes, so Nyoka can get knocked out easily, but luckily she defies raging fires? This is an example of how inconsistencies abound in serials, nevertheless we still enjoy the thrills of these action-dominated chapter plays.

Abu and Nyoka find out from the translation that the Shrine of the Evil Bird has the treasure. Actually, it is absurdly located in Vultura's palace where an altar once stood.

The members of the expedition get into a gunfight with Cassib's men. The digging in Vultura's palace leads them to find the treasure chest. A fight erupts in the Palace. Nyoka points her gun at Vultura. Nyoka shoots one of the men. After a prolonged and exciting battle between Nyoka and Vultura, Satan clumsily stabs Vultura by mistake. Larry arrives just in time to shoot Satan several times. Satan is unfazed as bullets had no effect on him until Nyoka fatally stabs him in the back.

Chapter Eleven:
Daredevils of the West (1943)

> "In this serial, she wore her hair tied back in a bun to fit under her Stetson. She liked the styling of the fringed jacket that she wore in the serial."
> - Mike Newton,
> *Classic Images*, January 1994

Aldridge joined Allan Lane, billed "King of the Serials" in her second serial. It was not her best time. She told Magers/Copeland that Lane "was pretty — and he knew it —if you know what I mean. Allan was handsome, but he was too stuck on himself." She told Newton that Lane was "too good-looking for his own good."

"That was a very trying time in my life. A friend of mine was killed in the service, my brothers were partially paralyzed, one in an auto accident (Ran), one from multiple sclerosis (John). Also my mother had to have an eye operation. My life was in a turmoil, so I don't recall much about *Haunted Harbor*" (Magers/Copeland Interview). Of course, this was between 1943 and 1944 (*Haunted Harbor* was released in 1944).

Newton said the serial's director John English told Aldridge: "Miss Aldridge, you'll be the only one there with all those men, and after a few weeks, you'll start to look good to them. If any of them bother you, please come see me."

Aldridge played a joke on him, she explained: "After three weeks, I came up to him and twisting my handkerchief and blushing, I said: 'Remember how you said I should come to you if I had any trouble with the men. Well, it's been three weeks, and you're starting to look good to me.

" 'I liked it when I got to kick or trip the stuntmen,' she says today. In *Daredevils* she even got to shoot one of the stuntmen, playing an outlaw, who was about to 'bump off' Allan Lane in a fight scene" ("White Hats and Black Hats" column on "Kay Aldridge: Queen of the Serials," by Mike Newton, *Classic Images*, No. 223, January 1994).

Overall, *Daredevils of the West* is less than satisfying when compared to *Perils of Nyoka* as regards to Aldridge not having as prominent and as heroic a role as Nyoka. Although the trailer again bills Aldridge as "Serial Queen" (and Allan Lane as "Serial King"), here her role is minor. It is disappointing that she does not play a dominant role in the action sequences as compared to Lane and the other men. In addition, Aldridge is the focus in only four of the eleven possible chapter cliffhangers.

The story tells of how land and cattle broker Martin Dexter pursues all possibilities to prevent the expansion of the stage line road owned by Foster Stage Co. The villainous Dexter says he does not want the "the 50,000 acres of the finest grazing land in the West" to be used by "a lot of tin-horned settlers following a stage road." June Foster (Kay Aldridge), daughter of the owner, is joined by Duke Cameron (Allan Lane) to find the identity of the villain.

Interestingly, two years later Aldridge would marry another Cameron – Arthur Cameron. Carey: "The fact that Allan Lane's character's last name is Cameron is pure coincidence, though oddly prescient."

Chapter One: Valley of Death

Early on June shows her ability to shoot the attacking Indians. She also shows her vulnerability as she is knocked out and nearly scalped. Turner and Ward rob the stage line carrying the Foster payroll. June is knocked out cold in the moving coach. Duke pursues the coach and he shoots the thief. The coach goes out of control as it unhinges from the horses. June awakes in the coach and covers her eyes just as it crashes into a mountain and explodes!

K.A. Cliffhanger: Yes.

Chapter Two: Flaming Prison

Screen title card reads: "DUKE CAMERON – Fails to save the payroll and attempts to rescue June from the runaway coach."

In the nick of time June escapes the coach before it crashes. Duke grabs her while she tries to climb to safety.

Turner is imprisoned. His cohort Ward manages to free him from the jail. Duke is trapped in a fire that starts in the jailhouse. The chapter ends with June and the others trying to save Duke from being burned to death!

K.A. Cliffhanger: No.

Chapter Three: The Killer Strikes

Screen title card reads: "WARD – Surprises Duke and the Sheriff and helps Turner escape from the Canyon City Jail."

Just before it is almost too late to save Duke, June gets the idea to knock the wall out of the jailhouse using the horses to pull a rope attached to the window. Duke escapes the fire just in time without any injury.

June insists on joining Duke in pursuit of the stage line payroll thieves, saying, "It's my stage road we're fighting for!" June shows her proficiency with a rifle as she wounds and kills some of the henchmen. The chapter ends with Duke seeming to get shot by the thieves!

K.A. Cliffhanger: No.

Chapter Four: Tunnel of Terror

Screen title card reads: "DUKE... Helps Red and June recover the stage line payroll and fights off their pursuers."

Unharmed, Duke along with Red seek the horses stolen by Turner and Ward. This leads them to a mine tunnel.

The chapter's finale has Duke and Red hiding in the first of two tunnel mine cars as they shoot at the henchmen. One of the henchmen throws a flame-ignited stick in the second mine car as the cars roll down the tracks. The chapter ends as the cars crash into the tunnel wall!

K.A. Cliffhanger: No.

Chapter Five: Fiery Tomb

Screen title card reads: "DUKE and RED. . . Trail the horses stolen by Ward and Turner, to a cave near Hidden Valley."

We find that Duke and Red avoided the crash by getting out of the runaway cars by grabbing roof timbers.

They recover the horses. Dexter has his men poison the lake water that the horses will drink from so they can get no further. June gets lassoed off her horse, and gets knocked out as a result of the fall. She is held prisoner by being tied to a chair at the Red Gulch Distillery. While Duke is fighting the henchmen, she warns him to avoid getting hit on the head with overhead barrels loosened by one of the men.

June unties herself, and kicks one of the henchmen in the face as she goes up a flight of steps. But then June gets knocked out as she is hit in the back of the head with a wooden beam thrown at her. The chapter ends as she falls into a vat of alcohol while flames around the vat engulf the distillery!

K.A. Cliffhanger: Yes.

Chapter Six: Redskin Raiders

Screen title card reads: "DUKE – Attempts to rescue June, who is a prisoner in the Distillery at Red Gulch."

Predictably Duke pulled June out of the vat, and they escaped the burning distillery just in time, and without any injury.

June uses her horse whip to fight off an Indian who jumped on her wagon fighting her with his tomahawk. When she turns around, the Indian throws the tomahawk and knocks her out. Duke jumps on her coach in an attempt to rescue her. He holds her in his arms as the coach goes off a cliff!

K.A. Cliffhanger: Yes.

Chapter Seven: Perilous Pursuit

Screen title card reads: "JUNE – Is attacked by Renegade Indians while bringing in guns to protect the Road Camp."

June and Duke are not hurt as the stagecoach actually fell over the cliff into a river. They swim to safety. Interestingly, neither looks wet nor seems disturbed by that traumatic experience.

The cliffhanger has Duke caught in a Hidden Valley explosion caused by a keg that was ignited!

K.A. Cliffhanger: No.

Chapter Eight: Dance of Doom

Screen title card reads: "WARD... Is aided by Turner in escaping from Duke Cameron who pursues them to Hidden Valley."

The Arapahoe Indians agreed by treaty to allow the stage road to cross the Indian reservation. Before the peace pipe is readied, Dexter's men antagonize the Indians by killing two of them. This makes the Indians angry. June and Red are held by the Chief, and they will die by fire if Duke does not find the perpetrators immediately. The Chief says that when the Sun clock's shadow reaches the tomahawk marker, they will be burned by fire.

This is perhaps the most suspenseful chapter with Aldridge at her very best here. Aldridge played to perfection this damsel in distress sequence. Her concerned glances and serious demeanor are most convincing. When Duke does not return in time, June and Red are tied together inside a stagecoach. A tousled-looking June declares, "This looks like the end, Red." Red: "Yeah, the death dance." Then the coach is set on fire. The chapter ends with June screaming!

One thing for sure is that Aldridge had a knack for the most convincing screams.

K.A. Cliffhanger: Yes.

Chapter Nine: Terror Trail

Screen title card reads: "DUKE – Races to the Arapahoe Reservation with Ward and Turner to save Red and June from death by fire."

Duke returns with the killers, Ward and Turner, just in time. Miraculously June and Red are rescued from inside the burning wagon uninjured. As a compromise to not kill those two responsible, the Chief holds the killers until the Commissioner can come to the reservation to help resolve the matter.

A fake Commissioner is placed in a stolen stagecoach. Duke and June separately pursue the coach. Duke is knocked off his coach in the path of an oncoming coach. The chapter ends as June frantically screams as her coach's horses are about to trample Duke!

K.A. Cliffhanger: No. (Some may say "yes" for although June is not in peril for her own life, she is not able to control the horses running over Duke).

Chapter Ten: Suicide Showdown

Screen title card reads: "DUKE - Attempts to capture the fake Commissioner who is escaping in the stolen stagecoach."

Apparently Duke did not get injured. The coach passed over him without touching. June: "Are you sure you're not hurt?" Duke: "Well the horses just clipped me."

To find out who is responsible for the attacks that delayed the building of the stage road, Duke seeks to trace money of large denomination found in the pocket of the dead fake Commissioner. The suspicion is on the lawyer Silas Higby as he had received five of the bills with the same numerical sequence. Duke's chase leads to the the old barn at Dead Man's Gully where a fight between Duke and Higby ensues. A fire starts which ignites the explosives, and the barn explodes!

K.A. Cliffhanger: No.

Chapter Eleven: Cavern of Cremation

Screen title card reads: "DUKE - Corners Higby in the old barn at Dead Man's Gully where the explosives are hidden."

Higby got killed, but Duke jumped out the window to escape before the barn exploded. Duke finds nothing incriminating when he searched Dexter's office. His papers at his ranch were removed and brought to Dexter who meets with Higby's attorney Maxwell. Duke follows the trail, and a fight ensues with Dexter at the Volcanic Caverns. This leads Duke to fall into the pit of fire after he got hit in the back!

K.A. Cliffhanger: No.

Chapter Twelve: Frontier Justice

Screen title card reads: "DEXTER - Meets Maxwell in the Volcanic Caverns to arrange for the sale of The Comanche Strip."

When Duke climbs out of the pit of fire, we learn that he did not fall all the way into the pit.

June shoots and kills two Indians. When June and Red's coach gets attacked and captured, Duke, dressed again in his Calvary uniform, rescues them. Duke jumps out the window as Dexter, Turner and Ward get trapped in a building that explodes.

With the enemies of June Foster's stage line dead, her stage gets through in the race for the fastest time. Now her company, Foster Stage Company, has won the road franchise. The serial ends happily with Duke saying to June: "Well June, you did it!" June to Duke: "You mean we did it!"

Chapter Twelve:
Haunted Harbor (1944)

"Kay didn't care for her acting in the serial. [K.A.:] 'I seemed awfully prissy.' "
- Mike Newton,
Classic Images, January 1994

As noted earlier, Aldridge's third and final serial, *Haunted Harbor*, re-released as *Pirates' Harbor*, was made at a time when she had many personal troubles.

For the first chapter of this serial which involved a rescue in a storm, Aldridge complained: "The water was cold and my clothes and hair were ruined." She also said that she was unhappy with her acting.

Unfortunately and again, the fan looking to see the derring-do of Aldridge's Nyoka will be disappointed with this serial. Here she is barely given a chance to be more than the typical serial female which means she has little to do, except for the times when she is a weak damsel in distress. Newton: "The plot did not give Kay the same importance to take on the villains as she had in the previous serials."

Overall, *Haunted Harbor*'s plot does not focus much on Aldridge as compared to *Perils of Nyoka*. However this serial, directed by Spencer Bennet and Wallace Grissell, does feature Aldridge in twice as many cliffhanger endings (eight of the possible fourteen) as compared to *Daredevils of the West*. But, just as with the latter, she does not play much of a role here. Again she does not live up to the Serial Queen billing as her part is minor.

The story simply involves island natives being scared by a fake sea monster. The search to find the reason for why they are being scared is what moves the hero Jim Marsden (Kane Richmond) to action.

Chapter One: Wanted for Murder

The story begins with a deal that went sour which leads to Jim Marsden's search for a killer named Carter (Roy Barcroft). Early on we learn the secret that Kane is really Carter. His cohorts are Gregg (Kenne Duncan) and Snell (Bud Geary).

Aldridge as Patricia Harding makes her first appearance towards the final minutes of the chapter. A hurricane is pounding her sloop. Jim helps her remove her injured father from the boat. The chapter ends as the heavy rains cause the crumbling rocks to come tumbling down supposedly trapping Jim and Patricia!

K.A. Cliffhanger: Yes.

Chapter Two: Flight to Danger

Screen title card reads: "JIM MARSDEN – Fights his way through a tropical Hurricane to rescue Patricia Harding and her father from their wrecked sloop."

We find out that Jim and Patricia swam to safety just before the rocks from the cliff came down. On Jim's schooner, Patricia tells her story that she's been living on the sloop. This is one of the brief but best moments, as Aldridge appears engaging.

The chapter ends as Patricia's car goes out of control when she ducks to avoid being shot at. Certain death looms when Patricia is unexplainably knocked out unconscious, and her car with the injured native Chief's son Kassim goes down a steep hill, rolling over uncontrollably!

K.A. Cliffhanger: Yes.

Chapter Three: Ladder of Death

Screen title card reads: "PATRICIA HARDING and JIM MARSDEN – Hope to learn from Kassim why the natives refuse to work near the Haunted Harbor."

Incredibly Patricia climbs out of the overturned vehicle without any injury despite the car's multiple turnovers.

The chapter ends as Jim is climbing up a cliff in pursuit of Carter's men. His ladder is cut and pushed off the cliff and he plummets to the ground!

K.A. Cliffhanger: No.

Chapter Four: The Unknown Assassin

Screen title card reads: "JIM MARSDEN and Yank are ambushed by Carter's men on their way to Haunted Harbor."

The ladder lands back onto a rock formation so Jim avoids the fall to the ground, and he jumps to safety.

Patricia sees the murder of her father. Her reaction is limited to her initial shock ("Father!") when she discovers him lying on the floor. The killer (Gregg) takes her hostage, and she is brought to Dark Canyon and bound to a chair. Jim arrives. However, while the fight is on, in a Serial Queen moment, Patricia somehow manages to untie her hands and free herself from the chair and escapes.

And in a moment of perfect timing, the chapter ends as Gregg and Snell push their car down a rocky road into Jim and Patricia's moving car. It explodes!

K.A. Cliffhanger: Yes.

Chapter Five: Harbor of Horror

Screen title card reads: "JIM MARSDEN – Has rescued Patricia Harding, but they are closely pursued by Carter's men." Jim and Patricia jumped out of their car just before the collision occurred.

They need to find Carter to clear Jim's name and to find the killer of Patricia's father. At times Aldridge's charm makes the serial better than it would be without her. Here in one scene, she tenderly asks Jim to let her stay on the island and not go back to the States so she can get justice.

To rescue Jim, Patricia fires her pistol. She then throws ignited dynamite overboard just in time, which saves Jim's life. Jim and Patricia head on a speedboat to Haunted Harbor.

As in the upcoming conversation (as well as in many other scenes in this serial), Aldridge's southern accent is quite apparent. There are times when she tried to minimize it.

Probably the most thrilling and ridiculous moment in the entire serial occurs now. The following exchange occurs on a speedboat:

Patricia: "Now that we're nearing it I'm getting sort of a queer feeling, a kind of sort of a premonition of evil."

Jim: (laughs) "You're thinking of all those stories you've heard. Don't let it get you." Some time passes as they move closer to the harbor.

Patricia: "Haunted Harbor certainly seems quiet and peaceful enough."

Jim: "Yeah."

Then an obviously fake, mechanical sea serpent appears.

Patricia: "A sea serpent!"

[Carey observed, "Sea serpent it is, but it always looked like a big frog to me."] Jim shoots at it with his rifle and Patricia shoots at it with her pistol. Unbeknownst to them their bullets have been replaced with blanks. The sea serpent goes back down in the water.

Patricia: "Do you think you killed it?"

Jim: "I don't know. But I'm sure I hit it."

Then the sea serpent reappears. When it shoots steam out of its mouth, Jim shoots again, and it goes down under the water. Once again the sea serpent rises again.

Jim: "The bullets don't seem to have any effect on it."

It reappears again and Jim still continues to shoot at it. Then for no apparent reason Jim dives in to water. A surprised Patricia screams "No!"

A frantic Patricia screams, "Jim! Jim!" The chapter ends with the sea serpent rising out of the water breathing out steam.

K.A. Cliffhanger: No. (Again some may argue otherwise, but it is only Jim that is in peril as he disappeared in the water).

Chapter Six: Return of the Fugitive

Screen title card reads: "PATRICIA HARDING and JIM MARSDEN - Set out to uncover the mysterious Terror of Haunted Harbor."

We learn that Jim is safe as he swims back when the sea serpent disappears. Patricia helps him back into the boat.

Another moment of pure Kay Aldridge modeling charm occurs now. When discussing their dilemma back onshore, Patricia, with hand on hip cutely asks: "Jim, what can you do against creatures that live at the bottom of the sea?"

Patricia is told she is protecting Jim, a wanted murderer. She is being forced to tell where Jim is. This is the chapter where

Patricia gets knocked out twice. A scuffle with the henchmen means that she bangs her head and is knocked out cold.

Jim sees through the window that they are getting some water to revive her. She wakes up and she starts to fight again as Jim comes in and fights the two henchmen. She bangs against a wall and is knocked out again. She awakes just after Jim knocked both guys out. Again this often-used plot device keeps her from being able to fight and be heroic.

A gunman fires bullets at the door apparently killing Patricia and Jim!

K.A. Cliffhanger: Yes.

Chapter Seven: Journey into Peril

Screen title card reads: "While Jim Marsden waits for Patricia Harding to contact Galbraith, she is being held prisoner by Lawson."

Patricia and Jim avoided being shot as they went through another door. Instead one of the henchmen (Neville) got killed. Credit for saving their lives inadvertently goes to Patricia as she stopped Jim from walking out that door – to avoid being seen.

A $5,000 reward is offered to find Jim dead or alive. Patricia tells Jim not to associate with someone: "By now the police'll know you hid at the inn. They'll watch his every move. It's too dangerous." Although Aldridge tried to sound concerned, it seems unconvincing.

The henchmen try to get Jim inside a cave. A fight ensues. Patricia is helpless as the fighting goes on. She is grabbed and pushed and she is easily knocked out again.

Apparent here and elsewhere is the limitations of poor dialogue which leaves little room for the actors to do much, as when the fight is over and she awakes...

Jim: "Are you alright, Patricia?"

Patricia: "I'm all right."

They drive off and are being chased by another car, bullets being fired at them. They switch to a twin engine plane to escape the bullets. The henchmen plant land mine charges. Jim and Patricia's plane flies over them.

The chapter ends as several charges are detonated as the plane comes into landing mode seemingly destroying the plane, Jim and Patricia!

K.A. Cliffhanger: Yes.

Chapter Eight: Wings of Doom

Screen title card reads: "DRANGA – Tells Carter that Jim and Patricia are returning from Amoa by plane."

Of course Jim and Patricia missed the explosive charges.

Jim sets a trap for Dranga which leads him to Carter's hide-out. Dranga pilots a plane and he is shot while landing his plane. The out-of-control plane taxis into the cabin where Jim is fighting Carter's henchman. The cabin explodes!

K.A. Cliffhanger: No.

Chapter Nine: Death's Door

Screen title card reads: "JIM MARSDEN – Attempts to capture Carter and his men, who do not know Dranga is flying to warn them."

Jim is safe as he jumps out of the cabin's window just in time to avoid the plane's explosion.

There are some exciting scenes with Patricia riding on horseback. She is pursued, and she gets off to jump into a lake. She gets caught on the side, and so she is lassoed by the henchmen. Gregg offers Jim a deal to exchange the kidnapped Patricia for Dranga. However, Greg and Carter do not know Dranga is dead.

Patricia is gagged and tied to a post. Jim impersonates the supposedly injured Dranga. A fight ensues when Jim reveals he is not Dranga.

The chapter ends as the terrified Patricia's eyes bulge as she sees the air drill is aimed at her. Then the air drill is fired!

K.A. Cliffhanger: Yes.

Chapter Ten: Crimson Sacrifice

Screen title card reads: "While Patricia Harding is threatened with death by the air drill, Jim Marsden, disguised as Dranga, attempts to rescue her."

Of course Patricia avoids the air drill as she ducks when it is fired. Alright, so here is one time when her reflexes are excellent for she ducks.

Carter learns finally that Dranga was killed in a plane crash. Carter spies on them with Snell planting a wireless Dictaphone in Jim's bungalow.

The native Chief gives them the gift of a monkey. Jim says he'll give the Chief a gift of a portable radio the following day. Gregg plans to rig the radio so it explodes so as to get Jim in trouble with the natives. Greg hooks up an oscillator in the radio. He explains that when it heats up by the radio tubes, it will trigger the firing pin.

The radio blows up shortly after Jim and Patricia give it to the Chief. The hut with the Chief is destroyed.

A stunned Patricia asks, "What caused it?" We too are shocked by this sudden and horribly violent death of the Chief. It is one of the most disturbingly memorable scenes in any serial as we know what will happen next, and unbearably the suspense mounts as the Chief enjoys the music on the radio. This is reminiscent of a sequence in Alfred Hitchcock's *Sabotage* in which a boy is carrying a package with a bomb. In both cases, we know it is going to blow up soon!

Even before it exploded the natives think it is a devil box with evil forces. As Jim is blamed for slaying their chief, June pleads, "Please, please, you must listen!" Jim is condemned to death by being burned at the stake. The natives hold back Patricia who tries to get loose so she can free Jim. A convincingly terrified Patricia watches the unfolding horror, and the chapter ends as she screams!

K.A. Cliffhanger: Yes.

Chapter Eleven: Jungle Jeopardy

Screen title card reads: "JIM MARSDEN – Gives the native chief a radio, in which Carter's men have secretly planted a deadly explosive device."

As Patricia is being held back watching the fire burn around Jim, she saves him by grabbing the head tribesmen's gun, and reveals her Annie Oakley-like perfect shot as she shoots the ties holding Jim to the stake. Patricia aims the gun at the tribesmen: "Tell your people if they move I'll shoot!" For this brief moment Aldridge's Patricia here is clearly the heroine and Serial Queen just as much as Nyoka was.

Jim is unbound and runs over to Patricia. She secures their escape, and they drive off.

The chapter ends as Jim is lured into a spiked jungle trap that falls on him when he releases it!

K.A. Cliffhanger: No.

Chapter Twelve: Fire Trap

Screen title card reads: "JIM MARSDEN - Is tricked into a deadly ambush, set by the natives who believe he murdered their chief."

Jim stopped the trap's fall with a branch just in the nick of time as he falls and triggers it.

As Patricia goes to save the gold shipment she is trapped in a truck. She bangs her head against the inside of the truck wall when it takes off and she gets knocked out. Yes, she is knocked out again! Anyone counting?

Jim pursues the truck. When it stops, a gunfight ensues. Patricia awakes just as the gas tank is leaking, and a fire begins to envelop it.

The chapter ends as she is trapped inside the burning truck. She screams repeatedly, again convincingly. The truck explodes apparently with her inside!

K.A. Cliffhanger: Yes.

Chapter Thirteen: Monsters of the Deep

Screen title card reads: "PATRICIA HARDING – Is locked in the truck in which Snell attempts to escape with the stolen gold."

Patricia breaks through the driver's compartment escaping just before it explodes.

Gregg is hoping he can destroy Jim and his schooner with a mine. The sea serpent is used to lead him to enter the minefield. Jim dives to find that the sea serpent is a mechanical device controlled onshore by wires. Jim finds his lost schooner "The Dolphin," which had a million dollars of gold bullion aboard.

Gregg is about to blow up Jim's schooner when he sees in his control station screen that Jim is salvaging near the sunken lost ship. As they search for Jim, Patricia and Tommy enter the control station. Patricia is told by Tommy to keep the henchmen covered while he takes Gregg and an assistant's gun. She drops the gun when she accidentally holds it in front of some ray. Then she runs to get the gun, and instead she is knocked out against a wall by a henchman.

Repeatedly, unlike Nyoka's derring-do, Patricia is conveniently and unfortunately kept down by plot devices to keep her from fighting. Unbelievably, she doesn't even throw a chair.

Gregg shoots Tommy, and blows up Jim's schooner. The chapter ends as an explosion disconnects Jim's oxygen supply!

K.A. Cliffhanger: No.

Chapter Fourteen: High Voltage

Screen title card reads: "JIM MARSDEN – Attempts to salvage the wreck in Haunted Harbor while Tommy battles desperately to prevent Gregg from blowing up their schooner."

Jim's schooner was not hit and so he is saved as his men quickly pull him up onboard. Apparently Carter wants to scuttle the lost schooner so he can steal its valuables. It's why they want to keep the natives from the area.

Patricia exhibits a look of relief when she hears the henchmen say that Jim is safe. She remains tied in a chair in the control station. Jim learns that Tommy and Patricia are captured.

Snell gets blown up by a car bomb that was intended for Jim. Carter orders that the control station should be blown up. "What about the girl?" asks the cohort. Gregg radios, "Leave her there she knows too much." Patricia fidgets in the chair as she tries to loosen the ropes when she hears that.

Jim enters the control station. Patricia screams, "Jim!" We get close-ups of a scared Patricia bound in the chair as a fight ensues. You would think that Jim would have untied Patricia as soon as he arrived and saw her bound? No, for then perhaps she would be able to help in the fight. Or maybe not, as she would probably get knocked out again!

A fire starts in the control station near the crates marked "HIGH EXPLOSIVES." As Jim is fighting a henchman, the crates explode. The chapter ends as we see the entire control station destroyed!

K.A. Cliffhanger: Yes.

Chapter Fifteen: Crucible of Justice

Screen title card reads: "JIM MARSDEN – Arrives just in time to save Patricia from death in the explosive-laden control station."

The gun battle ends as the henchmen die. Actually, Patricia screams the obvious: "Jim, the explosive's on fire!" Then Jim finally unties Patricia just in time before the building exploded.

Jim figures it all out. Carter murdered Voorhees and he kept everyone away so he can get the valuable gold from the sunken ship "The Dolphin" by planting mines and manipulating the mechanical sea monsters.

The serial's twist is that Carter figures that people do not know he's Carter as they think he is Kane. Unbeknownst to anyone, he already emptied all the gold from the ship. Jim captured Gregg and brought him to Kane (who really is Carter). Jim thinks Gregg is really Carter – the man behind the Haunted Harbor hoax as well as the man who murdered Voorhees.

As we know that Kane is really Carter, Kane says it is unbelievable Gregg is Carter, but Kane goes along with it. Then he frees Gregg when Jim leaves. Kane tells Gregg that since Jim believes Gregg is Carter – what will close the door on the case is if "Carter" is dead. So Kane shoots Gregg.

When Jim and Patricia return upon hearing gunshots, Kane says he shot Gregg in self-defense. Jim plays along with this but he realizes something is amiss for he sees the rope that bound Gregg nearby on the floor.

However, Jim walks in Kane's cave as Kane explains to another henchmen of his real identity. Kane gets knocked out, but then grabs a rope attached to a bucket of hot boiling liquid. He screams in terror as he pulls the rope, emptying the hot liquid on his face and body, thereby scorching himself to death. Whether Kane's act was accidental or intentional can be debated.

The rest of the gang are imprisoned. Jim's name is cleared. He is thanked and returned to be the master of his schooner. Jim says he could not have succeeded without Galbraith or his friend Yanks, but that goes double for Patricia.

The serial ends as Patricia and Jim are all smiles when they go off to a special dinner ordered by Yanks. Seeing the two go off happily together, Galbraith tells Yanks (who was going to join the two): "Jim don't need no more help now."

After three serials, Aldridge retired and passed the title of Serial Queen on to Linda Stirling, who would do twice as many serials as Aldridge.

Due to the constraints of the storylines given to her characters, in no way did Aldridge live up to the title of Serial Queen in *Daredevils of the West* or *Haunted Harbor* with the same viewer satisfaction as in *Perils of Nyoka*.

Chapter Thirteen: Afterword

Without any pretense or being puffed up about her abilities, Aldridge may have best summed up the limitations of her acting. In an article "Kay Aldridge May Fix Home Near Lyells; Is Thrilled over Pictures in *Life* Magazine" by Edith Lindeman, Aldridge observed: "Of course, being a Serial Queen does not mean that I'm a great actress, but then, I never was anyway."

Lindeman acknowledged Aldridge's claim to fame and memory, without realizing it then, specifically: "Kay is too modest to add that she is one of Hollywood's 10 most beautiful girls, in which she doesn't need to be a great actress. . . . She's a nice thing, this Katharine Aldridge, and the nicest part about her is that Hollywood, fame, money, stardom, adulation and all the other thrilling material things haven't spoiled her. Maybe she isn't the 'greatest actress in the world,' but, to my way of thinking, she's something better, a charming young woman."

The view that producers over at Fox and Warners had of Kay Aldridge as a mere society girl that served as brainless eye candy really kept her from reaching any height that she may have achieved. Aldridge's own reflections ring true about how if only she got a good small part with the right director, it could have paved the way to a real career. Also, her acting could have gotten better with the proper guidance.

For example, her more serious and even heroic demeanor exhibited in the Republic serials showed she could be more than just window dressing. However, the limitation in those productions is that the serials, albeit designed as juvenile fare, did not have the sophisticated writing and other aspects to really develop anyone's talent. Unfortunately, dialogue in serials is sparse and plots leave the characters with much to be desired emotionally or psychologically.

Nevertheless, Aldridge's character of Nyoka has come to be a filmic representation of the strong woman always in charge and capable of surviving without much need of a man. In short, she has been seen as a feminist icon in a world where women are still hoping to forever extinguish all of the gender politics and conventions that put men in a superior position in the universe.

Unarguably, Nyoka does stand tall in that regard. Although she exhibits some moments of fear and helplessness, as when she cries for help from Larry, these were brief and life-threatening moments when Vultura and her henchmen had put her at a decided disadvantage. But fear and helplessness is not indicative of her full nature. Most often it is her traits of fearlessness and compassion that dominated her character.

But given the chance, the photogenic Kay Aldridge may have been a more familiar name nowadays, and become more than the iconic female heroine from *Perils of Nyoka*.

Nevertheless, we will always have the thrills gone by of Kay Aldridge and the serials.

APPENDIX:

Bibliography

Part One and Part Two of this book rely predominantly upon newspaper articles from *Brooklyn Daily Eagle, Chicago Daily Tribune, Los Angeles Times, New York Times, Wall Street Journal,* and *Washington Post.*

Alan G. Barbour, *Saturday Afternoon At the Movies: 3 Volumes in 1*, New York: Bonanza Books, 1986.
Carey Cameron, *Memoirs of a Southern Belle*, Camden, Maine: Unpublished Scrapbook, 2014.
Evelyn S. Ward, with an essay by Peter Matthiessen, *The Children of Bladensfield*, New York: Viking Press, 1978.

Sources used to compile the credits included:

Feature Films, 1940-1949, A United States Filmography by Alan G. Fetrow, McFarland, 1994.
The Films of 20th Century-Fox, A Pictorial History by Tony Thomas and Aubrey Solomon, The Citadel Press, 1979.
Grand National, Producers Releasing Corporation and Screen Guild/Lippert, Complete Filmographies with Studio Histories by Ted Okuda, McFarland, 1989.
Hollywood Song, The Complete Film & Musical Companion, 3 volumes, by Ken Bloom, Facts on File, 1995.
Leonard Maltin's Classic Movie Guide, 2nd edition, edited by Leonard Maltin, Plume, 2010.
The MGM Story, The Complete History of Fifty-Seven Roaring Years by John Douglas Eames, Crown, 1982.
The Paramount Story by John Douglas Eames, Crown, 1985.
The Republic Pictures Checklist, Features, Serials, Cartoons, Short Subjects and Training Films of Republic Pictures Corporation, 1935-1959 by Len D. Martin, McFarland, 1998.
70 Years of the Oscar, The Official History of the Academy Awards by Robert Osborne, Abbeville Press, 1999.

Sound Films, 1927-1939, A United States Filmography by Alan G. Fetrow, McFarland, 1992.

Those Fabulous Serial Heroines, Their Lives and Films by Buck Rainey, The Scarecrow Press, Inc., 1990.

The United Artists Story by Ronald Bergan, Crown, 1986.

Vitaphone Films, A Catalogue of the Features and Shorts by Roy Liebman, McFarland, 2003.

Foreword to the scrapbook "Memoirs of a Southern Belle"

When my mother, Katharine Aldridge Cameron Tucker Nasland, died on January 12, 1995, the material from her brief but splashy career as model, cover girl and actress, came into my possession. The material – consisting of whole magazines, loose photographs, store displays, movie publicity stills, lobby cards, letters, scraps of diaries and loose pages in which Katharine (hereafter known as K.A.) recounted some of the history of her career – were contained in numerous dusty cardboard boxes. Though I had seen what I thought of as "most" of the material while she was alive, I started to uncover images and written material that I had never seen before.

The images – some spectacular, others charming, others embarrassing, the majority of them emblematic of American popular culture before and during World War II – compelled me to want to examine the contents of every one of the boxes, thoroughly. They also compelled me to want to share them with friends, and with family members ranging from those who had vivid memories of her to those who had no memory of her at all, but had shown a curiosity about K.A. and her career.

The written material – from gossip columns and articles, and from letters written by her or to her, from friends, family and fans – I found equally compelling, and soon realized that, even though there was practically no order to the images, the written material, together with my own memory of what my mother told me, could be a tool to help me organize the images into a kind of narrative describing the arc of K.A.'s 9-year career and its life-long consequences.

A good portion of the material I found in the dusty cardboard boxes had been glued onto pages. The pages I recognized as having belonged to albums that my sister, Melissa, and I, and my brothers, Arty and Scott, had been very used to when we were little. They were albums that K.A. would show to various guests who would show up at the various houses where we lived, sometimes after a lot of urging, other times after no urging at all. The albums were so poured over they eventually fell apart around the time I (the youngest of K.A.'s 4 children) became a teenager.

One of the albums was green leather and had a title on the cover, Memoirs of a Southern Belle. It had been made by K.A.'s friends, Maizie, a.k.a. Alice Boyer. Maizie had been K.A.'s roommate [at] the Studio Club in Hollywood. The Studio Club was a hotel for aspiring actresses. The other album had been made by Elsie West, K.A.'s classmate from the first school K.A. ever attended (which K.A. didn't get to until she was in 5th grade).

This album had 3 compilers who can be named: Maizie and Elsie and myself, though my work would not have been possible without the efforts of Maizie and Elsie, who clipped and pasted at the time the images and articles were appearing and which might not have been collected otherwise. 90-year-old Elsie, in addition (when I had nearly completed organizing the material I had, and who has since died), sent me a box of approximately 150 fan letters. At first I thought I couldn't get through the 70-year-old letters, but I started to read them and was hooked. I had spent months looking at K.A.'s images, then suddenly, thanks to the letters, I was discovering the effect of the images had, on unknown men and women, boys and girls, from all walks of life. Space prohibits me from including as many letters or excerpts of the letters as I would have liked; I have had to limit the selection to the most representational or curious or touching (or nervous-making) among them.

In the summer of 1995 I attempted to get to the bottom of the dusty cardboard boxes, but the material was too interesting and required too much time. I began to organize the material, then it was time to leave Maine for the busy life I had. Then my husband, Giovanni (an Italian Diplomat) retired, we were able to move to the United States, our daughters, Enrica and Francesca, entered college, the tenant who rented Mother's house (now our house) in Camden, Maine moved out and I found myself, for the first time since getting married, with the time and space to throw myself back into the boxes. I had heat installed on the side porch, set up 5 tables on it and started playing a vast game of "Concentration" with the images of K.A. – from a time when she was younger than her grandchildren and step-grandchildren are today -- as my playing cards. This is the result.

Carey Cameron – Camden, Maine 2013

Letter by Kay Aldridge to her mother Cornelia Ward Aldridge:

Please note all spelling is presented exactly as Aldridge typed it. The entire letter is typewritten except the date, which is scripted. The Swedish actress she refers to ("and I can't pronounce it") is....the lovely lady who changed her name to Ingrid Bergman.

Sunday Evening
June 11th, 1939

Dearests:

Tis Sunday evening and my first chance in a week to write you all the exciting things that have been happening to me too fast to give me time between to put them in paper to you.

Last Wednes'day Mrs. Zanuck, wife of the head of Fox, invited me to a private dinner party tonight to meet the Marajaha of Capopouli of India (sp of course). She sent her car and chauffeur for me. I wore my accordion pleated blue chiffon with jacket and hair up. I was one of the first arrivals the only guest ahead of me was standing in the living room when I arrived. I walked right up to him and said: "Are you the Marajaha?" I know he was much too attractive to be he and my remark had the desired effect. He grinned admiringly and said with an Austrian accent that melted my heart: "No but won't I do? I'm Baron Hubert Pontz." I said: "Oh Herbert Pants. . what a sweet name. . . are you a phony baron? So with this start we were inseparable for the rest of the evening except for a little work Loretta Young put in on him. It turned out that he is a real baron not rich but dead attractive and one of the best winter sportsmen in his country over here doing something about establishing a winter resort like Sun Valley or sumpin, I was the only woman at the party who was not a star or the wife of an executive. I sat at a table with Mrs. Gary Cooper who is herself very lovely and the one woman whose the right one for him, it seems for he came over to the table and said something aside to her that just made you know that he really cares for her.

They have a little girl now named Maria. Gary Cooper has the most marvelous smile I have ever seen on a man. Delores Del Rio looked beautiful as always and so did Loretta Young. Annabella was there with husband Tyrone Power. The Marajaha himself is dark but not negroid looking quite distinguné but 65 is too old for me... he did sort of look at me with a gleam for both he and his son are both lady's men and they say he thinks nothing of bequeating thousands of aches or a ruby or two to any pair of waiting arms but not for me these old boys. The baron took me home via the party via the Trocadero where we did some very funny waltzing in true old Vienna style...... he kissed my hand and now I know what hand kissing can be ... terrific! I would like to have kissed him but demurred cause he is so attractive that I reckon they come easy to him and then I hardly knew him though I always feel almost from the first that I know a person very well. He is leaving tonight for Arazona but will be back Tuesday....he called just now to say goodby. But I have two Austrians in my life now ....the other is named Kurt Scherff and he runs a shoppe (very snooty) called Lenz of Austria... I met him as a customer myself and was later introduced to him socially and he is really the most wonderful dancer I have ever danced (with whom), He is fun too cause he says he has no heart. I warned him against myself being foreign and emotionally I was afraid he would get serious about me so I explained to him that my friendly manner was really just me and that he must under no condition get serious about me but that I do enjoy dancing with him and he is fun to go out with it. He just laughs at me and says you are very nice .. pretty nice... but as I have no heart.

The Marajaha invited me to dinner party he gave last night at the Trocadero.... called for me himself.... and the funny part is I kept him waiting because I was being sewn into this dress I wore by a dressmaker who made it for me. Think of it: "His Imperial Highness waiting for me." I made him late for his own party and instead of making up a false excuse told everybody the truth and they all had a good laugh out of it.

[second page]

This dress I wore is of the loveliest dress I have ever owned. I saw a sketch of it in the Original designs at this Lenz of Austria shoppe. This wonderful woman I know who sews beautifully took one look at this sketch and made it for me at half the price they would have charged. Kurt Scharff (who owns the shoppe) could not tell it from one of their own makes. It is made from starched white chiffon. It has a set in yoke neck tyrolian style, the yoke is outlined by a ruffle and the neck has a high ruffle around it. The bodice is sherred and the skirt has 17 yds around the bottom. The sleeves are enormous sort of bishop sleeves with tight writ-struffles. It is called angle dress and that is what it looks like in this transparent material. Oh yes I have 7 crystal buttons down the front. I wore a gardenia in my hair as my only ornament and everyone remarked they had never seen me look as well. I wear it over a heavy satin slip the dress is so sheer. You'd just love it. . . . .I'm going to be photographed in it for you. Luckily it is not in style so it can never go out of style. The material I got 20% off cause the dressmaker's daughter works at the store.

From the Marajaha's party I went to the phoney prince Michael Romanoff's party at the Clover Club. Everyone knows he is a phoney but [he[has such a wonderful sense of humor about himself that people like to have him around. He has made me the "Lady Katharine". . . .you would be so amused to hear his perfect oxford accent and he really is up on everything. People try to trip him [up] all the time on the Russian aristocracy or Eaton or Oxford but he can even name his class mates. He has read everything. He even had nerve enough to say of the "Mar[a]jaha". . . . "that phoney. . .that pseudo visiting potentiate I'll throw him out." He said once to me: "You know what people call me don't. youth at dirty little bastard (with broad A) who thinks he's a prince." His party was too crowded to be fun so we went back to the Marajaha's.

About my carreer. . . .I have been assigned a small part in "Falling Stars" with Don Ameche and Alice Faye in Technicolor. I have two quite nice scenes in it . .I play an actress of the Theda Bara era. It is a story about the development the moving picture industry. I wear an evening dress in one scene and in the other a very

Queen of Sheba costume covered by ropes of pears and fancy headresses. Odd part for me but gives them a chance to see me in technicolor. You see this star business step by step. Tomorrow I'm going to make a fool of myself may be. I am going to ask David Selznick to test me for the part of Mrs. Max DeWinter in Rebecca. Folk say I couldn't look it but I can. . .the girls say I am too lively and self assured. . . .that she was homely. But I say she wasn't really homely and they wouldn't have her so on the screen anyway. She was awkward. . my newess to the screen makes me that way anyway. I bet you think I couldn't too but I am going to try. The girl has to be an actress to depict all those feelings about Rebecca that can't be screened . . . . I think it will make a wonderful movie and if I could get the part it would help make me to live down what everybody is predisposed to think because I was a model . . . . that I am a photogenic doll. I shall ask for the test even if he laughs at me and it. Pray for me. Even a great actress can not play a part to which she is physically unsuited . . . .and if they feel that I am they won't even test me. We shall see, Today I met the most really lovely girl I have ever seen. Her name is Swedish and I can't pronounce it . . .she is brought here to play in the movie "Intermezzo." She is 5'8." . . . . sort of my coloring but with a complection so beautiful that she made mine look like a hide. The most winsome and exquisite face you can imagine. She is married and has an eight month old baby. Her husband is a doctor and likes her success.

   I think it is thrilling that you are going to drive out to see me with Bernard. And of course, you are. It is the chance of a lifetime. Having lost your tegumental integrity some 25 years ago I think it is foolish to even care what folk think or say. I think it is the grandest idea I have ever heard. Perhaps I could drive back with you but I'll not be East to drive out here with you. I would want you to pay your own overnight expenses and some of your meals and can certainly afford to give you this myself.

List of Magazine Covers:

The Brooklyn Daily Eagle reported that Aldridge appeared on her 50th magazine cover as of February 13, 1944. However, she might have been on even more. Here is a list of the known covers as chronicled by Carey:

January 1937: *Redbook*
March 1937: *Redbook*
April 1937: *Ladies Home Journal*
April 1937: *The American*
May 1937: *Redbook*
April/May 1938: *You*
September 5, 1938: *Life*
October 1938: *Delineator*
October 1938: *Love and Romance*
October 1938: *True Romances*
December 1938: *Redbook*
March 1939: *Redbook*
March 27, 1939: *Life*
June 1939: *Redbook*
July 30, 1939: *True Experience*
August 1939: *Ladies Home Journal*
September 1939: *Redbook*
September 1939: *True Experience*
December 25, 1939: *Life*
1939: *Polynesian*
March 1940: *Redbook*
March 26, 1940: *Look*
March 1940: *Click*
September 15-26 1940: Unknown Russian magazine?
June 1941: *True Confessions*
June 1941: *Ladies Home Journal*
June 1941: *The Saturday Evening Post*
February 1942: *Redbook*
February 1942: *Coronet*
July 19, 1942: *This Week – Los Angeles Times*
August 1942: *Cinelandia*
March 1943: *McCalls*
June 27, 1943: *This Week – Los Angeles Times*
September 1943: *Redbook*
November 1943: *Cosmopolitan*
November 28, 1943: *Sunday Mirror*
November 29, 1943: *America's Alertmen*
April 1944: *Redbook*
April 1944: *Country Gentleman*
May 1944: *Facts*
July 1944: *Collier's*
Date Unknown: *Redbook*
Date Unknown: *Modern Romances*
Date Unknown: *True Experiences*
45. Unknown
46. Unknown
47. Unknown
48. Unknown
49. Unknown
50. Unknown

Print Advertising:

The following products are some of many products that Aldridge did advertising work:

Camel Cigarettes
Old Gold Cigarettes
Chesterfield Cigarettes
Lucky Strike Cigarettes
Model Smoking Tobacco
Raleigh Cigarettes
Ipana Toothpaste
Pepsodine Toothpaste
Dr. Lyon's Tooth Powder
Iodent
Listerine Toothpaste
F. Karl Beckh & Co. (Furrier)
Judy Bend Blouse
La Jade Beauty Shoppe
Knox the Hatter, New York
Pepperell Manufacturing Company, Boston, MA (maker of Lady Pepperell Sheets, blankets, broadcloths, etc)
Sunshine Krispy Crackers
Cinema Cake Makeup
Chanel
Dupont Cellophane
Texaco Fire Chief
Chrysler
LifeBuoy Soap
Naphta Soap
Woodbury Cold Cream
Bayer
SSS Hair Tonic
Wild Root Hair Tonic
Jergens
Ponds Cold Cream
Ticonderoga Pens
Tangee Lipstick
Sears Roebuck
Philo Film
Noxzema
Blue Waltz Perfume
Drene Shampoo
Roux Oil Shampoo
Spry Vegatable Shortening

Film Studios:

Studio Breakdown for Aldridge's movies:

Walter Wanger –1
MGM – 2
20th Century Fox - 11
Warner Brothers - 3
Republic Pictures – 3
Columbia – 1
RKO – 1
PRC - 2

CREDITS

Feature Films:

***Vogues of 1938* (1937)** D: Irving Cummings.

Warner Baxter, Joan Bennett, Helen Vinson, Mischa Auer, Alan Mowbray, Jerome Cowan, Alma Kruger, Marjorie Gateson, Dorothy McNulty [Penny Singleton], Polly Rowles, Georgie [George] Tapp[s], Virginia Verrill, Fred Lawrence, Gloria Gilbert, The Olympic Trio, The Wiere Brothers (Harry, Herbert, Sylvester), Maurice Rocco and Dotty Saulter, The Four Hot Shots, Victor Young and His Orchestra, Marla Shelton, Hedda Hopper, Roman Bohnen, Kay Aldridge, Judith Barrett, Jean Acker, Irving Bacon, Dick Elliott, I. Stanford Jolley, Dennis O'Keefe, Jason Robards Sr., Frank McGrath.

A New York fashion industry leader (Baxter) has trouble with his wife (Vinson) when she drains his money to put on a glamour show. Aldridge makes her film debut in an unbilled part as Katherine, a model. Screenplay by Bella and Samuel Spewack. Choreography by Seymour Felix. Produced by Walter Wanger. Portions filmed in New York City.

Songs
"(Turn On That) Red Hot Heat" (Louis Alter; Paul Francis Webster)
"That Old Feeling" (Sammy Fain; Lew Brown) (Academy Award Nominee)
"Lovely One" (Manning Sherwin; Frank Loesser)
"Lady of the Evening" (Alter; Webster)
"King of Jam" (instrumental) (Alter)
"Jingle Bells" (James Pierpont)
"Anchors Aweigh" (Charles A. Zimmerman; Alfred Hart Miles; R. Lovell)
"The Moonlight Sonata" (Ludwig Van Beethoven)
"Fall Fashion Show" (Alter; Webster)
"Siboney" (Ernesto Lecuona; Dolly Morse)
"Aloha Oe" (Queen Liliuokalani)
Additional Academy Award Nomination
(Art Direction) Alexander Toluboff.

Music by Borris Morros, (Victor Young).
Released on September 17.
(108 minutes/Western Electric Mirrophonic Recording/Technicolor/video/DVD)
Walter Wanger Productions/United Artists

Rosalie (1937) D: W.S. Van Dyke II.

Nelson Eddy, Eleanor Powell, Frank Morgan, Edna May Oliver, Ray Bolger, Ilona Massey, Billy Gilbert, Tom Rutherford, Clay Clement, Virginia Grey, George Zucco, Oscar O'Shea, Jerry Colonna, Janet Beecher, William Demarest, Tommy Bond, Kay Aldridge, Roy Barcroft, Lane Chandler, Rush Hughes, Jean Muir, William Tannen, Phillip Terry, Pierre Watkin.

Eddy and Powell become involved in a star-crossed romance and Ruritanian court intrigue amid lavish musical numbers. Aldridge (again unbilled) plays a lady in waiting. Screenplay by William Anthony McGuire, from the Broadway play he co-wrote with Guy Bolton. McGuire also produced. Choreography by Albertina Rasch and an unbilled Dave Gould. Portions filmed at the US Military Academy, West Point, New York.

Songs
"Who Knows?" (Cole Porter)
"I've a Strange New Rhythm in My Heart" (Porter)
"Night and Day" (Porter)
"Rosalie" (Porter)
"Why Should I Care?" (Porter)
"Spring Love in the Air" (Porter)
"In the Still of the Night" (Porter)
"It's All Over But the Shouting" (Porter)
"To Love or Not to Love" (Porter)
"Danse Russe (Allegro Giusto)" from "Petrouchka" (Igor Stravinsky)
"Polovetsian Dances" (Aleksander Borodin)
"Caucasian Sketches, Opus 10" (Mikhail Ippolitov-Ivanov)
"Second Movement (Allegro Con Grazia)" from "Symphony No. 6 in B Flat, Pathetique, Opus 4" (Pyotr Ilyich Tchaikovsky)
"Goodbye Forever (Addio)" (Francesco Paolo Tosti)
"The *WP* March" (John Philip Sousa)

"The Stars and Stripes Forever" (Sousa)
"El Capitan" (Sousa)
"Semper Fidelis" (Sousa)
"Parade" (Herbert Stothart)
"Gaudeamus Igitur" (traditional, composer unknown)
"The Wedding March" (Felix Mendelssohn-Bartholdy)
"Oh Promise Me" (Reginald De Koven; Clement W. Scott)
"M'Appari Tutt'amor" from the opera "Martha" (Friedrich von-Flowtow)
"Anchors Aweigh" (Charles A. Zimmerman; Alfred Hart Miles; R. Lovell)
"On, Brave Old Army Team" (Philip Egner)
"The Caisson Song" (Edmund L. Gruber)
   One of the 15 top-grossing films of 1937-38.
   Music by Roger Edens, Merrill Pye, George Stoll, Herbert Stothart.
   Released on December 24.
   (122 minutes/Western Electric Sound/video/DVD)
   Metro-Goldwyn-Mayer

"A girl in every room—and a man on every mind!"
***Hotel for Women* (1939) D: Gregory Ratoff.**
Ann Sothern, Linda Darnell, James Ellison, Jean Rogers, Lynn Bari, June Gale, Joyce Compton, Elsa Maxwell, John Halliday, Katharine [Kay] Aldridge, Alan Dinehart, Sidney Blackmer, Amanda Duff, Ruth Terry, Chick Chandler, Ivan Lebedeff, Charles C. Wilson, Mary Healy, Herbert Ashley, Gregory Gaye, Kay Linaker, Amzie Strickland, Charles Trowbridge.

Darnell travels to the big city hoping to see her boyfriend, but he has moved on to other interests. She finds lodging in a hostel that caters to single girls. From there she builds a career as a model. Aldridge plays Melinda Craig. Screenplay by Kathryn Scola and Darrell Ware, from a story by Elsa Maxwell and Scola. Produced by Raymond Griffith and Darryl F. Zanuck.

Song
"Whistle a Little Old Melody" (Elsa Maxwell)
   Music by (David Buttolph, Cyril J. Mockridge).
   Released on August 4.

(83 minutes/Western Electric Mirrophonic Recording)
Cosmopolitan/20th Century-Fox

Here I Am A Stranger (1939) D: Roy Del Ruth.

Richard Greene, Richard Dix, Brenda Joyce, Roland Young, Gladys George, Katherine [Kay] Aldridge, Russell Gleason, George Zucco, Edward Norris, Henry Kolker, Richard Bond, Robert Shaw, Robert Kellard, Charles C. Wilson, Harry Hayden, Minor Watson, Frank Coghlan Jr., Robert Lowery, Delmar Watson.

Greene, brought up in England, has never met his real father. That changes when the young man travels to America. He discovers that his dad (Dix) is a recovering alcoholic, but their meeting proves to be an impetus for Dix's further rejuvenation and Greene's growth as a man. Aldridge is Lillian Bennett. Screenplay by Milton Sperling and Sam Hellman, from a story by Gordon Malherbe Hillman. Produced by Darryl F. Zanuck and Harry Joe Brown.

Music by Louis Silvers, (David Buttolph).

Released on September 29.

(83 minutes/Western Electric Mirrophonic Recording)
20th Century-Fox

Free, Blonde and 21 (1940) D: Ricardo Cortez.

Lynn Bari, Mary Beth Hughes, Joan Davis, Henry Wilcoxon, Robert Lowery, Alan Baxter, Katherine [Kay] Aldridge, Helen Ericson, Chick Chandler, Joan Valerie, Elyse Knox, Dorothy Dearing, Herbert Rawlinson, Kay Linaker, Thomas E. Jackson, Richard Lane, Frank Coghlan Jr., Jerry Fletcher, Edward Cooper, Dorothy Moore, Gwen Kenyon, Mickey Simpson, Ruth Clifford, George Meeker, Robert Ryan, John Wald.

Bari and Hughes have differing approaches in finding love and happiness; unfortunately for one of them, the road of romance leads to jail. Aldridge plays Adelaide Sinclair. Screenplay by Frances Hyland. Produced by Sol M. Wurtzel. A sequel to *Hotel for Women* (1939).

Music by Samuel Kaylin.

Released on March 29.

(67 minutes/RCA High Fidelity Recording/DVD)
20th Century-Fox

"Yippee! We're together! Jane Withers—Gene Autry ridin'. . .singin'. . .ropin'. . .shootin'. . .and singin' some more!"

Shooting High (1940) D: Alfred E. Green.

Jane Withers, Gene Autry, Marjorie Weaver, Frank M. Thomas, Robert Lowery, Katharine [Kay] Aldridge, Hobart Cavanaugh, Jack Carson, Hamilton McFadden, Charles Middleton, Ed Brady, Tom London, Eddie Acuff, Pat O'Malley, George Chandler, Budd Buster, George Chesebro, LeRoy Mason, 'Snub' Pollard, Henry Wills, Hank Worden, Champion (a horse).

A film crew shooting a movie about an old west sheriff goes on location to where the lawman lived and meets his grandson (Autry). The grandson gets a job as stand-in for the actor playing the sheriff, but young Withers plots to make sure Autry gets the lead role for himself. Aldridge plays Evelyn Trent. Screenplay by Lou Breslow and Owen Francis. Choreography by Nicholas [Nick] Castle and Geneva Sawyer. Produced by John Stone and Sol M. Wurtzel.

Songs
"Wanderers" (Felix Bernard; Paul Francis Webster)
"Shanty of Dreams" (Johnny Marvin; Gene Autry)
"Only One Love in a Lifetime" (Marvin; Autry; Harry Tobias)
"Little Old Band of Gold" (Charles Newman; Fred Glickman; Autry)
"On the Rancho with My Pancho" (Harry Akst; Sidney Clare)
"Bridal Chorus (Here Comes the Bride)" from "Lohengrin" (Richard Wagner).

Music by Samuel Kaylin.
Released on April 26.
(65 minutes/RCA High Fidelity Recording/video/DVD)
20th Century-Fox

Girl In 313 (1940) D: Ricardo Cortez.

Florence Rice, Kent Taylor, Lionel Atwill, Katherine [Kay] Aldridge, Mary Treen, Jack Carson, Elyse Knox, Joan Valerie, Dorothy Dearing, Dorothy Moore, Jacqueline Wells [Julie Bishop],

Charles C. Wilson, William B. Davidson, Lenita Lane, Lillian Porter, Alice Armand, Gladys Costello, Adrian Morris, Lee Phelps, Charles Williams, Evalyn Knapp, Pat O'Malley, James Flavin, Ralph Dunn, Eddy Chandler, Rex Evans, Iris Wong, Laura Treadwell, Grace Hayle, Edward Cooper, Billy Wayne, Mantan Moreland, Iva Stewart, Florence Wright, Bess Flowers, Cyril Ring.

Aldridge is featured as Sarah Sorrell in this crime drama about a jewel theft and the investigation led by an undercover female cop (Rice) who infiltrates the gang. Screenplay by Barry Trivers and Clay Adams, from a story by Hilda Stone. Produced by Sol M. Wurtzel.

Music by Emil Newman, David Buttolph, Cyril J. Mockridge, Alfred Newman.

Released on May 31.

(56 minutes/DVD)

20th Century-Fox

"50,000 sailors...can't go wrong!"

Sailor's Lady **(1940) D: Allan Dwan.**

Nancy Kelly, Jon Hall, Joan Davis, Dana Andrews, Mary Nash, Larry [Buster] Crabbe, Katharine [Kay] Aldridge, Harry Shannon, Wally Vernon, Bruce Hampton, Charles D. Brown, Selmer Jackson, Edgar Dearing, Edmund MacDonald, William B. Davidson, Lester Dorr, George O'Hanlon, Matt McHugh, Peggy Ryan, Ward Bond, Barbara Pepper, Gaylord [Steve] Pendleton, Eddie Acuff, Pierre Watkin, Paul Harvey, Emmett Vogan, Kane Richmond, Irving Bacon, Cyril Ring, John Kellogg, James Flavin, Marie Blake, Tom Seidel, Charles Tannen, Charles Trowbridge.

Comedy about Navy man Hall planning to marry girlfriend Kelly after his hitch, but she already has adopted a child. Aldridge is Georgine. Screenplay by Frederick Hazlett Brennan, from a story by Frank Wead; Lou Breslow and Owen Francis contributed additional dialogue. Produced by Sol M. Wurtzel.

Music by Samuel Kaylin.

Released on July 5.

(66 minutes/RCA High Fidelity Recording)

20th Century-Fox

"Merry Miss Mixup!"

Girl from Avenue A (1940) D: Otto Brower.

Jane Withers, Kent Taylor, Katherine [Kay] Aldridge, Elyse Knox, Laura Hope Crews, Jessie Ralph, Harry Shannon, Vaughan Glaser, Rand Brooks, Ann Shoemaker, George Humbert, Wade Boteler, Edgar Dearing, Rex Evans, Edward Gargan, William Haade, Charles Judels, Carole Mathews, Pat O'Malley, Dick Rich, Eddy Waller.

A young girl (Withers) brought up in the streets is adopted by a family whose son is a writer. The child's capers inspires him to pen a play. Aldridge plays Lucy. Screenplay by Frances Hyland and an uncredited Albert Ray, from the play "The Brat" by Maude Fulton. Produced by Sol M. Wurtzel.

Song
"Let Us Dance at the Waldorf" (Emil Newman).
  Music by Emil Newman, (Cyril J. Mockridge).
  Released on August 9.
  (73 minutes)
  20th Century-Fox

Yesterday's Heroes (1940) D: Herbert I. Leeds.

Jean Rogers, Robert Sterling, Ted [Michael] North, Katherine [Kay] Aldridge, Russell Gleason, Richard Lane, Edmund MacDonald, George Irving, Emma Dunn, Harry Hayden, Isabel Randolph, Pierre Watkin, Frank Sully, M.J. [Mike] Frankovich, Don Forbes, Bert Roach, Matt McHugh, Truman Bradley, George Meeker, Frank Coghlan Jr., Mary Field, James Flavin, John Kellogg, Elyse Knox, June Wilkins.

A doctor (Sterling) looks back on his college days, when he was part of the football team. His dalliance with Aldridge (as Janice Mason) almost ruins his chances to be with his true love (Rogers). Screenplay by Irving Cummings Jr. and William Counselman Jr., from a *Saturday Evening Post* magazine serialized novel by William Brent. Produced by Sol M. Wurtzel.

  Music by Emil Newman, (Cyril J. Mockridge).
  Released on September 20.
  (65 minutes)
  20th Century-Fox

"Sing and swing the Hit Parade tunes of tomorrow!"
Down Argentine Way (1940) D: Irving Cummings.

Don Ameche, Betty Grable, Carmen Miranda, Charlotte Greenwood, J. Carrol Naish, Henry Stephenson, Katharine [Kay] Aldridge, Leonid Kinskey, Chris-Pin Martin, Robert Conway, Gregory Gaye, Bobby Stone, Charles Judels, The Nicholas Brothers (Fayard, Harold), Thomas and Catherine Downing, Pepe Guizar, The Flores Brothers, Six Hits and a Miss, The Carmen Miranda Band [Bando de Luona], Edward Fielding, Edward [Eddie] Conrad, Fortunio Bonanova, Armand Kaliz, Frank Puglia, Elena Verdugo, Frank Yaconelli.

A South-of-the-Border romance takes place when American Grable vacations in Argentina and meets handsome horse-breeder Ameche. Aldridge plays Helen Carson. Screenplay by Darrell Ware and Karl Tunberg, from a story by Rian James and Ralph Spence. Choreography by Nick Castle and Geneva Sawyer. Produced by Darryl F. Zanuck and Harry Joe Brown. Portions filmed at Metropolitan Airport, Van Nuys, California.

Songs
"Down Argentine Way" (Harry Warren; Mack Gordon) (Academy
  Award Nominee)
"South American Way" (Jimmy McHugh; Al Dubin)
"Nenita" (Warren; Gordon)
"Two Dreams Met" (Warren; Gordon)
"Mamae Yo Quero" (Vincente Paiva; Jararaca Paiva; Al Stillman)
"Bambu" (Alimirante [Henri Que Foreis]; Valdo De Abreu)
"Sing to Your Senorita" (Warren; Gordon)
  Additional Academy Award Nominations
  (Cinematography—Color) Leon Shamroy, Ray Rennahan.
  (Art Direction—Color) Richard Day, Joseph C. Wright.
  Music by Emil Newman, (Cyril J. Mockridge).
  Released on October 11.
(90 minutes/Western Electric Mirrophonic Recording/Technicolor/video/laserdisc/DVD
  20th Century-Fox

Golden Hoofs **(1941) D: Lynn Shores.**

Jane Withers, Charles 'Buddy' Rogers, Kay Aldridge, George Irving, Buddy Pepper, Cliff Clark, Philip Hurlick, Sheila Ryan, Howard C. Hickman, Stanley Blystone, Margaret Brayton, Robert Conway, Mary Field, Bess Flowers, Eugene Jackson, Etta McDaniel, Sam McDaniel, Jackie Searl, Robert Shaw, Frank Sully, Fred 'Snowflake' Toones, Minerva Urecal.

Withers' grandfather has to sell the trotting-horse farm that has been in the family for years. The new buyer (Rogers) has a mind to turn the farm into a facility for training racehorses. Withers, who has a crush on the young man, attempts to change his mind. Aldridge is Cornelia Hunt. Screenplay by Ben Grauman Kohn, from a story by Roy Chanslor and Thomas Langan. Choreography by Nick Castle. Produced by Walter Morosco and Ralph Dietrich.

Song
"Consider Yourself in Love" (Walter Bullock; Harold Spina)
  Music by Cyril J. Mockridge.
  Released on February 14.
  (67 minutes/RCA Sound System)
  20th Century-Fox

> "Aboard a treasure ship Chan battles his most elusive adversary...the ghost of a pirate 100 years dead!"

Dead Men Tell **(1941) D: Harry Lachman.**

Sidney Toler, Sheila Ryan, Robert Weldon, [Victor] Sen Yung, Don [Donald] Douglas, Katharine [Kay] Aldridge, Paul McGrath, George Reeves, Truman Bradley, Ethel Griffies, Lenita Lane, Milton Parson, Stanley Andrews, Pat Flaherty, Tim Ryan, Brick Sullivan, Charles Tannen.

Oriental detective Charlie Chan (Toler) joins a treasure hunt after an elderly lady is scared to death by the specter of a pirate. Aldridge is seen as Laura Thursday. Screenplay by John Larkin, based on characters created by Earl Derr Biggers. Produced by Walter Morosco and Ralph Dietrich.

Music by Emil Newman, (David Raksin).
Released on March 28.

(60 minutes/RCA Sound/DVD)
20th Century-Fox

"Hold everything for that wonderful whirlwind of gobs, gals and glee!"

Navy Blues (1941) D: Lloyd Bacon.

Ann Sheridan, Jack Oakie, Martha Raye, Jack Haley, Herbert Anderson, Jack Carson, Jackie C. Gleason, William T. Orr, Richard Lane, Hardie Albright, John Ridgely, The *Navy Blues* Sextette (Katharine [Kay] Aldridge, Georgia Carroll, Marguerite Chapman, Peggy Diggins, Loraine Gettman [Leslie Brooks], Claire James), Howard da Silva, Byron Barr [Gig Young], Adele Mara, Charles Drake, DeWolf [William] Hopper, Ralph Byrd, George O'Hanlon, Walter Sande, Richard Travis, Frank Wilcox.

Gobs and gals chart an eventful course for Hawaii in this musical-comedy-romance. Aldridge is part of a six-girl performing ensemble. Screenplay by Jerry Wald, Richard Macauley, and Arthur T. Horman, from a story by Horman. Choreography by Seymour Felix. Produced by Hal B. Wallis. Portions filmed at San Diego Naval Base, California and Honolulu, Hawaii.

Songs
"Navy Blues" (Arthur Schwartz; Johnny Mercer)
"When Are We Going to Land Abroad" (Schwartz; Mercer)
"Hawaiian Party" (Schwartz; Mercer)
"In Waikiki" (Schwartz; Mercer)
"You're a Natural" (Schwartz; Mercer)
"Old Honolulu" (instrumental) (Schwartz; Mercer)
"My Bonnie Lies Over the Ocean" (H.J. Fuller)
"Sailing, Sailing Over the Bounding Main" (Godfrey Marks)
"Columbia, the Gem of the Ocean" (Thomas A. Beckett; David T. Shaw)
"Turkey in the Straw" (traditional, composer unknown)
"Semper Paratus" (Van Boskerck)
   Music by Heinz Roemheld, Ray Heindorf, Leo F. Forbstein.
   Released on September 13.
   (108 minutes/RCA Sound)
   Warner Brothers

"Jimmy Durante—Phil Silvers they're funny! Jane Wyman she's a honey! With the *Navy Blues* Sextette (they're in the Army wow!) Swell music, too!"

You're In The Army Now (1941) D: Lewis Seiler.

Jimmy Durante, Phil Silvers, Jane Wyman, Regis Toomey, Donald MacBride, Joseph Sawyer, Clarence Kolb, Paul Harvey, George Meeker, Paul Stanton, William Haade, John Maxwell, Etta McDaniel, The *Navy Blues* Sextette (Kay Aldridge, Peggy Diggins, Loraine Gettman [Leslie Brooks], Marguerite Chapman, Georgia Carroll, Alice [Alix] Talton), Matty Malneck and His Orchestra, Charles Drake, Harry Lewis, Jack Gardner, Armando & Lita, Murray Alper, Dick French, Sally Loomis, David Newell, Weldon Heyburn, Anthony Caruso, Roland Drew, Bill Erwin, James Flavin, William Hopper, Olin Howland, Patrick McVey, Marc Platt, Dick Wessel, Gig Young.

Military comedy about two vacuum cleaner salesmen (Durante, Silvers) who find themselves drafted into the Army. Aldridge re-teams with the gals from *Navy Blues*. Screenplay by Paul Gerard Smith and George Beatty, with assistance from Fred Niblo Jr. and Louis Quinn. Choreography by Matty King. Produced by Bryan Foy and Ben Stoloff.

Songs
"I'm Glad My Number Was Called" (Charles Adler; George Kelly)
"I'm an Army Man" (Jimmy Durante)
"Whirlaway" (Durante)
"You're in the Army Now" (Isham Jones; Tell Taylor; Ole Olsen)
"My Wild Irish Rose" (Chauncey Olcott)
"Der Erlkonig" (Franz Schubert)
"Valse des Rayons" (Jacques Offenbach)
"Sweet Georgia Brown" (Maceo Pinkard; Ben Bernie)
"Happy Birthday to You" (Mildred J. Hill; Patty S. Hill)

Music by Howard Jackson.
Released on December 25.
(79 minutes/RCA Sound)
Warner Brothers

"The humor of Hope…the zoomph of Zorina…the merriment of Moore…the musical magic of Irving Berlin!"

Louisiana Purchase (1941) D: Irving Cummings.

Bob Hope, Vera Zorina, Victor Moore, Irene Bordoni, Dona Drake, Raymond Walburn, Maxie Rosenbloom, Phyllis Ruth, Frank Albertson, Donald MacBride, Andrew Tombes, Robert Warwick, Charles LaTorre, Charles Lasky, Emory Parnell, Iris Meredith, Catherine Craig, Jack Norton, Sam McDaniel, Kay Aldridge, Katherine [Karin] Booth, Alaine Brandes [Rebel Randall], Barbara Britton, Brooke Evans, Blanche Grady, Lynda Grey, Margaret Hayes, Louise LaPlanche, Barbara Slater, Eleanor Stewart, Jean Wallace, Frances Gifford, Edgar Dearing, William Wright, Tom Patricola, Dave Willock, Donald Kerr, Joy Barlowe, Patsy Mace, Douglas Dean, John [Bud] Hiestand, Floyd Shackleford.

When an investigating senator looks into the seamier side of state politics, a less-than-honest operator (Hope) steers him into a scandal. Comedy-satire with Aldridge as Louisiana Belle. Screenplay by Jerome Chodorov and Joseph Fields (additional dialogue contributed by Barney Dean and Louis S. Kaye), from a story by B.G. DeSylva and a Broadway play by Morrie Ryskind. Choreography by Eddie Prinz. Produced by Harold Wilson and Buddy G. DeSylva.

Irving Berlin Songs
"Lawyer's Letter"
"Girls Opening Chorus (It's News to Us)"
"You're Lonely and I'm Lonely"
"Louisiana Purchase"
"It's a Lovely Day Tomorrow"
"You Can't Brush Me Off"
"Fools Fall in Love"
"Dance with Me Tonight at the Mardi Gras"
"The Lord Done Fixed Up My Soul"
"Sex Marches On"

Academy Award Nominations
(Cinematography—Color) Harry Hallenberger, Ray Rennahan.
(Art Direction-Interior Decoration—Color) Raoul Pene du Bois; Stephen A. Seymout.

Music by Robert Emmett Dolan, Walter Scharf, Leo Shuken.

Released on December 31 (one of the 21 top-grossing films of 1941-42).

(98 minutes/Western Electric Mirrophonic Recording/Technicolor/video/DVD)

Paramount

Perils Of Nyoka (1942/serial) D: William Witney.

Kay Aldridge, Clayton Moore, William Benedict, Lorna Gray [Adrian Booth], Charles Middleton, Tristram Coffin, Forbes Murray, Robert Strange, George Pembroke, George[s] Renavent, John Davidson, George [J.] Lewis, John Bagni, Ken Terrell, Kenneth [Kenne] Duncan, Arvon Dale, John Daheim, Duke Taylor, Tom Steele, Iron Eyes Cody, Forrest Taylor, Yakima Canutt, Art Dillard, Augie Gomez, Bud Wolfe, Robert Barron, Emil Van Horn, Herbert Rawlinson, David Sharpe, George Plues, John Bleifer, Joe Garcia, Henry Wills, Al Kikume, Steve Clemente, Carey Loftin, Jay Silverheels, Ace (a dog), Professor (a monkey).

Chapters

1. Desert Intrigue
2. Death's Chariot
3. Devil's Crucible
4. Ascending Doom
5. Fatal Second
6. Human Sacrifice
7. Monster's Clutch
8. Tuareg Vengeance
9. Buried Alive
10. Treacherous Trail
11. Unknown Peril
12. Underground Tornado
13. Thundering Death
14. Blazing Barrier
15. Satan's Fury

When Nyoka Gordon's father goes missing in the jungle, she joins a dangerous archaeological expedition venturing into the area where he disappeared. Aldridge stars as Nyoka. Aldridge's stunt double was David Sharpe. Screenplay by Ronald Davidson, Norman S. Hall, William Lively, Joseph O'Donnell, Joseph Poland, and an unaccredited Taylor Caven. Produced by William J. O'Sullivan. Portions filmed at Corriganville (Ray Corrigan Ranch), Simi Valley, California, and Iverson Ranch, Chatsworth, California. Re-released in 1952 as *NYOKA AND THE TIGERMEN*. Later re-edited into a television feature "*Nyoka and the Lost Secrets of Hippocrates*".

Music by Mort Glickman, (Arnold Schwarzwald).
Released on June 27.
(261 minutes/RCA Sound/video/laserdisc)
Republic

"New face—same Falcon—as fiction's famous sleuth hands down a heritage of mob hate to the Falcon's brother."
***The Falcon's Brother* (1942) D: Stanley Logan.**
George Sanders, Tom Conway, Jane Randolph, Don Barclay, Cliff Clark, Edward Gargan, Eddie Dunn, Charlotte Wynters, James Newill, Keye Luke, Amanda Varela, George [J.] Lewis, Gwili Andre, Andre Charlot, Mary Halsey, Charles Arnt, Richard Martin, Kay Aldridge, Georgia Carroll, John Dilson, Ludwig Donath, William Forrest, Marten Lamont, Wilbur Mack. The Falcon (Sanders) needs help on a wartime espionage case in South America, so he calls in his able sibling (Conway) to assist in thwarting an assassination plot. Aldridge is seen as the Victory Gown model and a Spanish girl. Screenplay by Stuart Palmer and Craig Rice, based on a character created by Michael Arlen. Produced by Maurice Geraghty.
Music by Roy Webb, Constantin Bakaleinikoff.
Released on November 6.
(63 minutes/RCA Sound/DVD)
RKO Radio

***Something To Shout About* (1943) D: Gregory Ratoff.**
Don Ameche, Janet Blair, Jack Oakie, William Gaxton, Cobina Wright Jr., Veda Ann Borg, Jaye Martin, Lily Norwood [Cyd Charisse], James 'Chuckles' Walker, The Teddy Wilson Orchestra, Kay Aldridge, The Bricklayers (Leonard Gautier and his performing dogs), David Lichine, James 'Buster' Brown, Charles Judels, Edward Gargan, Charles Williams, Gregory Ratoff, Cliff Clark, Harry Harvey, Eddy Waller.
Press agent Ameche needs to rid himself of a no-talent star (Wright) and finds an opportunity with pretty Broadway hopeful Blair. Aldridge appears as a showgirl. Screenplay by Lou Breslow and Edward Eliscu, from a story by Fred Schiller; adapted by George Owen. Produced by Gregory Ratoff.

Cole Porter Songs
"You'd Be So Nice to Come Home To" (Academy Award Nominee)
"Through Thick and Thin"
"I Always Knew"
"Something to Shout About"
"Lotus Bloom"
"Hasta Luego"
"It Might Have Been" (instrumental)
"I Can Do Without Tea in My Teapot" (instrumental)
   Additional Academy Award Nomination
   (Music—Scoring of a Musical Picture) Morris Stoloff.
   Music by Morris Stoloff, Victor Schertziner, Gil Grau, John Leipold, David Raksin.
   Released on February 25.
   (93 minutes)
   Columbia

"Renegade Indians. . .strike from ambush against these fearless trailblazing western pioneers!"

Daredevils Of The West **(1943) D: John English.**
   Allan Lane, Kay Aldridge, Eddie Acuff, William Haade, Robert Frazer, Ted Adams, George [J.] Lewis, Stanley Andrews, Jack Rockwell, Charles Miller, John Hamilton,
   Budd Buster, Kenneth Harlan, Ken [Kenne] Duncan, Rex Lease, Chief Thundercloud, Duke Green, Eddie Parker, Tom Steele, Jack O'Shea, George Magrill, Al Taylor, Edmund Cobb, Joe Yrigoyen, Bill Yrigoyen, Babe BeFreest, Herbert Rawlinson, Edward Cassidy, Ralph Bucko, Ken Terrell, Chief Many Treaties, Pierce Lyden, Rodd Redwing, Tom London, Jay Silverheels.

Chapters

1. Valley of Death
2. Flaming Prison
3. The Killer Strikes
4. Tunnel of Terror
5. Fiery Tomb
6. Redskin Raiders
7. Perilous Pursuit
8. Dance of Doom
9. Terror Trail
10. Suicide Showdown
11. Cavern of Cremation
12. Frontier Justice

Crooked cattleman Frazer opposes the efforts of Lane, Aldridge (as June Foster), and Acuff to construct a road through the Comanche Strip. Aldridge's stunt double was Babe DeFreest. Screenplay by Ronald Davidson, William Lively, Joseph Poland, Joseph O'Donnell, and Basil Dickey. Produced by William J. O'Sullivan. Portions filmed at these California locations: Alabama Hills in Lone Pine and Iverson Ranch in Chatsworth.
Songs
"Oh, Susannah" (Stephen Foster)
"Camptown Races" (Foster)
Music by Mort Glickman, (Walter Scharf).
Released on May 1.
(196 minutes/RCA Sound/video/DVD)
Republic

"The musical extravaganza that tops Great Ziegfeld glory!"
***DuBarry Was A Lady* (1943) D: Roy Del Ruth.**
Red Skelton, Lucille Ball, Gene Kelly, Virginia O'Brien, Rags Ragland, Zero Mostel, Donald Meek, Douglass Dumbrille, George Givot, Louise Beavers, Tommy Dorsey and His Orchestra, Andrew Tombes, Ava Gardner, Marilyn Maxwell, Clara Blandick, Lana Turner, The Pied Pipers, Kay Aldridge, Hazel Brooks, Kay Williams, Dick Haymes, Jo Stafford, Buddy Rich.
Nightspot attendant Skelton, who has eyes only for singer Ball, falls unconscious and dreams he is Louis XVI—with Lucy as the famed courtesan Madame DuBarry. Aldridge is Mrs. McGowan. Screenplay by Irving Brecher, from the 1939 play by B.G. DeSylva, Herbert Fields, and Cole Porter. Choreography by Charles Walters. Produced by Arthur Freed.
Songs
"DuBarry Was a Lady" (Burton Lane; Ralph Freed)
"Well, Git It" (composer unknown)
"Do I Love You, Do I?" (Cole Porter)
"I Love an *Esquire* Girl" (Roger Edens; Freed; Lew Brown)
"Ladies of the Bath" (Edens)
"Katie Went to Haiti" (Porter)
"Madame, I Love Your Crepes Suzettes" (Lane; Freed; Brown)

"Song of Rebellion" (Edens)
"Friendship" (Porter)
"Thinking of You" (Walter Donaldson; Paul Ash)
"A Cigarette, Sweet Music and You" (Roy Ringwald)
"Do You Ever Think of Me?" (Harry D. Kerr; Earl Burtnett)
"Sleepy Lagoon" (Eric Coates; Jack Lawrence)
"You Are My Sunshine" (Jimmie Davis; Charles Mitchell)
"Salome" (Edens; E.Y. Harburg)
"I'm Getting Sentimental Over You" (George Bassman; Ned Washington)

Music by Georgie Stoll, (Daniele Amfitheatrof, Mario Castelnuevo-Tedesco, David Raksin).

Released on August 13 (box office: $3,496,000).

(101 minutes/Western Electric Sound/Technicolor/video/laserdisc/DVD/AFI Laugh Nominee)

Metro-Goldwyn-Mayer

"See bold daredevils defy the evil that plagues Haunted Harbor!"

Haunted Harbor (1944/serial) D: Spencer

[G.] Bennet, Wallace [A.] Grissell. Kane Richmond, Kay Aldridge, Roy Barcroft, Clancy Cooper, Marshall J. Reed, Oscar O'Shea, Forrest Taylor, Hal Taliaferro [Wally Wales], Edward Keane, George J. Lewis, Kenne Duncan, Bud Geary, Robert Homans, Duke Green, Dale Van Sickel, Tom Steele, Rico de Montez, Robert J. Wilke, Fred Graham, Jack O'Shea, Ken Terrell, Eddie Parker, Bud Wolfe, Carey Loftin, Jay Silverheels.

Chapters
1. Wanted for Murder
2. Flight to Danger
3. Ladder of Death
4. The Unknown Assassin
5. Harbor of Horror
6. Return of the Fugitive
7. Journey into Peril
8. Wings of Doom
9. Death's Door
10. Crimson Sacrifice
11. Jungle Jeopardy
12. Fire Trap
13. Monsters of the Deep
14. High Voltage
15. Crucible of Justice

When a banker is murdered, Richmond is framed for the crime and sets out on a peril-laden quest to clear his name and recover a cache of gold that was sunk with a schooner. Aldridge co-stars as Patricia Harding. Screenplay by Royal [K.] Cole, Basil Dickey, Jesse Duffy, Grant Nelson, and Joseph F. Poland, from the novel by Dayle Douglas [Ewart Adamson]. Produced by Ronald Davidson. Portions filmed at these California locations: Iverson Ranch, Chatsworth, and Sherwood Forest. Re-released in 1951 as *Pirates' Harbor*.
Music by Joseph Dubin, (Mort Glickman, Walter Scharf).
Released on August 26.
(243 minutes/RCA Sound/video/DVD)
Republic

"He was a one-man army—she a one-girl blitz!"
***The Man Who Walked Alone* (1945)** D: Christy Cabanne.
David [Dave] O'Brien, Kay Aldridge, Walter Catlett, Guin 'Big Boy' Williams, Isabel Randolph, Smith Ballew, Nancy June Robinson, Ruth Lee, Chester Clute, Vivian Oakland, Vicki Saunders, Robert Hartzell, Charles Williams, Frank Melton, Donald Kerr, Eddy Waller, Don Brodie, Tom Dugan, William B. Davidson, Dick Elliott, Jack Raymond, Jack Mulhall, Charles Jordan, Tom Kennedy, Paul Newlan, Lloyd Ingraham, Elmo Lincoln, Myra [Mira] McKinney, Dick Raymond, Eddie Hall.
Comedy-drama centering on the developing relationship and mystery between wealthy Aldridge (as Wilhelmina Hammond) and O'Brien, the hitchhiker she hires as her chauffeur. Screenplay by Robert Lee Johnson, from a story by Christy Cabanne. Produced by Leon Fromkess and Christy Cabanne.
Song
"Say It with Love" (Jay Livingston; Ray Evans; Lewis Bellin)
  Academy Award Nomination
  (Music—Scoring of a Dramatic or Comedy Picture) Karl Hajos.
Released on March 15.
(65 minutes/Western Electric Sound/video/DVD)
Producers Releasing Corporation

The Phantom Of 42nd Street (1945) D: Albert Herman.

Dave O'Brien, Kay Aldridge, Alan Mowbray, Frank Jenks, Edythe Elliott, Jack Mulhall, Vera Marshe, Stanley Price, John Crawford, Cyril Delevanti, Paul Power, Harry Strang, Robert Strange, Budd Buster, Pat Gleason, Milton Kibbee.

When an actor is killed during the performance of a play, a theatrical critic (O'Brien) turns sleuth to find the murderer. Aldridge co-stars as Claudia Moore. Screenplay by Milton Raison, from the novel by Raison and Jack Harvey. Produced by Martin Mooney and Albert Herman.

Music by Karl Hajos, (Walter Greene).

Released on May 2.

(58 minutes/Western Electric Mirrophonic Recording/DVD)

Producers Releasing Corporation

Short Subjects:

Meet The Stars #1: Chinese Garden Festival (1940) D: Harriet Parsons.

Kay Aldridge, Vera Vague [Barbara Jo Allen], William Bakewell, Beulah Bondi, The Brewster Twins (Barbara, Gloria), Georgia Carroll, Charles Coburn, Dolores Del Rio, John Garfield, Rita Hayworth, Mary Beth Hughes, Dorothy Lamour, Mary Martin, Patricia Morison, Ona Munson, Cliff Nazarro, Gertrude Niesen, Maria Ouspenskaya, Mary Pickford, Walter Pidgeon, Charles 'Buddy' Rogers, Cesar Romero, Rosalind Russell, Tom Rutherford, Jane Withers, Anna May Wong.

Narrated by Harriet Parsons.

Various Hollywood stars (including Aldridge) turn out for a gala benefit for war-torn China. The fete is held at Pickfair, home of Mary Pickford and husband Charles 'Buddy' Rogers. Produced by Harriet Parsons.

Released on December 24.

(9 minutes/RCA Sound)

Republic

The Playgirls **(1941) D: Jean Negulesco.**

Navy Blues Sextette (Kay Aldridge, Leslie Brooks (formerly Lorraine Gettman), Georgia Carroll, Marguerite Chapman, Peggy Diggins, The Playgirls Band (Claire James, Cathy Lewis), The Ryan Sisters.

Three all-female acts take to the bandstand and provide musical entertainment.

Songs
"Liebestraum, No. 3" (Franz Liszt)
"You Again" (M.K. Jerome; Jack Scholl)
"Oh, My Darling Clementine" (Percy Montrose)
"Yankee Doodle" (traditional, composer unknown)
  Released in November.
  (1 reel)
  Vitaphone/Warner Brothers

Unusual Occupations **(1947) D: Robert Carlisle.**

Kay Aldridge, Candice Bergen, Melissa Cameron, Georgia Carroll, Nancy Coleman, Barbara Correll, Charles Correll, Charles J. Correll, Dottie Correll, Richard Correll, Brian Donlevy, Judy Donlevy, Nora Eddington, Mia Farrow, Patrick Farrow, Deirdre Flynn, Richard Howard, Kay Kyser, Kimberly Kyser, Alana Ladd, Dorothy Lamour, Gloria May, Maureen O'Sullivan, Gail Patrick, Luana Patten, Maureen Reagan, Michael Reagan, Cheryl Rogers, Linda Rogers, Ann Rutherford, Edith Taylor, Pamela Ward.

The highlight of this featurette is Gail Patrick's Enchanted Cottage, a boutique that caters to children of Hollywood stars (such as Melissa Cameron, daughter of Aldridge). Also, a daisy grower who develops tinted daisies and a woman with her 3-D seaweed art. Written by George Brandt. Produced by Jerry Fairbanks.

Songs
"I've Been Working on the Railroad" (traditional, composer unknown)
"Old McDonald Had a Farm" (traditional, composer unknown)
"Three Blind Mice" (traditional, composer unknown)
"Shoo, Fly! Don't Bother Me" (Frank Campbell; Billy Reeves)
  Music by Edward Paul.

Released on August 30.
(11 minutes/Magnacolor)
Paramount

Stage Appearances:

"Dancing in the Streets" (play) circa 1943.
  Mary Martin, Kay Aldridge.
  Musical produced by Vinton Freedley.

"Over 21" (January 3 to July 8, 1944) D: George S. Kaufman.
  Ruth Gordon, Harvey Stephens, Kay Aldridge, Carroll Ashburn, Jessie Busley, Eddie Hodge, Philip Loeb, Dennie Moore, Beatrice Pearson, Tom Seidel, Loring Smith.
  A middle-aged man (Stephens) quits his job as a newspaper editor to be in the war. With the help of his loving wife (Gordon), he tries to make the grade in military officer training school. Broadway comedy with Aldridge as Miss Manley. Written by Ruth Gordon. Produced by Max Gordon.
  (221 performances)
  Music Box Theatre

Radio Appearances:

True or False (Blue) circa December, 1938.
  At this time I cannot pin down the exact date; if it aired in December, the possible dates are 12/12 or 12/19. Newspaper listings list other quiz participants for 12/5 and 12/26.
  Host: Dr. Harry Hagen. Announcer: Glenn Riggs.
  Six *Redbook* magazine 'cover girls' (Kay Aldridge, Anita Colby, Peggy Farley, Libby Harben, Virginia Judd, Betty Ribble, and substitute Jane Charlton) are pitted against six deacons of a Brooklyn, New York Baptist church.

Maxwell House Coffee Time (NBC) November 27, 1941.
  Stars: Frank Morgan, Fanny Brice, Hanley Stafford. Announcers: John Conte, Harlow Wilcox. The Meredith Willson Orchestra.

Frank has a tall tale about being descended from pilgrim Miles Standish. Baby Snooks (Brice) tries to find out if Daddy (Stafford) is really attending the opera "William Tell" or going for a 'night out with the boys' at a smoker. Snooks and her friend Red sing a duet. The guest tonight is cover girl and movie player Kay Aldridge.

Kraft Music Hall (NBC) December 17, 1942.

Star: Bing Crosby. Vocalists: The Charioteers, The Music Maids. Announcer: Ken Carpenter. The John Scott Trotter Orchestra.

The 90-voice Choral Society sings "The Prince of Peace". Bing's other guests tonight are Trudy Erwin, once of the Music Maids and now soloist with Kay Kyser's Orchestra; Kay Aldridge, movie Serial Queen; Edgar Buchanan, Hollywood character actor; and Lieutenant (junior grade) Frances E. Shoup of the WAVES.

Blind Date (NBC) August 12, 1943.

Host: Arlene Francis.

Six servicemen vie for dates with three glamorous females from the entertainment and modeling worlds. The soldiers (unseen by the ladies and vice versa) do so by explaining their best personal traits in a two-minute conversation. Afterwards, the women choose the men they like best from the six. It is pin-up girl night with three lovelies: Kay Aldridge, cover girl; Florence Robinson, radio actress; and Delma Bryon, actress-model.

www.ingramcontent.com/pod-product-compliance
Lightning Source LLC
Chambersburg PA
CBHW071436150426
43191CB00008B/1144